SECOND REVISED EDITION

UNDER THE SIDEWALKS OF NEW YORK

THE STORY OF THE GREATEST SUBWAY SYSTEM IN THE WORLD

A passenger deposits her token and joins millions of other passengers who daily travel under the sidewalks of New York. [New York City Transit Authority— NYCTA]

SECOND REVISED EDITION

UNDER THE SIDEWALKS OF NEW YORK

THE STORY OF THE GREATEST SUBWAY SYSTEM IN THE WORLD

Brian J. Cudahy

FORDHAM UNIVERSITY PRESS
New York • 1995

First published in 1979 by The Stephen Greene Press, Inc.
Revised edition published in 1988
Second revised edition published in 1995 by Fordham University Press
Fourth printing, 2000

Library of Congress Cataloging-in-Publication Data
Cudahy, Brian J.
   Under the sidewalks of New York : the story of the greatest subway system in the
   world / Brian J. Cudahy. — 2nd rev. ed.
      p.   cm.
   Includes bibliographical references (p.   –   ) and index.
   ISBN 0-8232-1618-7
   1. Subways—New York (N.Y.)   2. Local transit—New York (N.Y.)
I. Title.
TF847.N5C75   1995
388.4'28'097471—dc20   95-18861
                                              CIP

Printed in the United States of America

CONTENTS

"Nobody will deny that rapid transit is needed. That it is practical has been proved. Yet although the need and the practicality for rapid transit are among the obvious things that admit of no doubt, there has seemed to be no end of the hindrance in securing it."
—NEW YORK EVENING POST
June 4, 1877

The Thirty-fourth Street station on the ex-BMT Broadway line. [Author]

PREFACE TO THE SECOND REVISED EDITION

Under the Sidewalks of New York first appeared in 1979, the 75th anniversary of the opening of the city's original subway. It was published by Stephen Greene Press of Brattleboro, Vermont. A substantially revised edition was brought out in 1988, by which time Stephen Greene Press had become part of Viking Penguin. What follows is a further revision and updating; it is being published by Fordham University Press as part of its concentration in matters pertaining to regional history.

I have retained the book's original Introduction, as well as a Preface that was prepared for the 1988 version. What remains to be added here are those things that should be said to highlight subway developments since 1988.

First, the New York subway system has two new routes today that it did not have when *Under the Sidewalks of New York* last appeared. A new tunnel under the East River linking Manhattan (East 63 Street) and Queens (Long Island City) opened for revenue service on October 29, 1989 (see page 149 for earlier information about this project); ground was broken in September 1994 to connect this East River tunnel with the IND Queens Boulevard line. The new tunnel brings the number of subway crossings of the East River to an even dozen—ten by tunnel, two by bridge.

In addition, a new two-level subway spur under Archer Avenue in the Jamaica section of Queens that opened in December 1988 now allows passengers to make easier connections between the city subway and the Long Island R.R. Both the city subway and the LIRR, incidentally, are operating arms of the same umbrella transport agency, the Metropolitan Transportation Authority of New York State.

Together, these two new lines are the only routes to be placed in service, thus far, from a once-grandiose plan of subway expansion that was unveiled with such enthusiasm in the late 1960s, but was subsequently scaled back in the face of fiscal reality (see pages 148–152).

In the way of rolling stock, two brand new experimental subway trains were designed, built, and formally unveiled in a ceremony on November 19, 1992; they are currently undergoing operational tests. One was built by Kawasaki for service on the ex-IRT lines, where slightly smaller and narrower rolling stock is required, while the second train was built by Bombardier to the somewhat larger specifications required on the now-combined lines that were once known as the BMT and the IND. (A further note: ex-IRT routes are those that are designated by *numerals* in the Transit Authority's current system of train identification, while trains operating on the combined system that was once the BMT and the IND are identified by *letters*. See page 132 for additional information on this whole business of train identification.)

The new trains are prototypes for the next generation of subway cars, equipment that will then become the backbone of the fleet as the system begins its second century of service less than a decade from now.

In the way of transit operations, the ex-BMT routes across the Manhattan Bridge have been significantly downgraded, as has trunk line subway service along the Broadway line that bridge trains served with such intense frequency once upon a time. Structural problems with the Manhattan Bridge itself, plus shifting patterns of employment in Manhattan and improved connections between what was formerly the BMT and IND divisions, have rendered the Broadway line less important than it once was, and I report this fact with absolutely no enthusiasm whatsoever. Indeed, I could go on at some length in describing what things were like when the BMT's Broadway line in Manhattan was served by five *(count 'em, five!)* different subway routes to and from Brooklyn: There was the Brighton Express—Times Square-to-Brighton Beach via bridge, red and green marker lights; the Brighton Local—Queens Plaza-to-Coney Island via tunnel, white and white marker lights; the Fourth Avenue Local—Queens Plaza-to-95 Street/Fort Hamilton, green and green marker lights; the Sea Beach Express—Times Square-to-Coney Island via bridge, red and white marker lights; and the West End Express—Times Square-to-Coney Island via bridge, white and green marker lights. Rush hour action at Times Square, where the three different express services had to change direction and head back to Brooklyn with virtually split-second timing, was quite something to see. Today, sad to say, there are just two local services operating along the ex-BMT Broadway route, the R line and the N line. Even the distinctive touch of color-coded marker lights has largely become a thing of the past.

Another casualty since 1988 was a short-lived extra-fare express service that linked midtown Manhattan and downtown Brooklyn with the Howard Beach station on the Rockaway line, where passengers boarded special buses for delivery to the various terminals at John F. Kennedy International Airport. The buses still connect the airport and Howard Beach, but today one must ride a regular subway train to get there, not an extra-fare express.

An interesting development that is now emerging from experimental phase to actual deployment promises to doom the familiar subway token as the system's medium of exchange. Electronic fare collection equipment is being installed at strategic points that will permit passengers to enter the system with coded magnetic cards from which pre-paid value will automatically be subtracted during the transaction. In addition to rendering tokens obsolete, such a system may also open up the way for two concepts the New York subway has never particularly embraced: subway fares that vary according to the distance a passenger travels, and subway fares that vary depending on the day of the week, or the time of day, a passenger travels. Stay tuned; this one is very much a work-in-progress.

Speaking of tokens and transit fares, time marches on; today the price of a single subway ride stands at a buck-and-a-quarter, a 25-fold increase from the nickel fare that prevailed on the subway from 1904 through 1947. It would be wise to develop no emotional attachments to the $1.25 subway fare, though; few predict it will last very long.

The subway has, unfortunately, not been free of mayhem in recent years. As crime of various sorts becomes more evident on the streets of New York, the underground environment of the subway can hardly be expected to remain untouched by it all. And then on August 28, 1991 the subway suffered its worst accident in over 50 years when a train on the Lexington Avenue line derailed near the Union Square station, bringing death to five persons.

The final point that I believe is worth citing in the way of updating the story of the New York subway is not something that is taking place on the transit system itself. It is happening on university campuses, it is happening in publishing houses and television studios, and it is happening at conferences and seminars. It is happening in print, and it is happening on film and on tape. The New York subway—this marvelous and complex mosaic of social and economic and technological and political and historical and artistic and personal reality—is being taken far more seriously today by a wider variety of authors and commentators than ever before. People are writing and talking about the New York subway not merely in terms of issues of immediate concern, like next year's budget for the Transit Authority, or how much money will be needed from Albany to avoid another fare increase, or whether labor and management will be able to agree on a new contract in time to avoid a work stoppage. People are paying attention to how the subway has impacted the growth and development of individual New York neighborhoods, and what kind of architectural trends subway designs have promoted, and what role the subway has played in the overall history of New York.

Consider: In May of 1991, the New York Transit Museum held a two-day seminar on subway history that drew participants from all across the country. For that matter, the museum itself is part of the same general phenomenon of a more widespread general interest in the subway that I am trying to describe. Located in an unused subway station adjacent to Borough Hall in Brooklyn, the Transit Museum is a marvelous cultural attraction that is a repository of artifacts, old and not so old, that document the transit history of New York. (A visit is highly recommended!)

In addition, new titles are continually appearing in book stores that deal with different aspects of the New York subways; these range from glossy photo albums that document the endless variety of the system's rolling stock to more in-depth analyses of the system's history and impact.

From a variety of books that have appeared since 1988, I would like to make special mention of two, and will later make a passing reference to a third. Jim Dwyer's *Subway Lives* (New York: Crown, 1991) is a Runyonesque account of people and incidents associated with the system, written by a *Newsday* reporter who long worked the "transit beat" for his paper and whose overall approach may best be described as irreverent. Clifton Hood's *722 Miles* (New York: Simon & Schuster, 1993), on the other hand, is an academic analysis of the subway from its turn-of-the-century beginnings through 1953. I trust I do Professor Hood no disservice by calling his work a most readable account.

The third title I would like to mention briefly is the republishing of a classic work originally brought out by the Interborough Rapid Transit Company to celebrate the subway's opening in 1904: *The New York Subway; Its Construction and Equipment* (New York: Fordham, 1991). In a spirit of "full disclosure," I suppose I should note that the introduction to this 1991 reprint was written by me, the author of this book.

And there's more. For example, the Institute of Electrical and Electronics Engineers (IEEE) publishes a highly regarded monthly magazine entitled *IEEE Spectrum.* The issue of April 1988 (Volume 25, No. 4) provides an extensive multi-article treatment of the New York subways.

Finally, in the summer of 1994, the best of several made-for-television documentary films about the subway was first shown. Entitled "River of Steel," it was produced by Kerry Michaels and Stuart Math. Watch for re-broadcasts of "River of Steel"—it's a marvelous production.

I do not mean to suggest, by the way, that all of this expanded interest in subway matters produces anything at all like uniformity of opinion. I myself, for example, happen to disagree with certain things said in some of the works I have just identified, and in some instances I feel my disagreement is rather fundamental. Far more important than any such disagreement, however, is the much larger fact that the issues involved have been elevated in public discourse and are being openly and seriously debated. If *Under the Sidewalks of New York* has played any role at all in promoting and furthering this discourse, it will have far exceeded whatever goals I had for it when it was originally published in 1979.

—Brian Cudahy
Burke, Virginia
April, 1995

PREFACE TO THE 1988 EDITION

The first edition of *Under the Sidewalks of New York* was published in 1979, a year that also marked the seventy-fifth anniversary of the opening of the very first subway line in New York City. Two questions arise on the occasion of the publication of this revised edition: How does this edition differ from the first? How has the New York City subway system changed over the intervening years?

First, the book contains a good deal of new material; tables and charts have been updated; new developments are discussed; some treatments of old issues have been altered in the light of new information; and the selection of photographs has been revised. I have also made an effort to include references and suggestions for further reading and study. And, sorry to say, there were some out-and-out mistakes in the first edition that had to be corrected.

If there is one issue on which I have changed my mind between the first and the revised editions, it is the role Mayor John F. Hylan (1918–1926) played in the history of transport in New York City. In the first edition, I made light of Mayor Hylan and dismissed him as a shallow entity. I was wrong in doing so. New York in the 1980s deserves to know more about Red Mike, and perhaps someday it will. Of course, none of this should prevent us from enjoying Hylan's style. The man was one of a kind, and even the most vivid imagination falls short of picturing how John Francis and the magic eye of television might have coexisted.

What about the subways themselves since the Diamond Jubilee of the Interborough Rapid Transit (IRT) System was celebrated in 1979? What can be said to be new there? Lots, actually, both trivial and otherwise.

In 1979, the classic cast-iron Interborough subway kiosk was nothing but a fading memory in New York. But guess what? Today a marvelous re-creation of the famous old design has been installed at the Astor Place station of the IRT Lexington Avenue line—and not as a mute memorial to a bygone age but as a functioning entrance to a functioning subway station. (The re-creation was built in Alexander City, Alabama, by the Robinson Iron Company and hauled to New York, in several pieces, aboard a flatbed trailer truck.)

The fare has gone up. It's a buck these days. And there's even a premium fare service on an express train that runs from Manhattan to the Howard Beach station in Queens, where riders can transfer to a bus for direct delivery to the various airline terminals at JFK Airport.

Without for a minute wanting even to risk throwing a jinx at anybody or anything, it may be possible today to say the graffiti battle is on the way toward being won. (I resist quoting Churchill here on "the end of the beginning," or whatever it was.) There are two large fleets of new subway cars running under the sidewalks of New York today that were unthinkable in 1979—not because they represent a technological breakthrough on the cutting edge of modern science but because they are a commonsense breakthrough that are less mechanically complex than their predecessors and are, in fact, a return to earlier and more time-tested designs and concepts. In the way of train identification, a revised system is now in effect on two of the system's three divisions, the BMT and the IND lines. The changes are probably a good idea—things had gotten quite confusing in the nomenclature department over the past few decades— but it has made a casualty of a colorful designation that had been a part of the lives of many New Yorkers for generations. Sad to say the GG train is no more! Oh, there's a new G train that runs from Forest Hills through Queens to South Brooklyn exactly like the old GG used to, but the GG itself is no more. Too bad, I say.

—Brian Cudahy
Burke, Virginia
January 1988

In today's subway nomenclature, the designation "BMT" receives no official recognition. Perhaps this is just as well, as the subway operations of what was once called the BMT have been effectively merged with those of the IND. Here, though, four decades ago, the BMT really was the BMT and it maintained its distinctive subway rolling stock at Coney Island Shops. [Author]

CHRONOLOGY

PERSONALITIES

SPRAGUE
[Smithsonian Institution]

BELMONT
[Brown Bros.]

HYLAN
[Author's collection]

QUILL [NYCTA]

WAGNER
[Author's collection]

LINDSAY [NYCTA]

RONAN [NYCTA]

1863	World's first subway opens in London
1870	First Manhattan el
	Beach pneumatic subway
1883	Brooklyn Bridge opens; cable railway service begins between Brooklyn and Manhattan
1885	First el in downtown Brooklyn
1888	First successful electric streetcar in Richmond, Virginia
1893	Proposal to expand Manhattan els turned down
1894	Rapid Transit Commission formed
	First electrified rapid transit in New York area on the Brooklyn, Bath & West End Railroad
1896	Brooklyn Bridge cable cars electrified
	Brooklyn Rapid Transit Company chartered
1897	Rapid Transit Commission presents plans for a subway
	America's first subway opens in Boston
1898	Amalgamation of Greater New York
	Frank Sprague perfects multiple-unit control
	Through BRT el service over Brooklyn Bridge
1900	Ground broken for subway
	Brooklyn els fully electrified
1903	Belmont acquires Manhattan els
	Manhattan els fully electrified
1904	First New York subway opens
1905	Interborough-Manhattan merger
	Manhattan – Staten Island ferry taken over by city
1906	Elsburg bill
1907	Rapid Transit Commission dissolved; state Public Service Commission assumes control of subway matters
1908	Interborough service to Brooklyn through East River tunnel
	Hudson & Manhattan Railroad (H&M) begins service between Hoboken, New Jersey, and Manhattan
	BRT el service over Williamsburg Bridge
1909	Ground broken for Fourth Avenue (Brooklyn) subway
1910	Penn Station opens for business
1911	Construction begins on upper Lexington Avenue subway
1913	Dual Contracts signed
1915	First Dual Contract lines in service
1917	Last New York (and U.S.) horsecar line
	John F. Hylan elected mayor
1918	Malbone Street wreck
	BRT enters receivership
1921	Transit Commission created
1923	BRT reorganized as BMT
1924	First Triplex delivered to BMT
1925	Ground broken for Independent Subway System
	Baltimore & Ohio – owned Staten Island Rapid Transit (SIRT) electrified
	James Walker defeats Hylan for mayor
1928	IRT loses fare case in U.S. Supreme Court

1931	Final elements of the Dual Contracts completed
	New IND cars run tests on the BMT
1932	IRT in receivership
	IND opens
	Walker resigns under fire; O'Brien becomes mayor
1933	Fiorello La Guardia elected mayor
1938	Sixth Avenue el abandoned
1939–40	New York World's Fair
1940	Ninth Avenue el and portions of Second Avenue el in Manhattan, and Fifth Avenue el and portions of Fulton Street el in Brooklyn, abandoned
	BMT and IRT under municipal ownership and operation
1941	Service inaugurated over the right-of-way of the former New York, Westchester & Boston Railway in the Bronx
	El service across Queensboro Bridge and remainder of Second Avenue el abandoned
1944	Brooklyn Bridge el service abandoned
1947	Fare raised to ten cents
1953	Transit Authority formed; fare raised to fifteen cents
	Long Island Rail Road's Rockaway line purchased for expansion of subway service
1955	Third Avenue el abandoned
1956	Rockaway line opens
1957	Last streetcars in New York
1960	First mechanical car washer
1962	H&M taken over by the Port Authority
1964	Federal grants available for mass transit
1964–65	New York World's Fair
1965	Long Island Rail Road leaves the private sector
1966	John Lindsay becomes mayor; thirteen-day strike begins on New Year's Day
	Fare raised to twenty cents
1967	Chrystie Street connection
1968	Metropolitan Transportation Authority assumes control
1969	Last BMT Standard withdrawn from service
	Myrtle Avenue el abandoned
	Last prewar IRT cars withdrawn from service
1970	Fare raised to thirty cents
1971	SIRT becomes part of MTA
1972	Fare raised to thirty-five cents
	Ground broken for Second Avenue subway
1975	Fare raised to fifty cents
1977	All prewar IND cars withdrawn from service
1979	Seventy-fifth anniversary of IRT
1980	Fare raised to sixty cents
1981	Fare raised to seventy-five cents
	Contract signed for first foreign-built cars, the R-62 units from Kawasaki Heavy Industries
1984	Fare raised to ninety cents
1986	Fare raised to one dollar
1990	Fare raised to $1.15
1992	Fare raised to $1.25

A marvelous re-creation of the old Interborough subway kiosk was recently installed at the Astor Place station on the IRT Lexington Avenue line. (Author)

INTRODUCTION

How can one begin to speak about the New York subway, an urban railway network of almost unfathomable dimensions? Daily it carries almost 4 million passengers. If the subway tokens these people drop in the turnstiles in one day were stacked one on top of another, they would tower 33,000 feet into the air—a genuine menace for aerial navigation. Placed edge to edge along the ground, they would extend from Times Square to Trenton, New Jersey. The system provides work for over 20,000 employees, requires a fleet of 6,500 subway cars to meet daily schedules, and spends over $100 million each year just for electricity! The police force that patrols the New York subway—just the subway *alone*—is the fifth largest in the country. Furthermore, as it is in no other city on earth, the subway of New York is intimately woven into the fabric and identity of the city itself. The number of Hollywood films with a New York setting that feature subway footage, for instance, includes several Academy Award winners. How many movies shot in London or Paris give us scenes on the Underground or the Metro?

New York's subway is not the oldest in the world—London had been operating its underground transit for forty-one years before New York opened its first line. The New York system lacks the electronic complexity of such modern operations as the Washington, D.C., Metro, or San Francisco's BART, and New Yorkers have few qualms in admitting that theirs is not the world's most beautiful subway. Indeed, it isn't even the biggest in terms of route miles; London beats out New York in this respect, 252 miles to 231. But New York carries more passengers than London—although fewer than Tokyo or Moscow—and it operates more subway cars than any other subway system—almost as many as London, Moscow, and Tokyo combined! The busiest day ever on the London Underground, on authority of the prestigious Guinness *Book of World Records*, was May 8, 1945, VE Day, when 2,073,134 passengers were accommodated. The New York single-day record is 8,872,244—the author among them, incidentally—achieved on December 23, 1946. Though not yet memorialized by Guinness, this is a record not likely ever to be broken, by New York or any other city.

Herewith a brief caveat: the term *subway* correctly and strictly refers to an underground urban railway. Nevertheless, precision in much New York terminology is likely to be subject to perpetual qualification. Thus, there are instances when New Yorkers call an elevated transit line a subway; then again, there are times when they don't . . .

By whatever terms, New York's rapid transit system is an enterprise of appropriate magnitude for the city it serves, a city where things superlative have long been regarded as ordinary—the Empire State Building, Grand Central Terminal, the 1927 Yankees, Tin Pan Alley, the Great White Way. And also the IRT, the BMT, and the IND.

PROLOGUE: THE SECRET SUBWAY

There is an odd and interesting "preface" to the subway saga, an episode that took place under the sidewalks of New York many years before the 1904 inaugural of today's subway system and that forms a counterpoint to the city-wide proportions that are the normally perceived attributes of Gotham's rapid transit. In February 1870, during the presidential administration of Ulysses S. Grant and less than a year after the country's first transcontinental railroad was completed, a small subway car began offering demonstration trips under Broadway between Warren Street and Park Place, a distance of 312 feet. In 1870 Thomas Edison was a twenty-three-year-old struggling inventor, and the subway vehicle was powered not by electricity but by pneumatic pressure. The twenty-two-passenger car was "shot," in effect, through the tunnel like a projectile.

This minuscule forerunner of the world's preeminent subway system was financed and built by Alfred Ely Beach, an individual of some historical significance who was, among other things, the publisher of *Scientific American* magazine. He did important research on hydraulic tunneling, but perhaps the most intriguing aspect of Beach's subway was that he was unable to obtain a conventional franchise for the line, and so he built the project in total secrecy. Transit planners today, who must ply their trade in an atmosphere of intensive public participation, can be forgiven any envy they feel for Mr. Beach.

Beach's construction crews worked in the dead of night and began their tunnel through the *basement* of Devlin's clothing store on Broadway at Murray Street. Dirt from the bore was smuggled out through the store in a manner not unlike that associated with the digging of escape tunnels in World War II prisoner-of-war movies.

The underground road was opulent—wall frescoes, a fountain, fine upholstery. But the secrecy surrounding the construction spoke eloquently of New York's political climate during Beach's day. William Marcy Tweed—the "boss" of New York politics—was outraged at what he saw as an affront, namely, Beach's initiative. Municipal approbation for a project such as Beach's subway was not difficult to come by. But it had to be obtained "according to Tweed," and in tune with Tweed's designs. Meanwhile, the independent-minded Mr. Beach was already talking about expanding his system into a city-wide transit network.

Tweed would have none of this. Although Beach's expansion plans received approval in the state legislature, Governor John Hoffman—Tweed's man—vetoed the proposal. Promptly thereafter, the short demonstration tunnel was closed. Out of sight became out of mind, and the pneumatic subway was soon forgotten.

Beach was a perceptive man. He recognized the emotional strain subway passengers might experience when traveling beneath the ground, an environment more identified with unsavory journeys from the realm of ancient mythology than routine trips around town. He sought to allay their anxiety by providing a grand piano in the waiting room of his underground railway. Too bad his system didn't survive another sixty-two years! For if it had, Beach's piano player could have added a most appropriate tune to his repertoire. Written by Billy Strayhorn of the Duke Ellington orchestra, it celebrated a major underground public work of *its* day and quickly became Ellington's theme song. It was called "Take the A Train."

The subway today is not without occasional musical interludes. From time to time, roving musicians entertain passengers with impromptu recitals on instruments conventional and otherwise, and, to the bane of their unwitting traveling companions, the owners of portable radios as big as sides of beef often feel compelled to subject everyone within earshot to whatever is on the top of the charts.

But despite all this, it is Beach's quiet piano recitals and Strayhorn's classic piece of jazz that set the proper tone for the story to follow, a story that unfolds . . . *Under the Sidewalks of New York.*

In 1912, workers building the Broadway subway (a segment of the Triborough System that was eventually absorbed into the BRT) exhumed the old Beach pneumatic subway near Warren Street. This photograph shows the brick-lined tunnel of New York's first, albeit forgotten, subway. (Robert L. Presbrey collection)

A later view of the City Hall station, departure point for the city's first subway train on October 27, 1904. The track here is still in daily use by Lexington Avenue locals, but the ornate station has been closed, and passengers must board trains at the nearby Brooklyn Bridge station. [NYCTA]

1

"I DECLARE THE SUBWAY OPEN"

IT WAS ANOTHER AUTUMN IN NEW YORK BUT ONE unlike any before or since. It was October 1904.

For the first time in the twentieth century, a New York baseball team gave the city's fans a major league championship. John McGraw's New York Giants finished the season with a 106–47 record, and his stellar pitchers Christy Mathewson and Joe McGinnity between them won the scarcely believable total of sixty-eight games. But unlike the previous fall when the National League pennant winner played the champs of the new American League in the first World Series, McGraw regarded the new league with undisguised contempt and wouldn't let his club participate.[1]

In world news that October, wire dispatches from the Far East competed for space on the front pages of the city's dozen or more newspapers, for the Russo-Japanese War was raging, a conflict that many historians claim was the first war that can be called "modern."

As October drew to an end, voters throughout the country were getting ready to elect as president in his own right the man who had assumed that office from the vice-presidency three years earlier when President William McKinley was assassinated in Buffalo, New York, by Leon Czolgosz, an anarchist. Theodore Roosevelt was the country's twenty-sixth president.

In 1904, the population of New York City was approaching 4 million. Over the next fifty years, the population would double, but with that increase, it would level off and stabilize. In 1904, though, the city was in the midst of a tremendous demographic updraft that was remaking the face of America into a land that was more and more urbanized, industrialized, and just plain big. During the fifty years leading up to 1904, New York's population had increased almost five-fold. Growth and movement to the cities, factories and machines, loss of self-sufficiency, and massive waves of immigration—these were the characteristics of the era.

In the fall of 1904, New York City was in but its sixth year of existence under a new municipal charter that had radically altered the political alignment of the region just a few years earlier. In 1904 the City of New York was no longer just Manhattan and the Bronx, as had long been the case, with Brooklyn and other places enjoying separate status as independent municipalities. Since the stroke of midnight that rang in the year 1898, New York City was a metropolis of five interlocked boroughs—Brooklyn, Queens, Manhattan, the Bronx, and Richmond, the last more often called by its popular name, Staten Island.[2]

The amalgamation of 1898 was—and remains—a significant social and political event, for it gave to a single governmental unit, the new and enlarged municipal apparatus, the potential for dealing effectively with what had already become the scandalous by-product of the new age of commercial expansion: tenement crowding and all of its attendant evils. The old New York City simply didn't have enough room, and although redrawing a few municipal boundary lines didn't bring any more low-density residential territory closer to the commercial centers of Manhattan, it did give a single political entity jurisdiction over a sufficiently encompassing piece of geography to allow long-term planning and perspective, not just short-term reaction to whatever crisis was at hand. And tenement crowding surely was a terrible crisis.

It has been estimated by those whose expertise allows them to speak authoritatively in such matters that on Manhattan Island in the area generally called the Lower East Side, the turn of the century saw population densities of 9,000 residents per acre, rates that have never been even remotely equaled anywhere else on the face of the earth . . . not in the slums of Calcutta, not in block after block of high-rise apartment buildings of a later era.[3] Providing escape valves so this mass of humanity could migrate to more wholesome areas further removed from the city's business and commercial districts had been a perennial goal in late-nineteenth-century New York. The Brooklyn Bridge opened for traffic on May 23, 1883. Its construction, first under the guidance of John A. Roebling, and then his son, Washington, took fourteen years and cost $15 million. In 1903, the Williamsburg Bridge was opened. Linking Brooklyn with Manhattan, both bridges offered a swift alternative to East River ferryboat travel. But land was the limiting factor in lower Manhattan, and travel within the city was becoming more and more hampered as New York's population continued to swell and its business and commerce continued to grow. Streets were hopelessly clogged; horse-drawn buggies, foot traffic, pushcarts, wagons, and even an occasional horseless carriage competed jealously and aggressively for maneuvering room.

Thus, in 1904, New York took a bold step that would face up to these problems and promote the orderly growth of the city thenceforward. At precisely 35½ minutes after 2 P.M. on Thursday, October 27, with Mayor George B. McClellan at the controls, a subway train pulled out of a terminal and carried passengers under the sidewalks of New York for the first time. Things haven't been the same since.

Much of the ornate design work that went into the city's first subway is still visible. This rendition of the *Santa Maria* identifies the Columbus Circle station. [Tom Nelligan]

The classic Interborough subway kiosk, cast iron and distinctive, has a clear touch of the Near East in its design. These ornate structures, once common all over Manhattan, were replaced with more ordinary designs beginning in the mid-1950s since it was felt their curb-side locations blocked the vision of pedestrians and motorists. This 1906 view is at the City Hall station. Notice the old Post Office building in what is now City Hall Park, and also notice that graffiti already adorns the handsome kiosk. [NYCTA]

A HOT TIME IN THE OLD TOWN

The day that subway service opened in New York was filled with unabashed revelry. Ceremonies began in the Aldermanic Chamber of City Hall with some 600 special guests present. After the oratory had run its course, McClellan stepped forward and said: "Now I, as Mayor, in the name of the people, declare the subway open."

The various speeches inside City Hall lasted beyond the scheduled 2 P.M. departure for the first train. As the official party of bewhiskered and silk-hatted dignitaries proceeded out of the building and down into the sparkling new subway station located adjacent to the seat of municipal government—and called City Hall station—whistles, bells, and sirens already were proclaiming the opening of the new line. Cynics may think it fitting that the city's first subway train was a half-hour late.

Up and down the route, New Yorkers clustered around the subway entrance kiosks. It was an unusual kind of celebration, since most could not see what was happening. Few, however, were unaware of the day's historic significance.

Mayor McClellan was presented with an inscribed, Tiffany-made solid silver

It's almost half-past 2 in the afternoon outside City Hall in New York on Thursday, October 27, 1904. A contingent of helmeted police heads for the kiosk and the entrance to the subway. The oratory is over; service is about to begin. [NYCTA]

control handle by the president of the Interborough Rapid Transit Company, the proud host of the event, to use on the inaugural trip.[4] With motor instructor George Morrison keeping a careful eye on the neophyte motorman, His Honor latched back the controller and fed 600 volts of direct current into the cars' traction motors. Subway service began.

Original plans called for the mayor to operate the inaugural train only a short distance and then let an Interborough motorman take over. But McClellan did not surrender the handles until the train reached 103d Street, five miles north of City Hall, so thoroughly did he enjoy his task. A single minor incident marred the trip. After leaving Brooklyn Bridge station and before crossing onto the express track from the local track, the train came to a noisy and abrupt stop, "as if it had hit some large stationary object," as one journalist put it. The fancy silver controller being used for the ceremonial trip did not fit properly. Consequently, it had hit the air brake valve, throwing the train into an emergency stop. Interborough technicians made adjustments, and the incident was not repeated.

THE ORIGINAL ROUTE

The city's original subway line began as a single track turnaround loop (see plan, below) under City Hall in downtown Manhattan but quickly expanded into a four-track line at the Brooklyn Bridge station, less than a mile away. Four tracks permitted the operation of both local and express service. The line proceeded north from Brooklyn Bridge under what were then known as Park Row, Center

October 27, 1904. The city's first subway train is about to leave City Hall station on its historic inaugural run. In the center is Mayor George B. McClellan, who handled the controls. E. P. Bryan, president of the Interborough, is to the right. To the left is Frank Hedley, a man who would hold the president's post in later years. [Brown Bros.]

the plans

Street, New Elm Street, Elm Street, Lafayette Place, Fourth Avenue, and Park Avenue to East Forty-second Street. A more practical line from downtown, in the opinion of some, would have been a tunnel under Broadway, New York's most famous and important thoroughfare. But property owners on that avenue were unconvinced of a subway's merit and managed to kill construction proposals in the courts. At Forty-second and Park, the site of Grand Central, a major express station was located, and the line turned west under Forty-second Street. The Grand Central of 1904 was not the current railroad terminal building, which was not completed until 1913. Cornelius Vanderbilt started running his New York Central and Hudson River Railroad trains out of what was originally called Grand Central Depot in 1869. His sanity was seriously questioned at the time for building his New York terminal on Forty-second Street, a site then so far north of the city's business and commercial districts.

Proceeding crosstown under Forty-second Street, the original New York subway line took another 90-degree turn at Times Square and headed north under Broadway. The name Times Square was coined just prior to the subway's opening when the *New York Times* opened its new office building at the site.[5] Previously called Longacre Square, the area adjacent to Forty-second Street and Broadway was becoming a major focus of the city's theatrical activity in 1904. Many enterprising showmen bought up property in the area and moved their operations uptown from such older theater districts as Twenty-third Street and Fourteenth Street.

The Interborough failed to anticipate the traffic potential to Times Square, though, and in 1904 it was a mere local stop. Eventually it would become the second busiest subway station in the city and one of the busiest in the world.

From Times Square the four-track line continued north under Broadway to 145th Street. With the exception of a fifteen-block stretch of track near 125th Street, the entire line was built underground. At 125th Street, a geological formation called Manhattan Valley cuts across the western portion of the island. Rather than tunnel below this depression, engineers let the subway emerge from below ground and vault across the valley on a viaduct.

One of the line's four tracks stopped just north of Ninety-sixth Street, but the other three continued north to 145th Street. A junction of importance was also located at Ninety-sixth Street where a two-track subway cut eastward, then north under Lenox Avenue, eventually reaching West Farms Square in the Bronx after tunneling under the Harlem River and onto an elevated viaduct. But neither this route nor a two-track line north of 145th Street was ready for service on October 27. The contract for the construction of New York's first subway called for considerably more trackage than that which opened on inaugural day; the City Hall–145th Street section was simply the first segment to be completed. The first addition to the original 9-mile route—an extension beyond 145th Street to 157th Street—opened a scant two weeks after the October 27 gala. Formally opened, that is. On Saturday, October 29, a temporary service was operated to the incomplete 157th Street station to accommodate fans attending the Yale-Columbia football game (which the Elis won, 34–0).

The inaugural special ran express to 145th Street, where it arrived at 3:01½ P.M., 26 minutes after leaving City Hall. The return trip ran as a local, making all stops, to allow dignitaries a chance to examine the beautifully executed station details. This took 41 minutes.

Immediately after the first train left City Hall, additional trains that had been backed up along the southbound tracks followed it into the loop terminal and

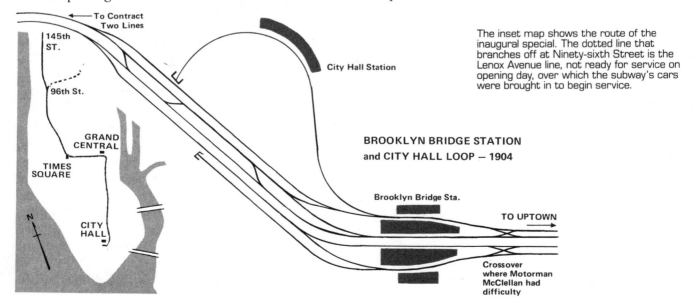

The inset map shows the route of the inaugural special. The dotted line that branches off at Ninety-sixth Street is the Lenox Avenue line, not ready for service on opening day, over which the subway's cars were brought in to begin service.

BROOKLYN BRIDGE STATION and CITY HALL LOOP — 1904

went into service for a select group of 15,000 invited guests. These riders sampled the line until 6 P.M. Then, after an hour's breather, the general public was allowed aboard. Some 150,000 New Yorkers tried out the line on its first evening of service, while dignitaries from the afternoon's ceremony retired to Sherry's for a testimonial dinner.

For the record—and it is an oft-repeated story—on one of the early "invitation-only" trains, a gentleman from Philadelphia named F.B. Shipley became the first man to offer his seat to a woman on the New York subway. Later, after the general public was allowed aboard, Henry Barrett of Forty-sixth Street noticed his $500 diamond horse-shoe pin was missing after he paid his fare at the Twenty-eighth Street station, the first recorded incident of a passenger's being separated from his property on the subway. Shipley's chivalry has been repeated in diminishing proportions, and Barrett's misfortune in increasing proportions, in the years since 1904.

Indicating how quickly the subway melded into the fabric of New York life, many of the 15,000 invited guests on the early trips decided to forgo the return trip to City Hall and instead got off at the stations nearest their homes. The ensuing scenes at the various subway exits comprised an ordinary evening rush hour as passengers emerged from the underground stations and headed home to supper in a manner that would be commonplace from then on.

Heavy crowds came to inspect the new subway on its first weekend of operation, and complaints immediately surfaced. At several stations built on curves, a large gap developed between the platforms and the subway cars. This problem was eventually rectified by the installation of a mechanical "sliding platform" that moved out to fill the gap as soon as the trains stopped. Another criticism concerned the advertising signs, which in the view of some beholders defaced the beauty of the stations. There were frequent complaints about crowding in the trains and stations, a problem the New York subways have yet to solve.

The stations were attractive in design and appointments. The construction contract was most explicit: "The railway and its equipment as contemplated by the contract constitute a great public work. All parts of the structure where exposed to public sight shall therefore be designed, constructed, and maintained with a view to the beauty of their appearance, as well as to their efficiency." Critics agreed these goals were amply met. A trade journal of the transit industry called the subway stations "dignified and artistic efforts of the highest order." One journalist called them "architecturally superlative executions."

In that first weekend of service, the subway had to cope with the first of its "problem" passengers, of a kind. According to the records of the Yorkville Court, Magistrate Breen presiding, one Michael Pollack was charged with being drunk and disorderly in public on October 29, a Saturday. He had been arrested the previous evening, and thirteen others were brought in on the same charge as well. Said Pollack to the judge: "Please, your honor, I rode from the Bridge to 145th Street and back in the tunnel. The dust was terrible, horrible, your honor. I had to take a drink to get it down."

This period postal card is a composite rendition of the new subway showing the ornate vaults of the City Hall station directly under the structure after which it was named. The station is a reasonable enough representation, although its proportions are a little off, but the subway car depicts nothing that ever ran under the sidewalks of New York. This card was mailed in New York in December 1907 to a man named Bob in Wollaston, Massachusetts. Its message reads: "Bad news, Bob, the subway's in a hole." [Author's collection]

The judge then asked if a single drink was responsible for the man's condition at the time of his arrest, to which the resourceful Pollack replied: "Oh, no. But one wouldn't do for that dust. I had to take six."

The case was dismissed with the suggestion that, in the future, the el might prove to be less dusty than the subway. The other thirteen, impressed by Pollack's performance, had exactly the same story to tell. And all won acquittal from the amused magistrate.

In the fall of 1987, eighty-three years after that inaugural weekend, 92-year-old Harry Lake of West Hartford, Connecticut, remembered what it was like to be an excited 9 year old whose father took him and his two brothers from their New Rochelle, New York, home to New York City just to ride the new subway. Lake, who later served with the U.S. Navy in two world wars, became the founder-publisher of a Brooklyn newspaper, and involved himself in real estate development in several states, remembered "how new and clean it was and how fast the trains ran. Everything even smelled new. And there wasn't any smoke and cinders like there used to be on the els."

But if 1904 and the opening of the subway marked the initiation of a new form of safe and swift local transport, it was also the year that gave New Yorkers the starkest possible evidence that new mobility and complex machines are not without attendant danger and risk. On the morning of June 15, 1904—with construction work on the new subway entering its final phases—a church group from the Lower East Side boarded a glistening white excursion boat at the foot of East Third Street and the East River. They were bound for a day's outing at Locust Grove on Long Island, but their sidewheel vessel, the *General Slocum*, never got them there. Fire broke out aboard the thirteen-year-old wooden steamer in the vicinity of Hell Gate. The captain maintained his helm as the fire gained headway, never trying to beach his vessel so passengers might flee the boat. The wind-whipped fire became a total conflagration that claimed 1,030 lives and stands as by far the worst tragedy ever to befall New York. May it ever remain so.

Horsedrawn transportation was commonplace in New York during the first decade of the 20th century, but alternatives were beginning to emerge. A battery-powered streetcar makes its way east along Cleveland Place, and an exit kiosk of the new Interborough subway tells of yet another dimension in urban transport now available below ground. The gentleman in the straw hat seems unimpressed by it all, though, and continues purposefully toward his destination on foot. [Author's collection]

A five-car train of Manhattan Railway
elevated cars, hauled by one of the line's
doughty little steam engines, heels into the
reverse curve at Coenties' Slip on a sunny
morning in 1894. Just a couple of hundred
yards ahead is the line's southern terminal
at South Ferry. Both Second and Third
Avenue els operated over this trackage.
[Library of Congress]

2

FROM STEAM TO ELECTRICITY

THE SUBWAY LINE THAT OPENED IN NEW YORK in the autumn of 1904 was not the first of its kind to operate in the world, or even the first rapid transit line to traverse Manhattan Island.

The world's first subway opened on January 10, 1863, in London, a steam-powered line that carried Queen Victoria's subjects on a 3.7-mile track between Farringdon Street and Bishop's Rock, Paddington. "The line may be regarded as the greatest engineering triumph of the day," commented the *London Times*. The New York subway doesn't even rank as the first subway in the United States. That honor belongs to Boston, where on September 1, 1897, trolley cars of the West End Street Railway began operating into the Tremont Street subway, adjacent to historic Boston Common. On June 10, 1901, the Boston Elevated Railway began running elevated trains into the same Tremont Street subway. The New York press, while sufficiently laudatory of Boston's initiatives, was visibly annoyed that any other city could accomplish such a major effort ahead of New York.[1]

The Beach effort aside, the first practical rapid transit line on Manhattan was a section of single-track elevated railway that opened for passenger service on February 14, 1870, almost thirty-five years before the first subway run. The line boasted a grand total of three wooden passenger cars that were propelled by a moving cable. When the line opened in 1870, it ran from Dey Street to Thirtieth Street. Eventually, it became part of the Ninth Avenue el.

Cable operations quickly proved unsatisfactory. The elevated company turned to the technology of standard railroading and began hauling trains behind diminutive steam locomotives. These little engines became a permanent fixture on the New York scene for more than twenty-five years. Both the cars and the locomotives of the elevated lines were essentially scaled-down versions of regular railroad equipment, although they ran on the standard track gauge of 4 feet,

8½ inches. At one time the elevated lines even interchanged freight cars with conventional railroads.

By 1880, elevated lines, or els, had been built down Ninth, Sixth, Third, and Second avenues. Also by 1880, operation of the els had become the responsibility of a single company, Manhattan Railways. Trains were powered by steam locomotives; they ran the length of Manhattan to South Ferry at the southern (or downtown) end of the island, where an armada of ferryboats made connections for points in Brooklyn, Staten Island, and New Jersey. (In later years, when the immigrant station was established on Ellis Island, many newcomers to America took, literally, their first steps in the New World as they walked from the ferry landing at the foot of Whitehall Street to the elevated terminal and a ride to the New World home of a friend or relative that was their destination).[2]

Manhattan Railways saw the entry to the New York urban transport scene of someone better known for his machinations in the world of intercity railroad finances. He is Jay Gould, a man who richly earned his reputation among America's high-rolling railroad chieftains of the nineteenth century. Together with James Fisk and Daniel Drew, he is said to have manipulated the gold market in 1869 for a personal gain of $11 million, although the actions brought on one of the nation's worst financial panics in the process. His leadership of the New York els, however, reveals more of Gould-the-careful-businessman than Gould-the-robber-baron.

The Manhattan els terminated at South Ferry, where passengers could transfer to various ferryboat lines for continuing on to Brooklyn, Staten Island or New Jersey. In the late 1890s, a steam locomotive prepares to lead its train out of South Ferry on a northbound trip. [Smithsonian Institution]

Various steam-powered el operations were started across the river in Brooklyn and Queens at about the same time. The Brooklyn Elevated Railroad operated its first train on September 24, 1883, the first such service in what is today the borough of Brooklyn.

In addition to the elevated lines, several networks of street railways crisscrossed Manhattan prior to 1904, but because these had to compete directly with street traffic, they can scarcely be called true rapid transit. The els, however, were a major league operation. In the last full year before the subway opened, Manhattan Railways carried more than 250 million passengers.

Steam power on the elevated lines, though, even in the 1890s, was a pronounced civic liability. The engines were sooty, messy, and noisy. They started fires in awnings, startled teams of horses, and in general wreaked havoc with efforts to lead a quiet and tranquil life. The press was vocal in decrying these conditions. "A major city should not suffer such indignities any longer," scolded one reporter.

An 1872 view of the Ninth Avenue el. Notice the drop-belly sides on two of the cars to ensure a better center of gravity and the small steam engine on the far end of the train. [Smithsonian Institution]

The crew of steam engine No. 173 poses for posterity at the northern terminal of the Sixth Avenue el. In the background can be seen, just barely, grandstands of the original Polo Grounds, home of John McGraw's New York Giants. The elevated structure where the engine sits survived to become the final segment of the original elevated lines in Manhattan to remain in service. [NYCTA]

Despite their drawbacks, the little engines had a definite charm. Unlike larger locomotives on conventional railroads, they did not have a separate tender for fuel and water, but rather carried coal in a bunker behind the cab, water in on-board tanks, and could operate equally well in either direction. The cab roof was decorated with a pair of colored disks by day and lanterns at night. By knowing the proper color codes, passengers could determine a train's destination and tell whether it was a local or an express before it entered the station. The stations themselves were jewel box masterpieces of Victorian gingerbread. Light danced into the waiting room through stained-glass windows. In winter months, the ticket agent was busy scooping coal into a potbellied stove to keep waiting passengers warm.

As the turn of the century drew near, many sensed that an effective replacement for steam power on the els was not only necessary but near. This new power promised to be clean, efficient, and silent, a type of energy that would truly fulfill the concept of urban transit: electricity!

At the Berlin Industrial Exhibition in 1879, Dr. E. Werner von Siemens demonstrated what is generally regarded as the first practical use of electricity to haul passengers. A series of experiments and demonstrations followed, and in 1880, Thomas Edison built a 10-horsepower (HP) narrow-gauge electric locomotive at his Menlo Park, New Jersey, laboratory.

Through the final two decades of the nineteenth century, continual efforts were also under way to develop an efficient replacement for the horsecar, the standard vehicle of the street railway industry. Naphtha engines and other exotic ideas were tried—unsuccessfully. Here, too, electricity would eventually win the day. Electricity would put the horses from the street lines out to pasture and send the steam locomotives from the els to the scrap heap.

Many complex engineering problems remained to be solved, however, before electricity could be successfully employed in a heavy-duty, multicar transit operation such as an elevated line. An Annapolis graduate named Frank Sprague did more than any other individual to upgrade the state of the art. Years later, Frank Hedley, who was president of the Interborough after World War I, said of Sprague: "It has rightly been said that he bears the same relation to electric transportation that Thomas A. Edison bore to electric illumination."

After earlier experiments by Sprague (including futile efforts to electrify the Manhattan elevated lines), an 1888 project in Richmond, Virginia—generally regarded as the world's first successful electric transportation installation— saw Sprague outfit an entire system of city streetcars with electric motors and an overhead wire system for power distribution.[3] But Sprague's most significant innovation in paving the way for electric-powered elevated trains and subways was the development of multiple-unit control. Multiple-unit control, as the name suggests, allows the motorman in the lead car of a multicar train to operate the motors of all cars from a single control station. By today's space-age standards, multiple-unit control may not seem notably outstanding, but Sprague's pioneering work gave the transit industry a technological breakthrough that was desperately needed. Sprague's success meant that trains could be lengthened or shortened at will and as traffic warranted. Only simple cable connections were needed to make, say, an eight-car train as easy and efficient to operate as a single car. In short, multiple-unit control made the change from steam to electricity more than merely having electric locomotives haul the same cars previously hauled by the steam locomotives. Each car would now contain its own power unit, all efficiently controlled by a motorman in the lead car.

How Sprague convinced the world of the value of multiple-unit control is itself an interesting story. The several elevated railway companies of Chicago had begun to electrify their lines, the original operational principle involving a motorized lead car hauling several motorless trailer cars. The city's oldest elevated, the Chicago & South Side Rapid Transit Railroad Company, was on the verge of replacing its steam engines with electric power and had elected to follow the lead of the other Chicago roads by using a power car and unpowered trailers. It was 1898, and Sprague had drifted somewhat out of the railway business and was devoting his hardly inconsiderable talents to various challenges associated with the deployment of electric elevators in the office buildings and hotels that were beginning to reach new heights in American cities. At one time, he worked out a circuit that could control a number of different elevators from a single

Manhattan in the age of the el! This is the Sixth Avenue line at West Thirty-third Street shortly after the turn of the century. The el trains and the streetcars have long since vanished from this scene, but the spot today contains, perhaps, the greatest concentration of electric railways on the face of the earth. They're all underground, of course—two city subway lines, a terminal of the trans-Hudson PATH System, and railroad trains of three operators heading to and from Penn Station and the East River tunnels. [Smithsonian Institution]

Of the four Manhattan els, the Third Avenue line lasted the longest. A five-car local threads its way northbound at East Thirty-fourth Street in April 1955. [Author]

location. Whether such a design had any practical application in the elevator business is problematic, but it did enable him to suggest a better idea to the management of Chicago's South Side L than the power car–trailer car system.

On July 16, 1897, on an experimental track outside the General Electric plant at Schenectady, New York, Sprague successfully demonstrated the workability of multiple-unit control. Later that same year, Sprague's concept was tested in Chicago on the South Side line . . . and then successfully deployed.

Thus, the way was cleared for the most daring and, ultimately, the most successful attempt to solve the growing congestion of New York streets. With electric power and multiple-unit control, an underground rapid transit line suddenly became more feasible than ever before.

Electric traction advanced with amazing speed. In 1900, management made the decision to electrify the entire Second Avenue el. By early 1903, all four Manhattan elevated lines were converted from steam to electric operation with multiple-unit-controlled cars.

Electricity progressed in other areas of the transportation industry as well. A serious rear-end collision in New York Central's Park Avenue tunnel in January 1902, caused by obscured visibility from steam locomotive exhausts, prompted state legislation prohibiting steam operation in the tunnels. Even prior to the accident, New York Central had begun to study the possible electrification of its Manhattan operations. In late 1906, electric equipment was phased into service. Meanwhile, New York Central's longtime rival, the Pennsylvania Railroad, was planning its own assault on Manhattan Island via a Hudson River tunnel and with electricity as a source of propulsion. With none but steam engines in its roundhouses, the mighty Pennsy was forced to terminate its trains from the west across the Hudson in Jersey City and transfer New York–bound passengers by ferryboat, a decided competitive disadvantage. Electric power brought the railroad smack into midtown Manhattan.[4]

Right: On March 14, 1903, the first spike was driven in the new subway at Columbus Circle, and a low-key ceremony was held to mark the event. Presiding (left to right) were John B. McDonald; William R. Wilcox, who would later become chairman of the state Public Service Commission; William Barclay Parsons; and Mayor Seth Low, who is holding the mallet used to drive home the silver spike. [NYCTA]

Left: August Belmont, the guiding influence behind the early Interborough. (Brown Bros.)

3

THE BIRTH OF THE INTERBOROUGH

NEW YORK WAS DETERMINED TO BUILD RAPID transit underground and even flirted with the possibility of steam-powered lines. As early as 1868, serious talks were under way concerning such projects. In 1872, Cornelius Vanderbilt incorporated something called the New York City Rapid Transit Company to build a "sub-surface rail road" in Manhattan, but the plan was dropped. Something of a formal move came on April 9, 1890, when Mayor Hugh J. Grant, acting under the provisions of legislation that had been passed back in 1875, appointed a commission to evaluate the question of rapid transit. The commission eventually recommended that a steam-powered line be built on a viaduct from the Manhattan end of the Brooklyn Bridge as far as Astor Place and then through a tunnel to Forty-second Street. That their advice wasn't heeded showed no slackening in the determination to go beneath the streets, for in 1893 the Manhattan Railway was rebuffed in a bid to construct additional elevated lines, despite an urgent need for new rail transit routes.

Passage of the state Rapid Transit Act of 1894 proved critical, as it sanctioned a wholly new idea—municipal construction of a subway system, a system that would then be leased to private interests for operation under a long-term contract. Previous subway proposals in New York had presumed construction by private interests, the same condition as had prevailed when the elevated lines were built. But a consensus was developing that the extraordinary cost of underground construction was beyond the ability of the private sector to finance.

The individual most identified with the passage of this important new law and the theme it introduced was Abram S. Hewitt, a late-nineteenth-century mayor of New York and often called the father of modern rapid transit. The law required a popular referendum by the city's voters before it took effect, as it was proposing a novel alteration to the fabric of municipal operations, and on November 6, 1894, that approval was resoundingly given. Of 184,035 votes cast on the issue, 132,647 were in the affirmative. New York voters had thus sanctioned the expenditure of public monies for rapid transit construction. Concurrent with this political development, of course, the perfection of electric traction for the powering of an underground transit line meant that progress was being made.

The 1894 law called for the formation of a new Rapid Transit Commission. Alexander E. Orr was its chairman; the panel included the city's mayor and comptroller as *ex officio* members and such other distinguished citizens as Seth Low and William H. Steinway. William Barclay Parsons was retained from the staff of the previous commission as chief engineer. Public hearings were held throughout 1896, and in 1897, Parsons presented plans for what would eventually become the 1904 Manhattan-Bronx subway. Many obstacles had to be overcome in the courts, such as the borrowing limit of the municipal government. But on January 15, 1900, bids were opened for the construction of the subway.

There were only two contending contractors. The company of John B. McDonald bid $35 million for basic line work and an additional $2.7 million for stations, beating out the Andrew Onderdonk organization. McDonald was experienced in tunnel work. He had constructed the Baltimore tunnels for the B&O Railroad, the nation's first mainline railroad electrification. But McDonald

The year is 1902, and the location is Astor Place. A crosstown streetcar heads for the Christopher Street ferry slip of the Hoboken Ferry Company, and workers have begun to excavate the right-of-way for New York's first subway. "Sidewalk superintendents" look on. [Robert L. Presbrey collection]

Subway construction seen from the Brooklyn Bridge el station looking south along Park Row, with City Hall to the right. Subway excavations are visible along both sides of the street. Notice the underground conduit between the running rails for the electric streetcars. Overhead trolley wires were prohibited in Manhattan. [Robert L. Presbrey collection]

ran into unexpected trouble obtaining security bonds, supposedly because certain street railway interests, who saw the subway as a threat, used their influence with the banking community to block approval. In order to obtain the necessary bonds, McDonald was forced to seek out a man whose imprint on the New York subways was to be firm and lasting.

McDonald formed a partnership with August Belmont, son of the North American representative of the Rothschilds, who had access through his father (August Belmont, Sr.) to virtually unlimited funds.[1] Belmont capitalized the newly formed Rapid Transit Construction Company at $5 million. On February 21, 1900, the firm signed a construction contract with the city through the Rapid Transit Commission. In early March 1900, construction began in Washington Heights, and on May 24 of the same year, Mayor Robert Van Wyck broke ground officially on the project in front of City Hall.

Something that is a little unclear many years later is what McDonald's original intentions were with respect to operating the new subway once it was constructed. The state legislation of 1894 under which the project was begun specified that the winning bidder agree not only to construct the new civil works on behalf of the city but also to operate it for a term of fifty years under a lease arrangement. (The lessee was required to supply such equipment as rolling stock, signals, and even a power house to generate electricity with its own funds.) The subway fare was fixed at five cents a ride for the term of the lease.

McDonald, whose experience extended to construction matters only, apparently originally planned to negotiate with another company, perhaps an existing New York street railway, to handle subway operations after construction was completed. But his joining forces with Belmont changed matters. On May 6, 1902, Belmont incorporated the Interborough Rapid Transit Company. Through this company, the McDonald-Belmont venture moved from a mere construction enterprise to becoming the operator of the new underground system as well. The Interborough's first general manager was a man by the name of E. P. Bryan; he came to New York after a stint as the general manager of the Terminal Railroad Association of St. Louis. Belmont himself served as the president of the new subway operating company.

Later in 1902, McDonald's firm was awarded an $8 million contract to extend the unfinished subway down lower Broadway, under the East River, and through downtown Brooklyn to the Long Island Rail Road terminal at Flatbush and Atlantic avenues. This addition was referred to as the "Contract Two" segment of the subway (the original work was known as the "Contract One" segment). In the same year, the Interborough signed a 999-year lease for all properties of the Manhattan Railway Company, the operator of all four elevated lines. The lease, which guaranteed a 7 percent return each year on the el company's stock, took effect on April 1, 1903. It meant the Interborough would become the operator of all rapid transit on Manhattan Island, both new subway and old elevated, enabling the company to plan integrated operations, especially in the less densely settled residential sections of the Bronx. A combined subway and elevated network would also offer stronger competition to the street railway lines. Belmont's action provided the Interborough with extensive rapid transit experience before the subway itself opened and eliminated by consolidation whatever competitive threat the elevated system represented for the new subway.

HOW TO BUILD A SUBWAY

The symbolic start on the project took place on May 24, 1900, when Mayor Robert Van Wyck presided at an official ground-breaking ceremony in front of City Hall. McDonald separated his own contract into fifteen subcontracts, which were then awarded to other firms. Different construction companies had responsibilities for different sections of line, in other words, and the McDonald-Belmont organization functioned in a supervisory capacity managing the overall effort. The trade press of the day described the construction as the "shallow excavation type," a technique similar to that which had been used on the Glasgow Central Railway and also the subways of Boston and Budapest. Crews dug out the right-of-way from street level, built a concrete and steel subsurface structure for the trains to run in, and then rebuilt the surface thoroughfare atop the tunnel. Tunneling methods varied according to the geography or the geology of a particular section. At times, molelike deep-bore tunneling—perfected on the London Underground—proved to be more practical than shallow excavation. Deep-bore tunneling had the advantage of not disrupting surface activity. If the ground through which a deep-bored tunnel was cut proved to be firm, the work was routine, and the finished bore merely had to be lined with concrete. But if the ground was soft, crews were forced to work in an artificially pressurized atmosphere within an airlock, and the tunnel was built with iron rings bolted together to form a secure, and even watertight, structure.

Shallow excavation work, or "cut-and-cover" construction as it later came to be called, was much more complex and costly than deep-bore tunneling. Engineer William Barclay Parsons, however, felt that the added cost of shallow excavation work would later be offset by reduced subway operating costs since systems of elevators would not be needed to bring passengers to the surface.[2] The problem with shallow excavation, though, was that it had to take place in an environment that was already pretty crowded. Sewer, gas, and water mains had to be diverted and then rebuilt as the work moved along. Often, there were no maps showing the precise location of these utility lines. The texture of the soil also presented a variety of problems. Quicksand was discovered in the Canal Street area, and at other places, construction crews had to blast through solid rock. On the west side of Fourth Avenue at Union Square, engineers found nothing but rock from street level on down, and on the east side of the same avenue, the first 15 feet of work required merely the removal of soft sand.

One of the most troublesome problems was the shoring and protecting of existing construction along the subway route. The elevated structures of the Manhattan Railway particularly caused trouble for Belmont's engineers. One ingenious solution of such problems was at the curve from Forty-second Street into Broadway at Times Square. The New York Times was erecting its new headquarters building at that site. The Interborough tunnel was literally run *through* the foundation of the newspaper building, although the supporting work for each is totally independent of the other.

A typical four-track section of tunnel, built by the cut-and-cover method, was 55 feet wide. Tracks—100-pound rail laid in 33-foot sections—were spiked to conventional hard pine cross-ties embedded in broken stone ballast. All curves were fitted with guardrails on the inside of the turn, and an outside third rail was mounted on top of insulators affixed to extra-long cross-ties. A wooden guard was installed over the third rail following a style developed by the Wilkes-Barre & Hazelton Railway in Pennsylvania, an added safety feature to ensure against accidental electrocution.

Track and ballast were installed atop a poured concrete floor, a slab generously treated with waterproofing compounds of several varieties. Between each set of tracks, as well as along the tunnel's outside walls, rows of steel I beams were erected on 5-foot centers, providing a reserved corridor for each of the four tracks, and firm support for the roof beams. Tunnel sidewalls were finished off in concrete, and the stand of beams separating the two express tracks, on which trains would pass in opposite directions, was cemented to provide the additional safety of a "crash wall" in the event of an accident or derailment.

The construction project endured its share of tragedy. On January 27, 1902, 6 men were killed and 125 hurt in a dynamite explosion. A tunnel cave-in on the east side of Park Avenue between Thirty-seventh and Thirty-eighth streets caused such damage to nearby property owners that an exasperated August Belmont found it easier to buy out the entire block for a million dollars than to attempt to indemnify specific liabilities. Ten men died in another cave-in during the fall of 1903.

Progress, though slow, was steady, and New Yorkers never grew tired of hearing about their new subway. Rolling stock was of special interest to potential passengers. The Sunday supplements devoted endless copy to describing the cars that would soon roll along the underground railway.

The first two subway cars to arrive in New York were experimental vehicles built by the Wason Manufacturing Company of Springfield, Massachusetts, cars that would "be made the basis for letting the contract for fitting the subway with rolling stock," according to the *Springfield Republican*. The newspaper was anxiously looking ahead to local jobs that the New York subway was sure to produce in the New England city. One of the experimental cars was called the *August Belmont*, later designated No. 3340 in the Interborough numbering sequence, and the other was the *John B. McDonald*, listed on the roster as No. 3341. Although neither car would ever run in regular passenger service, they established design features not only for the earliest production-model subway cars but for subsequent Interborough car orders until 1925—more than 2,500 vehicles. Wason delivered the first batch of regular cars to the Interborough in the summer of 1903. Because it had leased the elevated lines, the company had a full-fledged test facility at its disposal. On September 14, 1903, a five-car train of new subway cars took a demonstration run over the Second and Third Avenue elevated lines. By late fall, more than 200 of the original order of 500 cars were delivered from Wason and three other manufacturers that were sharing the order. They were quickly pressed into service on the Second Avenue el to test their mettle through the harsh winter months.

These cars came to be called the "Composites" because they were built of both wood and steel. Frames and structural members were all made of steel, but car sides were of wood. Officials repeatedly called attention to the layers of asbestos and other materials that made the cars "virtually fireproof." Good-looking cars inside and out, their white ash exteriors were finished in a deep, rich, wine color. The sides of the cars were slightly tapered, making them narrower at the top than at the bottom. They measured 51 feet, 2 inches in overall length, 8 feet, 11⅞ inches wide at the windowsills, and just a fraction of an inch over 12 feet high. Each car was equipped with fifty-two seats made of attractive rattan. To allay the qualms of passengers unaccustomed to riding through the darkness of underground tunnels, officials never failed to emphasize that each car was illuminated by twenty-six electric light bulbs. Another feature often

Construction scenes on the Interborough. *Right:* The Dyckman Street station in upper Manhattan. Immediately below, the curving arch elevated structure is at Broadway and West 125th Street, where the subway emerged from its tunnel to vault across Manhattan Valley. Center below, the underground steelwork is for the local station at Broadway and West Fiftieth Street. At bottom, Chambers Street near the southern end of the Contract One line. [All photos Robert L. Presbrey collection]

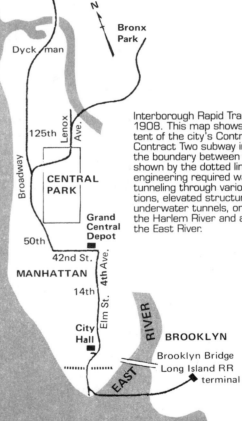

Interborough Rapid Transit Company, 1908. This map shows the full extent of the city's Contract One and Contract Two subway investments, the boundary between the two being shown by the dotted line. The civil engineering required was extensive: tunneling through various soil conditions, elevated structures, and two underwater tunnels, one beneath the Harlem River and another under the East River.

One of the Interborough's early experimental subway cars, the *John B. McDonald*. Although here identified as No. 2, the car was long carried on the Interborough roster as No. 3341. [NYCTA]

noted was a copper sheathing overlay that protected the lower reaches of the wooden car sides. A chief in the New York Fire Department, though, dismissed this as nothing but a coat of paint.

Following the design pioneered in Nos. 3340 and 3341, the Composites featured enclosed end platforms, or vestibules, and manually operated sliding doors. Actually No. 3341 had a trolley car–style folding door on one end, but it proved to be less desirable than the sliding variety and was never repeated. Something of an advance in the design of the Composites was the location of the motorman's station on the end platform, with the control apparatus protected by a full-length door when a given car was coupled into the middle of a train. Previously, as on the els' operating open platform cars, the cab had been squeezed inside the car behind the platform. To be certain the motorman's vision was not obstructed, admonitions were posted everywhere on the els: "Passengers Not Permitted to Ride on Front or Rear Platforms."

The city's original subway cars, the Interborough's Composites, were eventually banished to the elevated lines when it was felt their wooden car bodies represented a safety hazard in underground tunnels. The center door, and the fish-belly sill beneath it, were not part of car No. 2019 when it was new. [Author's collection]

One of the Interborough's early all-steel subway cars, the design developed by George Gibbs. Photograph of No. 3354 was taken at the Berwick, Pennsylvania, plant of its builder, the American Car and Foundry Company. A considerable amount of under-car electrical equipment had yet to be installed, and in later years the car's appearance would be significantly altered by the introduction of a midcar center door and a fish-belly center sill to compensate for the structural loss to the car body caused by the center door. [James E. Tebbetts collection]

FIRST ALL-STEEL SUBWAY CARS

The Interborough had toyed with another idea before signing the contract for the Composites in December 1902—an all-steel car. Electrical engineer George Gibbs, the resident genius on the Pennsylvania Railroad, was retained by Belmont to design such a vehicle. Gibbs later designed the Long Island Rail Road's first multiple-unit electric cars and almost all the electrical installations on the Pennsylvania itself. But car builders were reluctant to commit themselves to the idea. An all-steel passenger car had never been built before, and the industry was unwilling to experiment at a time when it had a heavy backlog of orders for conventional cars.

So the Composites were ordered to ensure that the new subway would have some rolling stock on opening day. But the Interborough refused to let the all-steel idea die. Thanks to Gibbs's good offices with the Pennsy, that line's Altoona Shops turned out No. 3342 and delivered it to the Interborough in February 1904, eight months before the subway opened. The car carries the distinction of being the first all-steel passenger car ever built.[3]

Officials needed to assure a wary public that there was no more danger of electrocution in a steel subway car than in a wooden one, and a fleet of 200 additional "Gibbs cars" was quickly ordered from the American Car and Foundry Co. Opening day saw 103 of them on the property, and the inaugural special that Mayor McClellan piloted was made up of the new all-steel rolling stock. With the exception of the original fleet of 500 Composites—which saw service only until 1916, when they were transferred to the elevated lines—wooden equipment was never again ordered for subway service in New York.

The Gibbs cars were basically like the composites. They featured the same enclosed end platforms, manually operated doors, and a convertible motorman's cab, but because of their all-metal construction, they lacked the interior warmth, not to say the luxury, that finished hardwoods gave to the Composites. They were powered by a pair of 200 HP motors, both mounted on one truck. The steel cars lacked, of course, the copper sheathing of the Composites, and they did not have tapered sides. Neither the original Gibbs cars nor the Composites were equipped with center passenger doors, a feature that became standard on the Interborough in later years. Consequently, these cars lacked the typical Interborough "fish-belly" side, which was necessary to give structural strength to a car whose side wall is cut out for a door. Because of the absence of a center door, eight sets of transverse seats were installed in the middle of the original subway cars. Expectedly, the all-steel Gibbs cars outweighed the Composites by 2 tons each. Both types were equal in length, although the Composites were a few inches wider. Performance statistics were impressive for the time. Both cars could attain a maximum speed of 45 mph. Electrical components were designed to permit a fully loaded train to accelerate at 1.25 mph per second on level track.

As opening day drew closer, interest in the subway gathered momentum. On January 1, 1904, Mayor McClellan took a group of VIPs on a handcar tour over the new line. Photographs taken of this trip have often been incorrectly captioned as the October 27 opening, and many journalists commented that the handcar operators, who were drafted from the ranks of subway construction workers, appeared unexpectedly dapper in the uniforms Belmont provided for the occasion. However, instead of using the term *construction workers*, newspapers usually identified the men simply as "Italians" and presumed readers knew who they were talking about. Such was the extent of ethnic consciousness in New York in 1904.

On April 15, Belmont and other officials toured the line behind a small steam engine rigged to burn oil instead of coal. On September 1, power was fed into the entire system from the Interborough's huge new Manhattan generating

New Year's Day 1904, a frigid day in New York, and a group of dignitaries are about to leave the City Hall station on a tour of the subway under construction, hauled by a handcar manned by subway construction workers. This photograph, often reproduced, has at times been incorrectly captioned as the subway inaugural on October 27, 1904. [NYCTA]

During the summer of 1904—straw hat season in New York—August Belmont took a group of VIPs on a tour of the subway and its associated elevated routes. The special was powered by a steam engine borrowed from the el lines, which is barely visible behind the second flatcar. Here the train pauses for a formal portrait at West 125th Street and Broadway. [NYCTA]

station at Eleventh Avenue and West Fifty-eighth Street, and Belmont led an official party on an inspection tour in a regular subway train. By September 6, as many as twenty trains were running simultaneously in the subway, testing the new line, and personnel were being instructed in equipment operation.

During construction, the Interborough repeatedly claimed the new line would travel from downtown Manhattan to Harlem in 15 minutes. Initial test runs were held to slow speeds until October 3, 1904, when a run was made from City Hall to Ninety-sixth Street, with 150 newsmen aboard, in 10 minutes, 45 seconds. The promise had been kept.

Fifty-four summers after Belmont's inspection tour shown in the photograph above, a northbound Broadway local drifts into the same station at West 125th Street. [Author]

R-21 unit No. 7243 leads a south-bound Broadway local into the station at 137th Street and Broadway in 1972, part of the original Contract One subway line that opened on October 27, 1904. Look closely at the station; the scourge of 1970-era graffiti is starting to appear! [Tom Nelligan]

A curious editorial in the *New York Times* on October 4, 1904, prior to opening day suggested that wooden cars would prove to be more popular with passengers than the steel ones. One reason stated was the clearly superior decor of the Composite cars; by contrast, the Gibbs cars were almost spartan. Another reason was perceived as safety. In the event of an accident, it was argued, rescue workers with axes could more easily gain access to a passenger trapped in a wooden car. A later disaster in Brooklyn proved, however, that the greater collision protection provided by steel equipment at the moment of impact is a much more important consideration.

As the inaugural drew near, many New Yorkers grew curious about rolling stock logistics. The Composites were providing almost all service on the Second Avenue el through the summer of 1904, but there was no physical track connection between the elevated line and the new subway. How would the cars get from the el into the tunnels? The solution: the cars were taken to the north end of Second Avenue, at the Harlem River, and placed aboard barges. They were then floated to the head of Lenox Avenue and run down a temporary ramp into the Lenox Avenue tunnel. Although this section of line did not open for regular service until November, track work had been installed, and the cars reached the City Hall–145th Street line via the Lenox Avenue branch.

After the gala opening, remaining segments of the original Contract One work were opened piece by piece. Service was extended to Bronx Park over the Lenox Avenue line and the Harlem River tunnel on November 26, 1904, and trains began to run to 242d Street and Broadway on August 1, 1908—a departure from original plans, which called for the northern terminal to be at Bailey Avenue adjacent to the Kingsbridge Station of the New York & Putnam Railroad. Service was extended down lower Broadway on the Contract Two phase of the project to South Ferry on July 10, 1905, and through the new East River tunnel to Brooklyn in January 1908. Trains reached Flatbush and Atlantic avenues by May that same year.[4]

4

COMPETITION FOR MR. BELMONT

THE SUBWAY RAN UP IMPRESSIVE STATISTICS DURING its first year of operation. A total of 106 million passengers rode the line at five cents a head. Brooklyn Bridge, expectedly, was the busiest station, recording some 18 million fares. Until the Interborough's Contract Two line down Broadway into the heart of the city's business district was opened in 1905, Brooklyn Bridge was the new subway's major station for all of downtown Manhattan. Furthermore, up a couple of flights of stairs from the Interborough's platforms at Brooklyn Bridge was a busy station where elevated trains from Brooklyn terminated after crossing the East River on the span, the only place where riders could conveniently switch from the Interborough subway to Brooklyn-bound el trains.

Uptown, the station at Times Square—quite unexpectedly—became very busy, the most popular local stop on the line, with 5 million fares paid during the subway's first year. A group of theater owners in the growing entertainment district unsuccessfully petitioned the Interborough less than a month after the line's opening to install crossover switches between local and express tracks near the station so express trains could also stop there. Belmont's concession was to have his conductors announce the stop as "Times Square" and not simply "Broadway and Forty-second Street."

A few problems emerged almost immediately. The Interborough was hit with an unpleasant strike of a week's duration during March 1905, the first of many work stoppages on the subway over the years. Effective ventilation of the stations was perceived to be a minor but continuing problem, especially during warm weather. Advertising posters on the station walls annoyed many sensitive New Yorkers who appreciated the finely executed mosaic work of the underground railway stops. Some even tried to imply that the bad air, such as it was, was actually caused by the presence of the advertisements.

On Joralemon Street in Brooklyn near the East River is a row house that looks a little different from others on the block. It has no windows, for instance, just heavy shutters. In actuality, it isn't a house at all but a cleverly outrigged air shaft for the Interborough's East River tunnel, which passes directly underneath. [Author]

Few issues in New York fail to admit of conflicting opinions, though. The advertising franchise for the Interborough stations was held by Artemas Ward, a great-grandson of General Artemas Ward, the Revolutionary War commander at Dorchester Heights. Defending the concept of subway advertising—and Ward too—in a speech before the Spinx Club in New York in early 1905 when the debate was raging, one Max Wineburgh delivered the following rebuke to the ad critics: "The worthy and eminently respectable gentlemen who are making all this outcry are simply out of touch with the times. The masses who struggle for existence, who produce the money upon which their leisurely critics live, get much of their information about what is going on in the business world through reading the signs arranged for their entertainment upon the walls of the subway."

There was a problem with loading and unloading the subway trains, especially during busy rush hours: the process took too much time. Eventually an additional set of doors in the center of the cars that were remotely controlled and electrically operated were cut into Interborough rolling stock. In later years, cars were designed and built with such doors, and eventually all passenger entry doors, center car as well as vestibule, were operated by remote control.[1] But when the subway opened in 1904, everything was manually operated and a separate conductor, or guard, was stationed between every two cars to open and close the doors manually and oversee the entry and exit of passengers. Once the doors were remotely controlled, fewer conductors were used on Interborough trains. Interestingly, in 1905, when the whole problem of remotely controlled doors was under discussion, one highly respected scientific journal examined the problem in detail and announced that it was totally impossible.

The local station at East Sixty-sixth Street and Broadway on the Interborough's Contract One line. Advertising posters proclaim the value of particular brands of ale and laxative; a machine is available to dispense chewing gum in several flavors; the clock on the wall says it's eight minutes before twelve; and a uniformed guard mans a "chopper box," a receptacle in which passengers deposit their pasteboard tickets. The guard also has the requisite lanterns at the ready to signal trains in the event of an emergency. [NYCTA]

When the extension down lower Broadway was opened as far as South Ferry in July 1905, the Interborough was able to improve its terminal procedures at the southern end of the line. The South Ferry station was built on a turnaround loop, which allowed inbound trains to be dispatched back uptown with greater flexibility. The South Ferry loop, however, was an engineering horror to construct. It came to within a few feet, literally, of Manhattan Island's shoreline, so that pumps ran continuously to keep the waters of Upper New York Bay out of the works. To add to the woe, the entire complex was directly under a large and busy elevated terminal, which had to be carefully shored up.

The new subway tunnel under the East River ran 1.2 miles from the Battery to the foot of Joralemon Street in Brooklyn. At midpoint, it was 95 feet below mean high water and 40 feet below the silty river bottom. Trains had to descend and then climb a maximum grade of 3.1 percent, a stiff one by railroad standards but no great effort for a multiple-unit electric train. The tunnel was the first long tube to carry any kind of regular passenger vehicles beneath tidewater in New York.

The city's first major river tunnel of any kind was the Ravenswood Gas Company's 8-foot-high tunnel under the East River between Long Island City and Manhattan, completed in 1894 as a conduit for gas mains. It was largely chiseled out of solid rock, while the subway crossing used the shield method of tunneling. The shield method involves a huge circular cutting bore through the soft material under the river and then lining the tunnel with iron rings from the inside. The entire operation must be carried out under a pressurized atmosphere. While the subway tunnel was being built, three eminent engineers made public a state-

When the Contract Two line was built down lower Broadway, less ornate kiosks were specified, such as these at Broadway and Rector Street, which provide access to the Wall Street station. This view was taken in 1906. [NYCTA]

ment warning that the tunnel would collapse like a deflated balloon when it was completed and depressurized. It hasn't yet, although one tale from the tunnel's building remains amazing to this day. In 1905, while the bore was under construction, a weak spot developed in the roof. Since the works were pressurized, the weak spot became not a cave-in but a blowout. One of the sandhogs working in the tunnel was sucked up by the developing cyclone and propelled through mud and water to the surface of the East River. He survived and was hale and hearty—but scared and wet—when pulled aboard a passing tugboat.

Had fortune been kinder to an earlier venture, a Hudson River tunnel might have been the city's first major underwater tube. A group headed by a man named Dewitt Clinton Haskin began work on a Jersey City to Morton Street (Manhattan) tunnel in 1874, but after a serious accident, the half-finished bore was abandoned and remained thus for over a decade. Eventually the tunnel was completed. It became part of William Gibbs McAdoo's Hudson & Manhattan Railroad and opened for passenger service in late February 1908, a few weeks after the Interborough's East River crossing was placed in service.[2] In another early effort, a trolley car tunnel was built under the East River between Manhattan and Queens in 1907, but, for reasons to be discussed in chapter 6, it did not open for passenger service until 1915 and then not as a trolley car tunnel. The Interborough's own Harlem River tunnel opened in 1904. It was considerably shorter than the East River crossing and was built in a shipyard and lowered into place— no minor engineering feat, but not of a sort to challenge the designation of the Joralemon Street tunnel as the city's first *major* underwater link.

SUCCESS BREEDS COMPETITORS

The success of the Manhattan-Bronx subway prompted talk of more lines. Groups and syndicates were rumored to be seeking financial support for all manner of new routes. As a matter of course, the Interborough continued to profess its own interest in handling future construction and operation, taking great pains to point out that the original line was a compromise on the city's real subway needs—a compromise dictated by the city's rigid debt ceiling, which restricted the amount of construction bonds that could be issued. If the audience was appropriate, Belmont did not hesitate to speak of what he called the city's "moral obligation" to award future construction and operation rights to the Interborough and the Interborough alone.

Belmont gave priority to a spur up Lexington Avenue from the Grand Central area and to additional construction along the lower West Side, especially after it became known that the Pennsylvania Railroad would build its huge New York terminal on Seventh Avenue at West Thirty-third Street. And the Interborough could well hanker after more subways, for in 1905 it appeared to be a truth beyond question that operating rapid transit in New York was a very lucrative business.

Finally, in 1905, one group did present a serious challenge to the Belmont interests for construction and operation rights to future lines. The Metropolitan Street Railway had managed in the years prior to 1900 to gain control of almost all surface car lines in Manhattan and a goodly number in the Bronx, too, either directly or through its parent corporation, Metropolitan Security. The only large surface operation to elude its grasp prior to 1900 was the Third Avenue Railroad. When that system went into receivership in 1900, it too was taken into the Metropolitan family. So, in 1905, the Metropolitan moved to get for itself the additional subway lines the city unquestionably would soon build.

The Rapid Transit Commission looked favorably upon the Metropolitan's proposals, principally because there was growing uneasiness with Belmont's de facto monopoly of Manhattan rapid transit. Both corporations soon presented roughly similar plans for additional subway lines. The Interborough was able to propose an expansion and extension of its original line, while the Metropolitan had to build a brand new system from scratch. Another difference was that the Metropolitan was reconciled to having the Interborough as a competitor. Belmont was not amenable to grant a similar concession.

That March, when details of the two rival plans became known, the press took sides. Some newspapers favored allowing Belmont to continue as the city's sole subway entrepreneur; others thought competition from the Metropolitan would benefit the city, its citizens, and the Interborough in the long run. From still other quarters came a different cry: municipal operation. The subways are an essential public service, like fire and police protection, it was argued; private interests should not be allowed to profit from them and, more important, should not be making important decisions about public needs with their eye primarily on the balance sheet.

Perhaps the person who championed this last position with more verve—
and more vinegar—than anyone else was a man who challenged George
McClellan for mayor in 1905 and came within an unexpected whisker of beating
him. He was a native Californian who had served in the U.S. Congress for a
time, ran for public office on several other occasions, published newspapers
that drove elected officials, from aldermen to presidents, to distraction, and
is perhaps best known through a fictional presentation Orson Welles created
in 1940 based on his life and called *Citizen Kane*. He was William Randolph
Hearst, a man whose 1905 mayoral candidacy was under the banner not of a
conventional political party but of something called the Municipal Ownership
League.

Hearst's position on municipal ownership was too radical for New York in
the first decade of the twentieth century, and instead less threatening proposals
were given consideration, proposals that continued to rely on private corporations to run subway trains in a profit-loss situation through tunnels they leased
from the municipal government. It was in this context that another potential
Belmont challenger emerged in April 1905.

The Brooklyn Rapid Transit Company (BRT) submitted a proposal to the Rapid
Transit Commission outlining a network of new routes that called for much
greater penetration of Manhattan from Brooklyn. The BRT operated both elevated trains and streetcars in Brooklyn and had been an unsuccessful bidder for
the Contract Two lines in 1902. (The genesis of the BRT will be examined in
more detail in chapter 5.) It suggested it was quite prepared to bid for the rights
to construct and operate the new routes it was recommending, and the
commission reported favorably on almost all of the company's suggestions and
agreed to include them in its own master plan for transit expansion. Even more
threatening to Belmont than the commission's acceptance of the BRT proposals
were the strong rumors around New York that the Brooklyn company and the
Metropolitan were on the verge of developing an alliance.

Some saw the commission's action as a body blow to the Interborough. Belmont's chief argument in his head-to-head battle with the Metropolitan for new
construction rights was that his was the only system that would and could offer
through service from the Bronx to Brooklyn. The Interborough already had one
line into Brooklyn under construction—it would open in 1908 (see map in
chapter 3)—and its expansion plans included additional mileage in Brooklyn.

Right: No. 3815 is a typical Interborough
subway car. Built by Standard Steel Car
Company in 1910, this unit was still hauling
passengers under the sidewalks of New York
forty-five years later. [Author's collection]

The Metropolitan had no desire to build into Brooklyn and presented as its trump card transfer privileges between its new subways and its existing network of street lines. Belmont thought he had the leverage he needed when he threatened not to operate any lines in Brooklyn unless the Interborough got exclusive rights in Manhattan. But the BRT's rumored consortium with the Metropolitan, coupled with the decision of the Rapid Transit Commission, dulled Belmont's bargaining edge in his efforts to stop the Metropolitan.

In mid-December, trading in both Interborough and Metropolitan stocks assumed irregular patterns, a reaction to rumors of high-level negotiations. Then on Friday, December 22, 1905, Belmont issued a simple, factual announcement. He had purchased the Metropolitan—lock, stock, and streetcars. As he had three years earlier with the lease of the elevated lines of the Manhattan Railway, Belmont demonstrated himself to be as resourceful as he was rich. He responded to challenge with a classic maneuver; he crushed the upstarts, emerging from combat without a scratch. Of note was a rumor, circulated earlier, that the BRT had been involved in the Wall Street dealings. Yet the Brooklyn firm was not a party to the final agreement and retained its autonomy, a matter that would later prove to be most important.

Belmont's bold stroke gave the advocates of municipal operation added fuel, and they began to speak out more strongly against private operation of the city subways. Hearst, perhaps the most vociferous foe of private operation, went so far as to petition the New York State attorney general to file suit to block the Interborough-Metropolitan merger. But Attorney General Mayer refused to bring action against Belmont, ruling that existing antimonopoly statutes were inapplicable to rapid transit firms. Belmont, on the other hand, expected no serious problems to arise from the merger: "There need be no public anxiety occasioned by the adjustment of transportation matters in New York City," he said.

Left and below: An interesting design variation among the Interborough's early rolling stock was a fleet of fifty cars, Nos. 3650–3699, built by American Car and Foundry in 1907 and 1908. These units featured a raised deck roof, much as contemporary trolley cars. In the photo at left, the car is still equipped with the early manual couplers that the Interborough quickly replaced with a newer automatic model. [Left: Brown Bros.; below: Author's collection]

SOUND AND FURY

August Belmont had firm views on the question of private versus municipal subway operation. Speaking before the Chicago Real Estate Board in January 1905, he proclaimed, "If associated with municipal ownership there is municipal operation of these properties, then I think the justifiable line of municipal activity has been overstepped."

Among Belmont's staunchest supporters was the *New York Times*. It continually backed the concept of private subway operation, even suggesting that the truest test of the real need for any proposed subway route was the "reasonable certainty of profit" by a private operator. The advocates of total municipal operation, spearheaded by the Hearst organization, made the counterargument that only subway construction in advance of actual need would be able to spur the development of outlying areas, adding needed valuation to the city's real estate tax rolls and allowing municipal growth to take place in an orderly and planned fashion. Growth rate figures of the Bronx after the original subway opened were often cited by municipal operation advocates. In presubway 1903, $6.5 million in building construction was begun in the borough. In 1905, construction had ballooned to $38 million, with the bulk of the increase credited to the presence of the subway.

In 1906, all arguments on private and municipal operation became largely academic. The Interborough-Metropolitan merger was consummated on March 6, 1906. Later that year, the state legislature enacted something called the Elsberg bill.

The original subway was *owned* by the city and *leased* to a private operator under a long-term agreement: the Interborough, which held a fifty-year lease for the Contract One lines and a thirty-five-year agreement on the Contract Two segment. The leases stipulated that the Interborough was to finance its own rolling stock. Both leases contained identical twenty-five-year renewal options. The Elsberg bill, named for a state senator from the Fifteenth District of New York City who was a strong municipal operation advocate, greatly shortened the length of lease the city could sign with private operators. The maximum term under the new law was twenty years, with a single twenty-year renewal option. Economically the new measure meant that any equipment investment would have to be amortized over a shorter term than before; thus, profits would be reduced by the expense of meeting payments on equipment bonds.

Belmont was quick to denounce the new law, saying it was designed to force municipal ownership and operation. The Rapid Transit Commission also stood adamantly and unanimously against it, but for a different reason. Instead of leading inevitably to municipal operation, the commission reasoned, the short-term leases meant that only the city's existing subway operator could afford to bid on new lines. The Interborough could risk the short-term lease because it already owned power houses, repair shops, and storage yards. George L. Rives, counsel for the commission, said: "It is manifest that under such provisions the city would get only such future subways as the Interborough Rapid Transit Company sees fit to build."

In the end, the Elsberg bill resulted in neither municipal ownership nor any new Interborough routes. Belmont continued to express interest in new lines, but the restrictive features of the Elsberg legislation, coupled with unfavorable economic conditions brought on by the panic of 1907, effectively discouraged any firm commitments by Belmont or anyone else. Total municipal operation was ruled out on practical grounds by the city's rigid debt limit and on theoretical grounds because public opinion was not yet ready to accept it.

Out of the Elsberg dilemma eventually emerged a highly detailed proposal for new rapid transit construction—the Dual Contracts, or Dual System—that would account for the building of the major portion of today's subway network. The Dual Contracts were signed in March 1913, seven years after the passage of the Elsberg bill and eight and one-half years after Mayor McClellan notched out the silver controller on the city's first subway.

The Dual Contracts were negotiated over a period of years and involved all the complexity, intricacy, and diplomacy of a major treaty between nations. The New York State Constitution had to be amended, legislation had to be passed, old regulatory agencies abolished, and new ones created. After the contracts were drawn up, two private transit companies and several arms of government had to adjudge them to be in their own best interests. Furthermore, the advocates of total municipal operation either had to be won over to the Dual Contracts idea or be politically outflanked in some other way. Court tests were complex and involved; at many stages, the Dual Subway System seemed destined to become just one more good idea that would never become a functioning reality. But the contracts were completed, thanks principally to the long and patient work of such people as William R. Wilcox, who headed up the state Public Service Commission (PSC) during most of the Dual Contracts talks, and former mayor Seth Low, who is credited with rescuing the negotiations on numerous occasions. Both William J. Gaynor and John Purroy Mitchel, the mayors who followed McClellan in City Hall, were active in their support of the evolving plan. But if any one man can be called the prime mover behind the Dual Contracts idea, it was Wilcox. He began the six years of talks when it became clear that the city's debt limit clearly ruled out large-scale municipal subway construction and operation, and the Elsberg law prevented the construction of new lines for private operation to meet the city's needs. George McAneny, Manhattan Borough president, was a key participant, as was Alfred Craven, chief engineer of the PSC, whose expertise on technological matters helped resolve many problems during the talks.

Oddly enough, Craven was dead set against subways of any sort some years earlier. Except it wasn't *this* Alfred Craven; it was his uncle, Alfred W. Craven, who served as the chief engineer of New York's Croton Aqueduct Board. When steam-powered subways were under discussion in the waning years of the nineteenth century, Craven-the-aqueduct-man objected to the very notion for fear

Action in the Interborough's shops. In the top view, rows of cars are undergoing repairs. The bottom photograph shows how a basic component such as a motor truck can be removed from a car for maintenance. The car itself can be reequipped with a substitute truck and returned to service. [NYCTA]

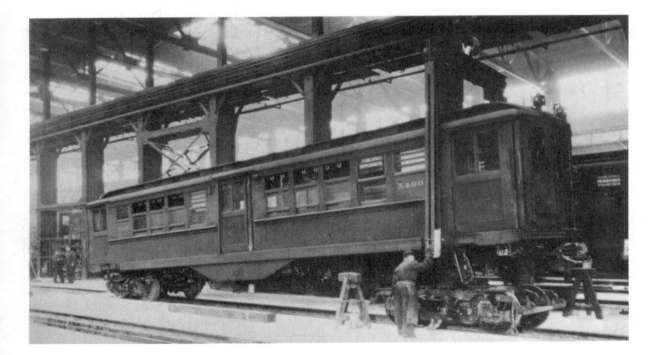

that the city's water supply system would be adversely affected. The younger Craven was appointed chief engineer of the PSC in 1910. Earlier he had been a division engineer on the staff of the Rapid Transit Commission, and it was he who was in charge of supervising construction of the Contract One line from East Forty-first Street and Park Avenue north to Broadway and West 104th Street, a segment that included the tricky passage "through" the *New York Times* building at West Forty-second Street and Broadway. As the massive Dual Contract project began to gear up in 1913, Alfred Craven, the son of a Civil War admiral and born in 1846, became the chief engineer in charge of the whole darn works.

Throughout the years when the Dual Contract negotiations were proceeding, other history-shaping events kept right on happening. Claiming he got there first, on April 6, 1906, Admiral Robert Peary "discovered" the North Pole. In 1911 a gentleman by the name of C. P. Rogers made the first transcontinental airplane flight. It was definitely *not* of the nonstop variety and took six weeks longer than if he had gone by train. In 1912, remains of a 50,000-year-old "Piltdown Man" were discovered in England, and scholars expounded at length and

A derby-hatted spectator observes activity in the Interborough repair shops in the early years. It is likely that the cars shown here are being outfitted with new automatic couplers, replacing the original Van Dorn models. [Brown Bros.]

with much profundity on the significance of it. (After World War II, "Piltdown Man" was proved to be a big hoax.) The New York Giants dominated the National League, and it is likely, if not a certainty, that officials struggling with technical matters in their subway negotiations from time to time called it a day after lunch and headed up to the Polo Grounds on the Ninth Avenue el to cheer on the home team. (Christy Matthewson never failed to win twenty games during the years the talks and negotiations were under way, and in 1908 he won thirty-seven, his career high. But that was also the year Chicago's Ed Walsh won forty-one games, the most ever by a pitcher in modern baseball.) In 1912, the *Titanic* sailed and sank. Through it all, subway plans continued to develop in New York.

Left: One of the original Gibbs cars has survived! Here is No. 3352 at rest on a storage track at the Seashore Trolley Museum in Kennebunkport, Maine, idle after a half-century of service.

Right: Owner James E. Tebbetts works at restoring No. 3352 to like-new condition. The center door and fish-belly sill have been removed, and except for the trolley pole—necessary for operation on Seashore trackage—the veteran is starting to resemble its 1904 appearance. (Both, R.T. Lane photos from James E. Tebbetts collection)

5

THE BRT, THE TRIBOROUGH SYSTEM, AND THE END OF INTERBOROUGH DOMINANCE

ONE OF THE DUAL CONTRACTS TRACTION operators was, naturally, the Interborough. August Belmont relinquished the line's presidency in 1907 to become chairman. (He would die in 1924 at the age of 71.) The company was then run by Theodore P. Shonts, a distinguished-looking gentleman who wore pince-nez glasses and sported a fine white moustache. Shonts was a longtime railroad man who came to the Interborough in 1907 after a stint as chairman of the Isthmian Canal Commission, the group responsible for building the Panama Canal. Before Shonts could be freed from his Central American assignment to take over the Interborough, though, the personal approval of President Theodore Roosevelt was required. Another important individual who spent many years on the Interborough Rapid Transit System in its early period was Frank Hedley. He joined the company in 1903 and advanced through just about every important post on the line. Indeed, it was Hedley who succeeded Shonts as president in 1919.[1]

As mentioned earlier, the other traction company to sign the Dual Contracts—the firm that was able to convince the city government and the Interborough too that more than one firm should run subway trains in New York—was the Brooklyn-based BRT. Chartered in 1896, the BRT was a complex union of many previously independent transport entities—as many as sixty separate horsecar, cable railway, trolley, elevated, and even short-haul steam railroad companies. Its operating territory was the western end of Long Island—today the boroughs of Brooklyn and Queens—and the many different companies and lines were gradually amalgamated and merged, with senselessly competitive routings eliminated. The early Interborough always operated in comparatively built-up urban areas, but the territory in which the BRT germinated included the densely populated sections of downtown Brooklyn, suburban residential areas such as Ridgewood and Flatbush, the rural precincts of Canarsie, and oceanfront resort communities in Brighton Beach and Coney Island.

Basically, the BRT ran two different kinds of transit operation: elevated lines and streetcars. The els, originally steam powered but converted to electricity at the turn of the century, funneled from outlying districts into two different sections, each of which can be called "downtown" in its own fashion. One, the area near Brooklyn's Borough Hall and the approach to the Brooklyn Bridge, was the "original Brooklyn," a city that grew and expanded over the years. The other "downtown" was once a city in its own right, the City of Williamsburgh,

A three-car train of open platform el cars curves gently from the BRT's Lexington Avenue line onto the three-track Broadway line. Both avenues—Lexington and Broadway—are names of thoroughfares in Brooklyn and Manhattan. This is Brooklyn! [NYCTA]

Interior view at the Park Row terminal where Brooklyn el trains terminated in Manhattan after crossing the Brooklyn Bridge. [Author's collection]

but lost its separate status in 1854 when it was amalgamated with the City of Brooklyn. (It also lost its terminal "h" at the turn of the century and has since been rendered "Williamsburg.") Each of these two downtown areas was also an important gateway to New York City, which is to say Manhattan, first by ferry-boat and later by bridge. People so destined became important customers for BRT streetcars and el trains.

In outlying districts, BRT "elevated" trains often ran on ground-level right-of-way much like a conventional railroad. Sometimes they even rolled onto Brooklyn streets and trundled alongside ordinary traffic, as streetcars did. Trains

Riders on the els sat on rattan-upholstered seats [left] and were kept informed about routings and destinations from metal plate destination signs [right]. [NYCTA]

Borough Hall, Brooklyn, in the days when the Fulton Street el rumbled overhead. The Manhattan els are certainly better known than those of Brooklyn, but the BRT and its predecessors operated an extensive network of such lines. Many were upgraded and became extensions of the Dual Contract subway network after 1913. [Author's collection]

drew electricity from a third rail while on the el structure but usually switched to an overhead trolley wire as a safety precaution when they descended to the surface. BRT el cars were also equipped with steps to use at suburban stations that lacked high-level platforms, not to mention mere street corners that were little more than trolley car stops.

The BRT reached into the Borough Hall section of Brooklyn with major trunk lines along Myrtle Avenue and Fulton Street. Feeder branch lines from these two els continued on out to places like Ridgewood and Coney Island. The twin downtown terminals for these several services were at the foot of Fulton Street, where passengers could transfer to a ferryboat that crossed the East River to the foot of a Fulton Street in Manhattan, and the large Sands Street Terminal, where one transferred to the cable cars that ran across the Brooklyn Bridge. The ferry, immortalized in Walt Whitman's poem "On Crossing Brooklyn Ferry," was pretty well doomed when the Brooklyn Bridge opened in 1883, although it hung on until 1924.[2] Once the els were electrified, it was reasonable to discontinue the bridge cable cars, electrify that trackage too, and run BRT el trains over the river to the Manhattan side—all of which happened in 1898. But this line was, of course, the BRT's first rapid transit landfall on Manhattan Island.[3]

The el that served Brooklyn's other "downtown" ran along Broadway—Brooklyn's Broadway, not Manhattan's more famous thoroughfare of the same name—from the East New York and Bushwick sections and terminated at a large ferry terminal that provided waterborne transfer service to many points on the Manhattan side. There were inland connections between the Broadway line and both the Myrtle Avenue and Fulton Street lines, and the Broadway el was a major conduit to and from Manhattan for people who lived in places like Bushwick, Ridgewood, and even farther out on Long Island. For that matter, long before the el reached the ferry terminal in 1889, a predecessor company of the Long

Motormen aboard open platform el trains worked from a cab back inside the car body, sometimes creating an impression that the trains were running themselves. Open platform trolley cars of the same era placed their motormen right out on the open platform with no protection from wind, cold, or driving rain. This is a 1955 view on Brooklyn's Myrtle Avenue line. Lead car No. 1334 was built in 1905–1906, a year or so after the Interborough's Contract One line carried its first passenger. [Author]

Island Rail Road, the South Shore Railroad, operated its trains to the foot of Broadway over city streets.[4]

As happened with the Fulton Street ferry that operated across the East River in the shadow of the Brooklyn Bridge, so did the opening of the Williamsburg Bridge in 1903 spell the end of the ferryboats that steamed out of the terminal at the foot of Broadway. The BRT would also route its Broadway-Brooklyn el trains over the Williamsburg Bridge into Manhattan (discussed shortly). The Williamsburg ferry company abandoned all service in 1908, and although three routes were temporarily revived under municipal auspices for various periods of time, the opening of the bridge in 1903 was the beginning of the end for the old double-ended steamers.

By 1910, the BRT had become a stable and prosperous operation. It had rebuilt and standardized its fleet of hand-me-down el cars and supplemented them with new equipment. Its car barns were tastefully decorated with whitewashed rock gardens that drew praise from the trade press—"this is how a railway should be managed." Its stock was the kind of issue conservative bankers and rich widows looked to with supreme confidence, although early in its history, the company was anything but highly regarded on Wall Street. In the teeth of the panic of 1907, the BRT had the financial muscle to float $60 million in bonds to underwrite capital improvements.

Despite the Elsberg law, some limited subway construction was begun after 1906 and prior to the Dual Contracts. A loop line linking the Manhattan terminals of the three East River bridges—the Williamsburg, the Manhattan, and the Brooklyn—was one such project. As early as September 1906, the Rapid Transit Commission was considering two proposals, one a subway and the other an el on the Manhattan portion of the route. The BRT lacked experience in subway operation and owned no genuine subway equipment. Since its Broadway el was already projected to run over the Williamsburg Bridge, through the loop, and back over the Brooklyn Bridge, the BRT recommended an el. Brooklyn residents, anxious to obtain rapid transit service into Manhattan, were impressed by the fact an el could be built more quickly than a subway. But the city government had the last word, and it wanted a subway. Thus, on September 16, 1908, the BRT reluctantly started running Broadway elevated trains from East New York and Canarsie across the Williamsburg Bridge and into a terminal at Delancey Street, a bona fide subway station. Once again Mayor McClellan handled the controls as the first official train left the underground Manhattan terminal at 9:55 A.M. In celebration of the event, bands played, firecrackers exploded, and orators decried the sorry state of New York subway expansion. The BRT had joined the Interborough in the subway business on Manhattan Island after a fashion, although in fact it was the *third* company to operate underground rapid transit into Manhattan. The Hudson Tubes had been running trains between Hoboken, New Jersey, and Manhattan since February 25, 1908.

The BRT's connection over the Williamsburg Bridge to Delancey Street was hardly a major accomplishment. Some purists would even argue that the BRT never really became a subway operator until it extended this line inland some years later. But it was the third transit line to cross the East River and link Brooklyn with Manhattan, and in due time it became a route of major importance. In 1908, however, it left "its passengers from Brooklyn at a point in Manhattan where almost nobody wishes to go," to quote the caustic words of a newspaper reporter.

Construction of the loop line continued at a sluggish pace so that not until August 1913, five months after the Dual Contracts were signed, had service been extended slightly over a mile to a new station under the Municipal Building near the Brooklyn Bridge. Even in 1913 the BRT had no steel subway cars and continued to use wooden elevated equipment in the Centre Street loop subway, much to the company's embarrassment.

A JOLT FOR MISTER B.

The BRT's real coup in the years before the Dual Contracts came when it was awarded operating rights for the Fourth Avenue subway in Brooklyn. As long as subways were discussed in New York, a line out to Bay Ridge seemed inevitable.

The obvious move would then be to tunnel under the Narrows and link Staten Island with the rest of the city. In October 1909, the Board of Estimate approved construction of the Bay Ridge segment of this route with an appropriation of $15.8 million, after a complex court action had determined that the city's debt ceiling was somewhat higher than previously thought. (The debt limit was, essentially, a percentage of the city's taxable real estate valuation, and the court ruled that a more liberal formula could be used in calculating a precise figure.) The Interborough appeared to be solidly entrenched for operational rights over the new line. After all, wasn't its Brooklyn line already a proved success? Interborough officials were understandably jolted when the BRT won the contract.

At an early stage of its construction, Brooklyn's Fourth Avenue subway was combined into a master plan called the Triborough Subway System. In 1907 a new state agency was created, the Public Service Commission, to assume jurisdiction over city subway matters from the 1894 Rapid Transit Commission, and the Triborough Subway System was a product of this new agency. Since construction was to take place under the limitations of both the Elsberg law and the city's debt ceiling, it was not the kind of robust and complete subway system most observers felt was needed. Basically, the Triborough System called for a north-south trunk line subway in Manhattan from South Ferry to the Harlem River that would run under Church Street, Broadway, Irving Place, and Lexington Avenue. This line would be fed in the Bronx by two new elevated branches, one into the Pelham Bay area and the other along Jerome Avenue. The Triborough Subway System would also have a crosstown line in downtown Manhattan under Canal Street from the Hudson River to the Bowery and then over the new Manhattan Bridge to Brooklyn, where it would join up with the abuilding Fourth Avenue subway there. This Fourth Avenue line would also be extended over two branches: by tunnel to Eighty-sixth Street in Bay Ridge and over an elevated line to Coney Island. Finally, there would be a large loop route in Brooklyn connecting the Williamsburg Bridge and the Centre Street line in Manhattan, where BRT el trains were already running, with the Fourth Avenue subway. This line would run under Lafayette Street and Broadway in Brooklyn.[5]

The Public Service Commission did not necessarily intend to exclude the Interborough from consideration as an operator of any portion of the new network, although the BRT had already been assured of the Fourth Avenue line in Brooklyn and, presumably, the Manhattan Bridge crossing into the Canal Street crosstown line. However, it was clear that there was no intention to link up the Triborough System with the city's original subway either. (The latter, incidentally, was generally referred to as the Elm Street subway in the days when the Triborough's proposed Broadway–Lexington Avenue alignment was in the news.)

Although construction had begun on several sections of the Triborough Subway System, before it was even close to being completed, it was absorbed into the far more comprehensive Dual System. Two interesting features of the Triborough proposal are worthy of attention because they greatly influence New York subway operations to this day.

First, the line across the East River into Brooklyn was to be over the new

Manhattan Bridge. This span had been proposed (and built) even before the Triborough concept emerged, at which time the BRT stated that it could connect the Brooklyn end of this bridge with its existing elevated network, an idea patterned after operations across the Brooklyn and Williamsburg bridges. Specifications were drawn up for a massive four-track el structure down Flatbush Avenue Extension to the Brooklyn end of the new bridge that would link up with both the Myrtle Avenue and the Fulton Street lines. But city fathers wanted no old-fashioned els for their new span. Thus, the Public Service Commission turned down the bid, proclaiming that Flatbush Avenue Extension was to be "a fine avenue, which the construction of the [elevated] railroad would frustrate." The timing was perfect. The developing Triborough plan was adapted so its subway tunnels could bring trains onto the new bridge from a connection with the new Fourth Avenue line. The importance of this decision may be more aesthetic than anything else. Had BRT el trains been connected to the Manhattan Bridge, they would have been abandoned by now, no doubt, and the span turned into a vehicles-only river crossing. But by hooking up with the subway network, rapid transit continues across the Manhattan Bridge, albeit at the price of extensive maintenance activity and much slower speed than a tunnel would have permitted. But the vista of Manhattan provided from the trains is priceless.

The second hand-me-down from the Triborough System was the tunnel dimensions specified for the rail network. Trains would run on standard gauge railroad track as on the Interborough—4 feet, 8½ inches between rails—but tunnels were to be built higher, wider, and with broader curves to allow suburban-type equipment from standard railroads to connect with the subway. Standard railroad cars could not squeeze into the more restrictive confines of the city's original subway. The Triborough decision was reached partly on the strength of the operational flexibility it would permit: through service someday between the city and the suburbs, it was hoped. The key reasons were economic and political, though. The Public Service Commission, which ultimately chose the larger tunnels, hoped to persuade a conventional railroad company to take over the entire operating responsibility for the new system, an intention it spelled out clearly in a letter to the city's Board of Estimate in January 1908.

The commission's hopes were never realized, and adopting "big railroad" dimensions for the Triborough System served only to create a second set of specifications for the New York subway that to this day prevents total interchangeability among lines. No railroad company became a serious contender for operating rights of the Triborough System, or even the later Dual Contracts, and no through city-suburban service ever developed. Oddly enough, the two places in New York where civil construction work was partially undertaken and where, if completed, might have led to joint subway-railroad operations involved the smaller Interborough system. (Interborough-sized cars could have operated over any standard gauge railroad, assuming electrical compatibility, raising further questions about the Public Service Commission's motives. Indeed, the Long Island Rail Road's initial fleet of electric multiple-unit cars, designed by George Gibbs, were nearly identical to the first fleet of steel cars on the city's oldest subway system, cars also designed by Gibbs.)

As to the two points where railroad-subway connections were envisioned, one is Grand Central Terminal, where tunnels on the lower level of that vast facility are but a knock-away wall removed from the Contract One Interborough line, and the other is the Long Island's depot at Flatbush and Atlantic avenues in Brooklyn. To this day, one can trace an alignment that leads onto the IRT's Brooklyn line from the bumper posts of the railroad terminal, and supposedly such a physical connection actually existed at one time, although there was never regular passenger service between the systems.[6]

Many eminent transit professionals took a dim view of this adoption of a second set of subway specifications in New York, granted that the larger dimension system, other things being equal, could carry more passengers per hour than the smaller. Among such critics was Frank Sprague, of multiple-unit fame. On October 17, 1910, he delivered a paper to the American Institute of Electrical Engineers in which he harshly criticized the Triborough plan, foreseeing that it would rule out integration of the new lines with the old 1904 subway.

The BRT's victory in clinching operating rights for the Fourth Avenue line was a choker for the Interborough. Once the Brooklyn company crossed the East River over the Manhattan Bridge, it would have additional access to Manhattan Island, territory the Interborough strongly felt was its private turf. And the BRT was destined to win again. In the midst of the Dual Contract discussions, it was suggested that the BRT's Fourth Avenue line should not only cross the East River and serve downtown Manhattan, as conceived in the earlier Triborough scheme, but also turn north and tunnel north up Broadway to the Times Square area, eventually to operate into Queens via another East River crossing. At this, the Interborough threatened to break off all negotiations. The older company by then had grudgingly conceded the BRT its toehold in downtown Manhattan, but giving the proposed Broadway line to the newcomer would be too painful an intrusion into Interborough country.

Nevertheless, the days when an all-powerful August Belmont could call every shot were over. City representatives responded to the Interborough break-off threat by blandly asking the BRT if it would be willing to assume operation of *all* the subway lines then up for consideration, including such obvious Interborough links as the upper Lexington Avenue spur. When the Brooklyn company responded "Yes!" the Interborough swallowed hard and gave in to the idea of mid-Manhattan competition.

(Subway explorers can find interesting evidence of the way these decisions progressed in the vicinity of today's Canal Street station on the BMT. The Broadway line begins at the southern tip of Manhattan Island as a two-track line out of the Montague Street tunnel from Brooklyn. It twists its way to the huge City Hall station and here becomes a four-track line—two local and two express—and continues north up Broadway, a line that was conceived as part of the Triborough System. But the two express tracks come to a halt at the north end of the Canal Street station, only one stop after City Hall. This obvious last-minute change of plans allows two tracks coming off the Manhattan Bridge that were originally to have tunneled west under Canal Street to a terminal near the Hudson River to turn north under the Broadway line and emerge in the alignment of the express tracks. Vestiges of the never-used Canal Street tunnel heading west of Broadway can be seen from the front window as a train coming off the Manhattan Bridge takes the curve at Canal Street.)

The Interborough had one last stand to make. The older company felt it had made all the concessions it could and attempted to block the construction of lower Manhattan "turn-back" facilities on the BRT's Broadway line. Service from Brooklyn to Manhattan, OK . . . if reluctantly so. But it wanted no pocket tracks to allow Broadway trains to reverse direction in lower Manhattan and head back uptown, thus providing the kind of Manhattan-oriented service that the Interborough felt should be its exclusive province.

Sorry again! Both the Whitehall Street and the City Hall stations were built to allow southbound Broadway trains to terminate, reverse direction, and become northbound without having to cross the river into Brooklyn first.

A relic of a bygone day—a metal sign advertising the BRT's Dual Contract plum, its Broadway line in Manhattan. [Author]

6

THE DUAL SUBWAY SYSTEM

THE DUAL CONTRACTS OF 1913 WERE agreements between the city and the two traction companies stipulating that the BRT and the Interborough would help in the financing of construction in return for attractive lease agreements. The Elsberg law had, by this time, been superseded by new legislation suggested during the Dual Contracts talks. The agreement worked as follows: the city's debt ceiling was raised by passage of a state constitutional amendment allowing municipal bonds to be sold to finance most of, but not all, the construction costs. The BRT and the Interborough both had to put up some of their own funds for construction and also were required to provide equipment for the new lines. In return, they were given forty-nine-year leases to operate the lines, leases to begin on January 1, 1917, the deadline for actual completion of the Dual System. Furthermore, the Interborough's earlier leases were rewritten to be coterminous with the Dual Contracts. The Centre Street loop, the Fourth Avenue subway, and other elements of the now-moribund Triborough System were also incorporated into the Dual Contracts arrangement.

Both the IRT, as Belmont's Interborough had come to be known, and the BRT were profitable ongoing operations prior to the Dual Contracts. The original IRT subway realized an annual profit of more than $6 million, and the BRT was clearing $9 million a year on its elevated lines alone. The new agreement stipulated that each company combine revenue from its Dual Contracts operations with revenue from established operations. Thus, the IRT would pool Dual Contracts money with its gross from the original subway—although, interestingly, not from the Manhattan elevated lines—and the BRT would pool its Dual Contracts funds with its el revenues—but not its surface line fares. Out of the resultant sum of money, each company's first obligation was to pay all operating expenses.

One feature of the Dual Contracts stirred up considerable disagreement and controversy: after paying operating expenses, each line was entitled to draw from gross revenues a sum of money in lieu of profits it had been making from its older operations, the precise amount being established by formula. The rationale for this clause was that the older operations were proved profitmakers for the traction companies and that they should not be denied this compensation after entering the Dual System. But opponents claimed this preferential system, so called, amounted to a guaranteed profit for private interests, at municipal expense. It became still another argument on behalf of total public operation of the subways.

Each line was required to service its own Dual Contracts bonds and to be responsible for meeting payments on the interest and principal of the city's Dual Contracts bonds, thereby freeing the municipal government from any direct financial liability. The city was lending its credit to the enterprise and would generate funds from the sale of bonds. But it would be the two transit companies that would pay off these bonds, out of subway-generated revenues. Finally, the city and the companies were ultimately to share equally any and all remaining profits.

The clause concerning operating expenses pointedly excluded any payment of rent to the city, only the *equivalent* of rent through meeting payments on the city's Dual Contracts bonds, and the city's share of the profits. But none of these monies need ever be paid out until the traction companies *first* received their *guaranteed* profit—and here was the nub of concern with the whole arrangement. This agreement was, assuredly, a distinct departure from the one signed originally between the Interborough and the city for the first subway. At that time, rental payment to the city for the use of its subway tunnels was required *before* the company could realize any profits.

Hindsight wisdom may be critical of the Dual Contracts, a pioneer effort toward incorporating private interests into a large-scale public works project. But the fact is that the city was totally unable to undertake such a massive transit project on its own; it had to have the cooperation of private enterprise and private investment. Private firms, on the other hand, could not go into the 1913 money market for financing without the guarantees provided by the Dual Contracts profit provisions.

Whatever their faults, the Dual Contracts were a major development, an extraordinary benchmark in the history of New York transit. Perhaps the most remarkable aspect of the Dual Subway System, as it came to be called, was that it offered more than a patchwork or piecemeal solution to a pressing municipal need—as the Triborough System would have been. It was a solution, or in retrospect, an attempt at a solution, that was total in its scope. Only a precious few other municipal undertakings can be so characterized.

The original cost estimate for the project was $302 million. By comparison, the Contract One subway cost $38 million. The Pennsylvania Railroad's New York Tunnel Extension bore a $116 million price tag when Penn Station opened in 1910, and even such a dramatic undertaking as Henry Flagler's Key West Extension of his Florida East Coast Railway in 1912 was modest in comparison with the Dual Contracts. The island-hopping line out from the Florida mainland cost $31 million. In the first quarter of the century, perhaps the most expansive era in world history for massive investment in transportation projects, only the Panama Canal exceeded the cost of the Dual Subway System, with an expenditure of $352 million. But it took a national government to build the canal, where the Dual System was the work of a mere city. Mere, indeed!

Perhaps it was the *Times* of London that had sufficient perspective for a balanced view: "After a long struggle against unprincipled politicians, self-interested financiers, and inefficient service, New York seems to have evolved a system of locomotion of which its citizens may well feel proud."

As to cost-sharing arrangements, the City of New York was to make by far the largest contribution, $164 million. This sum was for construction work only, and largely for underground subway construction. The Interborough and the BRT, the latter acting through the New York Municipal Railway Corporation, a newly formed subsidiary, put up $158 million between them ($77 million and $61 million, respectively). The two companies basically handled construction on their own surface and elevated sections of the Dual Systems and equipment for all the routes and lines. By including the value of previous city investments in things like the Fourth Avenue subway, public sector investment in the Dual Subway System quickly grew to almost $200 million.[1]

On Tuesday, March 18, 1913, the city Board of Estimate gave its final approval of the Dual Contracts, thirteen to three, and also voted an appropriation of $88.2 million for initial construction costs. The stage was thus set for the signing of the Dual Contracts, which took place next day, March 19, at the New York headquarters of the state Public Service Commission in the Tribune Building.

The contracts were designed for immortality! The city-BRT pact—known as Contract Number Four—was printed on fine parchment, ran to 226 pages, and was bound in a heavy red cover. The seal was attached with red ribbon. Edward E. McCall, who had succeeded Wilcox as head of the Public Service Commission just before the contracts were readied, signed the BRT agreement at nine minutes after noon. Then, in a gesture appreciated by all parties, he asked Wilcox to witness his signature. The former commissioner, who had just missed out on his dream of seeing the Dual Contracts through to the final stages, was thus given the honor of signing the documents.

Along with the BRT contract, additional certificates were signed outlining improvements on certain BRT elevated lines that would feed traffic into the subway. Technically, the BRT was not a signatory of the Dual Contracts at all. The New York Municipal Railway, a wholly owned subsidiary that the BRT created in 1912, was the signatory agency that actually entered into the pact with the city.

Interborough officials signed a 253-page document—Contract Number Three—bound in blue and secured with a blue ribbon. After the subway document was official, certificates for improvement to Interborough-controlled els were also signed. Before the parties headed off to a luncheon celebration, McCall characterized matters thusly: "New York has never met a problem too big for it. It never will."

BETWEEN THE SIDEWALKS OF NEW YORK

Above: Two Brooklyn streetcars when such vehicles were a mainstay of that borough's transportation network. [Author]

Above: A New York Railways streetcar pauses at the West Twenty-third Street ferry terminal. Notice the absence of conventional trolley poles; Manhattan prohibited such devices and forced street railways to use underground electric pickup. [Author's collection]

In their heyday, streetcars operated on virtually every major thoroughfare in New York. Indeed, the world's first streetcar—a horse-powered vehicle that welcomed its inaugural passengers in 1852—ran in New York.

As streetcars progressed in New York from horse-drawn vehicles, through a short period of cable operation, and on to electric traction, the local field eventually shaped up as three major operators—and several smaller ones.

In the first half of the twentieth century, upper Manhattan and the Bronx were served by the Third Avenue Railway, whose cream and red cars drew electric current from an underground conduit, not regular trolley wires, because a city law banned trolley wires in Manhattan. When Third Avenue cars operated into the farther reaches of the Bronx, and even Westchester County, they resorted to the industry's more conventional, and less costly, form of overhead power distribution.

A second streetcar operator was New York Railways. Its green cars were a Manhattan fixture in the middle to lower reaches of that borough. It, too, drew electric current from underground conduits.

In Brooklyn and Queens, the dominant street railway was a subsidiary of the BRT/BMT, and it was called, in its later days, the Brooklyn & Queens Transit Corporation (B&QT). No underground conduits were used here, just plain overhead trolley wire.

The Third Avenue system and New York Railways have evolved into the TA's subsidiary, known as the Manhattan and Bronx Surface Operating Authority, or MaBSTOA for short. MaBSTOA runs buses only, of course; Third Avenue's last streetcar vanished from New York streets by 1948. [Some of the company's Westchester streetcar lines lasted into the early 1950s.] New York Railways' green cars gave way to buses in the mid-1930s. The B&QT became a municipal responsibility along with its parent, the BMT, in 1940. Trolley cars hung on a little longer in Brooklyn than in Manhattan, but motorization of ordinary street railways was inevitable; the end came for B&QT trolley cars in 1956.

The last streetcar to carry revenue passengers in New York did so

Above: New York's last streetcar line operated across the Queensboro Bridge. Cars made a midriver stop to give passengers access to Welfare Island. [Author's collection]

Above: The BMT's subsidiary, the Brooklyn & Queens Transit Corp., ordered the first PCC cars, such as No. 1016, shown here arriving at Coney Island in the summer of 1954. [Author]

in 1957, and it wasn't a vehicle operated by any of the three major operators or their public sector successor. That's when one of the smaller trolley companies called it quits. Its longevity can be explained by its unconventional route. It linked Manhattan and Queens over the Queensboro Bridge, including a midriver stop where passengers could take an elevator down to Welfare [today's Roosevelt] Island. Until the island was physically linked to Queens by bridge, the streetcar was necessary since buses would have been hard pressed to manage the midriver stop.

The history and traditions of New York's trolley cars are long and colorful. The B&QT, for example, was instrumental in the development of the PCC streetcar. This product of the 1930s was a design developed jointly by several street railways as a failing industry's final effort to rejuvenate itself in a world growing more accustomed to petroleum-powered transport — motor buses as well as automobiles. The term *PCC car* derives from the group that developed the vehicle, the Electric Railway Presidents' Conference Committee,

ERPCC, or PCC in the coinage that quickly became universal. The B&QT provided testing facilities for the group's R&D team at one of its car barns and backed up its moral support with hard cash by ordering the first fleet of production model cars — one hundred of them. The new cars were introduced into service on October 1, 1936, and became fixtures on various B&QT lines for the next thirty years.

This would appear to be the end of the story of trolley cars in New York. But in developments that would have seemed impossible just a few years ago, there is now talk in several quarters of restoring streetcar operation in several parts of the city.

For further information on New York streetcars, see Frederick A. Kramer, *Across New York by Trolley: The Third Avenue Railway System in Manhattan, the Bronx and Westchester* [New York: Quadrant, 1975], and James C. Greller and Edward B. Watson, *Brooklyn Trolleys* [New York: N. J. International, 1986]. For specific information on Brooklyn's role in the development of the PCC car, see Stephen P. Carlson and Fred W. Schneider III, *PCC, the Car That Fought Back* [Glendale, Calif.: Interurban Press, 1980].

Above: In faraway California, there's a National League baseball team whose white home uniforms have blue script letters across the front of their shirts that say "Dodgers." The name, coined when that team played in Brooklyn, refers to the fact that denizens of the borough were constantly dodging the trolley cars that provided service along many thoroughfares. This is 1955 along the Church Avenue line. In one more year, there would be no more trolleys to dodge; in two, there would be no more Dodgers. [Author]

For many generations, the most popular streetcar in Brooklyn was a fleet of 535 cars like this one, identified as the 8000 series. Built in the 1920s, the breed lasted until 1954. No. 8477 is shown here on the McDonald Avenue line. The beer advertisement on the apartment house wall was also 100 percent Brooklyn; the company's original brewery was in the borough, and for many years it was a major sponsor of Brooklyn Dodgers broadcasts. [Author]

CUTTING UP THE PIE

The original S-shaped trunk line of the Interborough was to be split into two separate and parallel north-south routes, and the short stretch across Forty-second Street was to become a shuttle between Times Square and Grand Central. The S became an H, so to speak. Coming south on Broadway from the Bronx, a new line was to be built out of Times Square down Seventh Avenue to South Ferry. This line was to branch off below Chambers Street and tunnel to Brooklyn,

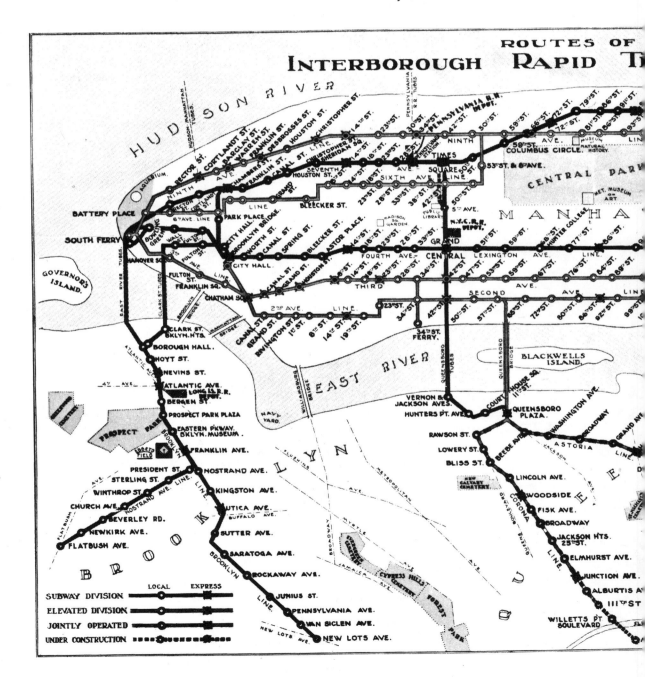

there to join the IRT's existing Contract Two line. Beyond the original terminal at Flatbush and Atlantic avenues, the Interborough would probe deeper into Brooklyn by running out Eastern Parkway to Brownsville with a spur under Nostrand Avenue to tap Flatbush. The long-discussed Lexington Avenue line was to tunnel up to the Bronx from Grand Central; the PSC had begun this line as part of the Triborough System even before the Dual Contracts were agreed upon because such a line was a necessity in any event. Construction had begun in July 1911. Triborough specifications were used on the project. Station

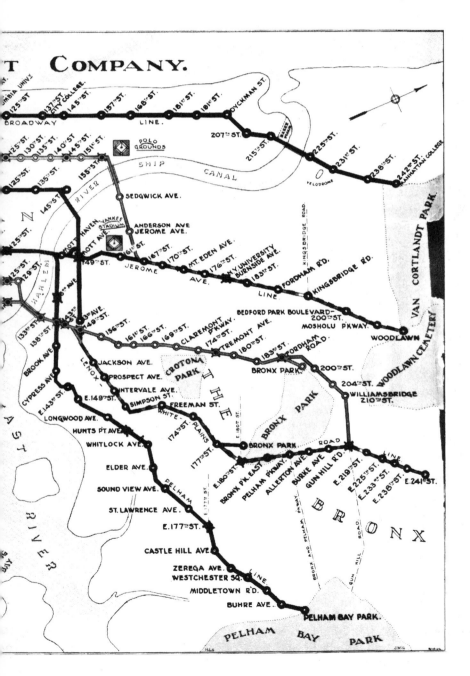

This 1924 map shows the style of artwork the Interborough long used for its subway maps. New Yorkers easily adjust to anything, but out-of-towners were often puzzled by the fact that the map's north-south axis runs from right to left. [Author's collection]

platforms later had to be equipped with steel extension plates to accommodate narrower IRT rolling stock that would be used on the line.[2]

The Interborough made its biggest gains in the Bronx. A long three-track elevated line up Jerome Avenue and another of equal size into the Pelham Bay section would feed the new Lexington Avenue subway; the original Contract One line to West Farms Square would extend to the Yonkers border at 241st Street and White Plains Road. In addition, the various el properties were to be improved and extended. In many cases, the original two-track lines were increased to three to permit a measure of express service.

A third, or express, track was often easy to install on the elevated structures because many of the original two-track routes had room in the middle for a third track. In order to avoid costly reconstruction, stations for the express trains were often built on a raised upper level, allowing the original tracks to retain their alignment below. This proved to be operationally sound as well because the upgrade into the station and the downgrade out of it provided gravitational pull to the stopping and starting of trains.

BRT's big plum was the Broadway line up Manhattan and over to Queens. This line was to be fed by a pair of tracks on the Manhattan Bridge and another pair in a tunnel under the East River from Montague Street in Brooklyn to White-hall Street in Manhattan. In addition, a second pair of tracks on the Manhattan Bridge was to feed the Centre Street loop. The loop then would swing into the Montague-Whitehall tunnel to Brooklyn. Earlier plans to connect the loop with the Brooklyn Bridge el line were dropped.

All BRT lines from Manhattan were to converge at an outsized junction in downtown Brooklyn at Flatbush Avenue Extension and DeKalb Avenue and from there proceed into residential sections of Brooklyn by way of two principal trunk lines. The Fourth Avenue subway—the leftover of the Triborough System—was to feed Bay Ridge and divide into four separate branches: the Sea Beach, the West End, the Culver, and the Fourth Avenue line itself. The other line out of DeKalb Avenue was to connect with the BRT's existing Brighton Beach line at Malbone Street near the entrance to Prospect Park and eventually connect again with the Sea Beach, West End, and Culver at Coney Island. Prior to the Dual Contracts, the Brighton line ran to downtown Brooklyn over a connection with the Fulton Street el at Franklin Avenue. The Sea Beach, West End, and Culver lines were former independent steam railroads that were electrified after they became part of the BRT complex. They connected with the elevated line that ran over Brooklyn's Fifth Avenue and into the Myrtle Avenue line at Hudson Street. Now they were to be upgraded to heavy-duty standards and become part of the subway system.

This group of lines was known, even in the days before the Dual Contracts, as the BRT's Southern Division. An Eastern Division, so called, embraced the lines that radiated out of the junction of the Broadway el and the Fulton Street el in East New York, a spot that was called Manhattan Junction before 1913 and Broadway Junction thereafter. Chiefly, the Dual Contracts mandated the improvement and extension of older elevated lines on the Eastern Division. In

On transit maps prepared to help passengers get around, the BRT, and its successor corporation, the BMT, oriented things with north to the top, where it's supposed to be. This 1924 edition was printed specifically for delegates to the 1924 convention of the Democratic party, held in Madison Square Garden, then located at East Twenty-third Street near the line's local station at that time. In sweltering summer heat, the "Dems" took 103 ballots to nominate John W. Davis—but for naught. Cal Coolidge whipped him in November. [Author's collection]

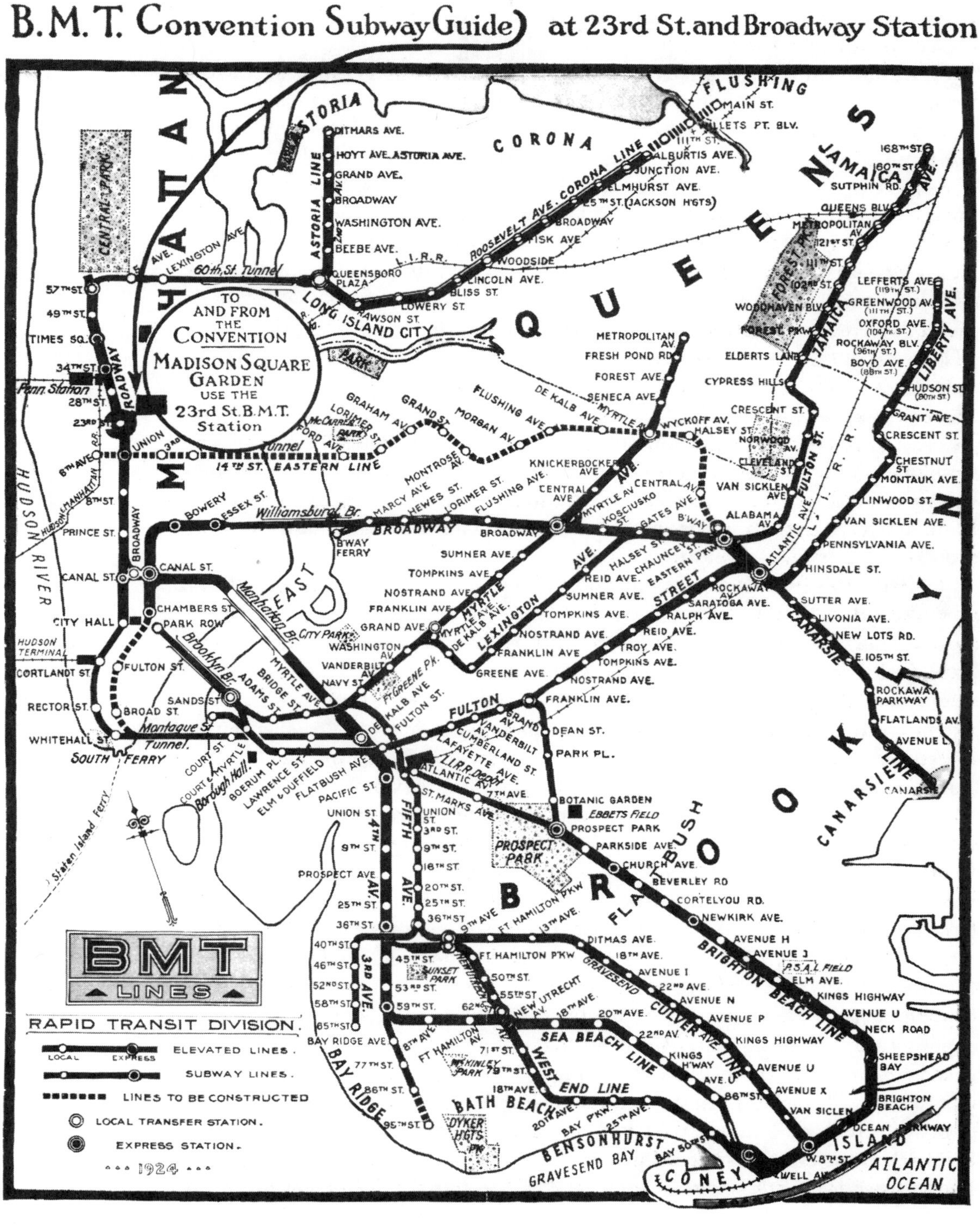

B.M.T. Convention Subway Guide) at 23rd St. and Broadway Station

TO AND FROM THE CONVENTION
MADISON SQUARE GARDEN
USE THE 23rd St. B.M.T. Station

BMT LINES ▲

RAPID TRANSIT DIVISION.

LOCAL · EXPRESS · ELEVATED LINES.
LOCAL · EXPRESS · SUBWAY LINES.
■■■■■ LINES TO BE CONSTRUCTED
◯ LOCAL TRANSFER STATION.
◉ EXPRESS STATION.

··· 1924 ···

later years, the cry was raised, not without basis, that this area was seriously slighted in the Dual System. However, one major new project was planned for the area: a line from East New York across the Bushwick section of Brooklyn, under the East River, and into Manhattan at Fourteenth Street. It was to be called the Fourteenth Street–Eastern line.

One additional Dual Contract provision stipulated that a pair of East River tunnels completed in 1907 to bring trolley cars from Queens into Manhattan be absorbed into the city subway system. One of the backers of this early project was William Steinway, the Long Island City piano manufacturer, and the tunnels have since been known as the Steinway Tunnels. A group headed by Steinway purchased fifty trolley cars from the Brill Company to begin service, but, after the first test run, a franchise dispute erupted. The tunnels sat empty until 1913, when they were made part of the Dual Contracts agreements, assigned to the IRT. Revenue subway service began in 1915.

The Steinway Tunnels extended from the Grand Central area in Manhattan to Long Island City. At Queensboro Plaza in Long Island City, the IRT planned to link up with the BRT, whose Broadway line was to tunnel under the East River to Queens from Sixtieth Street in Manhattan. Originally, the BRT planned to cross the river at this point on the Queensboro Bridge. When concern developed over whether the bridge could bear up under the weight of all-steel subway trains, the decision was for a tunnel instead. The bridge was used, however, by a line that connected with the Second Avenue el and ran only wooden el cars. The resulting junction, built on an elevated structure at the approach to the Queensboro Bridge, was a complex assemblage of traction lines. The Queensboro Plaza station was a two-level, eight-track facility, and from it two elevated lines were to extend into the residential sections of Queens—one to Astoria and the other to Corona—which, according to the Dual Contracts, were to be joint BRT-IRT operations. Also, the BRT was toying with plans to extend a crosstown el from Franklin Avenue and Fulton Street in Brooklyn across Greenpoint to tie in at the huge Queens Plaza terminal. This projected line was never formally part of the Dual System and, in fact, never materialized.

Soon after the contracts were signed, construction agreements were let out for bid. During the next decade, every borough except Staten Island was involved in developing the massive transit system. Besides the expected hassles over easements and other right-of-way problems, a rackety flap erupted when area businessmen learned that the BRT station at Times Square was to be—horrors!—a mere local stop. Merchant groups held meetings and proclaimed that they had not been consulted. Only through the efforts and tact of both transit companies plus the City of New York was a plan worked out to the satisfaction of all: a *superstation* at Times Square, a station that would include a large mezzanine area where passengers could transfer among the new IRT Seventh Avenue line, the BRT Broadway line, and the shuttle to Grand Central. The mistake of 1904 was not repeated; Times Square was made an express stop on all lines.

In 1913, the city felt it could not afford the disruptive traffic snarls caused by construction of the original subway. After an initial street excavation was

The cut-and-cover method of subway construction as used on the Dual System network called for building a temporary wooden "street" over the tunnel excavation and then allowing traffic to continue about its business as construction proceeded beneath. Occasionally, there were problems. On September 22, 1915, at Seventh Avenue between West Twenty-fourth and Twenty-fifth streets, the wooden "street" collapsed. A streetcar and a brewery wagon fell into the pit; eight people were killed in the mishap. [Brown Bros.]

made, it was roofed over by a temporary wooden "street" so that subway construction could continue while vehicles and pedestrians moved overhead. Although practical, temporary structures did not always prove to be safe. On the morning of September 22, 1915, eight New Yorkers were killed and more than one hundred injured when a dynamite explosion blew out a large section of the planked "pavement" of Seventh Avenue between Twenty-fourth and Twenty-fifth streets. A streetcar and a large brewery wagon fell into the subway excavation. On September 25 of the same year, a similar accident at Broadway and Thirty-eighth Street claimed one life. In July 1916, a Nostrand Avenue trolley car in Brooklyn fell into the IRT subway between Beverly Road and Tilden Avenue, without casualties, fortunately.

Construction methods for the Dual System were similar to those of the Contract One and Two lines. Subway portions were built either by the cut-and-cover or deep tunneling methods. Five new twin-tube borings under the East River were put through, including the never-used Steinway Tunnels. Add on the rapid transit tracks already on the Brooklyn, Manhattan, Williamsburg, and Queensboro bridges, plus the Interborough's original East River tunnel, and by 1920, ten rail connections linked Manhattan and Long Island.

Most underground routes of the Dual System were built as four-track lines, with all four tracks on the same level—an arrangement that can probably be called standard New York subway engineering. Express tracks are in the middle and local ones on the outside; express stations where locals also stop generally feature platforms between the local and express tracks headed in the same direction. An exception was the Lexington Avenue line between Grand Central and

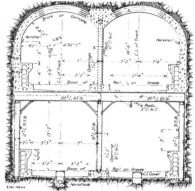

Left: Tunneling on much of the upper Lexington Avenue line was through solid rock. [Robert L. Presbrey collection]
Above: Cross-section of this line showing local tracks above and express below. [Author's collection]

East 125th Street, roughly, where the express tracks were put on a second level below the local tracks. The IRT's Brooklyn line beyond Atlantic Avenue is also a bit irregular; between Atlantic and Franklin avenues, the express tracks are largely, but not entirely, below the local tracks. One reason is that the BRT's Brighton Beach line has a tunnel under the same street as the IRT line for a portion of the distance, and there's not as much room as there should be. Between Franklin and Utica avenues, there are again two levels of track but with express and local in the same direction on the same level.

Virtually all local stations on the new Dual System lines of the BRT and the IRT were built to accommodate trains fully as long as the expresses, a departure from the original subway where it was presumed locals would, or should, be shorter than expresses.[3] Tile work and design in the new stations was considerably less ornate than the more artistic touches lavished on the Contract One and Contract Two routes.

More than half the mileage of the Dual Systems wasn't subway at all but built on elevated structures, embankments, or in open cuts . . . out-of-doors, in other words. Because of Dual Contract financing, construction of these "fresh air" portions of the systems was generally funded by the two operating companies, with city money reserved for the more costly subway elements. For that matter, Dual Contract investment in many of the nonsubway routes involved upgrading an existing transit line rather than the construction of something totally new.

The most common style of elevated structure called for a three-track right-of-way, and this allowed operation of express service, but in a single direction: inbound during the morning rush hour and outbound in the evening. The three-track configuration became popular because four tracks were too wide for the average New York street. Columns of support girders were usually erected di-

Left: Many older two-track elevated lines were originally constructed with room for a center express track, and the Dual Contracts called for upgrading these to three-track capacity. Stations on the new express track often proved a problem because engineers wanted to retain the external alignment of the line. The solution? Elevate the express track at express stations and build the platforms over the outside tracks. [NYCTA] *Right:* Construction proceeds on the open cut of the BRT's Sea Beach line in Brooklyn. [Robert L. Presbrey collection]

rectly in the road or avenue over which the line was built, providing a workable but far from ideal center corridor for various lanes of traffic. Streetcar lines, particularly, often operated inside a semiprivate right-of-way between the supports of the elevated lines, and the area was frequently left unpaved—or at least it was until automotive traffic became a more important user of the city's thoroughfares than streetcars. Then everything in sight was paved.

The Lexington Avenue line turned out to be a poser for IRT construction engineers. The older subway was under Fourth and Park avenues between Fourteenth Street and Grand Central. Among many plans drawn up for linking this route into the new upper East Side trunk line, one proposed that the new route continue southward on Lexington to Fourteenth Street, there to intercept the existing line. In the end, the connection was made at Grand Central—as envisioned when the Dual Contracts were signed—and the now-famous Forty-second Street Shuttle was put together out of the unneeded remains of the city's original subway. When the shuttle began its back-and-forth operations in September 1918, the chairman of the Public Service Commission, Charles Buckley Hubbell, proposed that colored bands be painted on station ceilings to guide passengers through the labyrinth of passageways and stairways at both Times Square and Grand Central. Later supplemented with lights, the bands have led confused millions—perhaps even billions—to and from the shuttle trains over the years.

Civil construction work on the IRT at Times Square was also quite tricky,

Three days before Christmas 1915, Times Square is alive with activity. Hobble-skirt streetcars were known as "Broadway battleships." Beneath all the surface traffic, workmen were busy building the Dual Contracts subway lines. A steam crane under the Fatima cigarette sign chuffs away, and there is wooden planking on the streets. [Robert L. Presbrey collection]

and some contemporary accounts say it was the most difficult design problem the whole Dual Subway System had to face. As at Grand Central, an existing line had to be connected to a new one. But what made Times Square such a challenge to Alfred Craven's crew was the simultaneous construction of a four-track BRT subway at the same location, plus the proximity of many tall buildings with extensive foundations.

As might have been expected, delays pushed back the opening of the various portions of the Dual Contracts lines. (Rarely has a New York subway opened on schedule.) Finally on Tuesday, June 15, 1915, a two-car BRT train ran tests on the Fourth Avenue line and across the Manhattan Bridge to the station under the Municipal Building on the Centre Street loop. The bridge itself had opened for vehicular traffic on New Year's Eve in 1909, and the subway tracks on the lower level were installed either just before or just after that date, but they were not tied in with any tunnel routes, since none existed. In 1912, arrangements were made for cars of the unusually named Manhattan Bridge Three Cent Line, a trolley company, to use the idle subway tracks on a temporary basis. Such service continued until 1915, when the streetcars were moved to the bridge's upper roadways. There they served until 1929, when the upper roadways were given over to the needs of the city's growing numbers of motorized vehicles.[4]

On Saturday, June 19, 1915, an elaborate eight-car ceremonial train, with city, state, and BRT officials aboard, ran from the Municipal Building in Manhattan to the West End Depot in Coney Island, over the Manhattan Bridge, and the Fourth Avenue and Sea Beach lines. Conspicuously absent was the city's mayor, John Purroy Mitchel. His Honor was upset because his invitation did not arrive until the night before. Thoroughly piqued, he passed up the BRT gala and went instead to the Brooklyn Navy Yard for the launching of the U.S.S. *Arizona*, a battleship fated to become a memorial to infamy at Pearl Harbor twenty-six years later.

The Fourth Avenue and Sea Beach lines, and the tracks over the Manhattan Bridge, opened to the public on Tuesday, June 22, 1915, the same day the Interborough opened the Steinway Tunnels for subway service. These lines were the first fruits of the Dual Contracts.

SETTING A STANDARD IN ROLLING STOCK

By 1915 the BRT had rectified its lack of steel subway equipment, a deficiency that had caused it such embarrassment when the Centre Street loop line began service in 1908. When the Fourth Avenue–Sea Beach segment opened, the BRT welcomed passengers aboard what has since proved to be as fine and durable a piece of railway rolling stock as this world has seen. Some 950 of these steel cars eventually took to the rails to form the backbone of the company fleet.

The cars were not put into service without some resistance. When BRT officials notified the state's Public Service Commission that they intended to design a new all-steel subway car, the state agency recommended that they instead modify the basic Interborough car to suit their needs—and pay the IRT a royalty for each unit. The BRT wanted none of this! In August 1913, the BRT sent plans to the commission for a distinctive new car, strongly influenced by the imaginatively designed Boston Elevated Railway cars on the new Cambridge subway.

A train of BRT Standards awaits a call to service in the Fresh Pond Yard in Queens. Letters "BX" on the end bulkhead of car No. 2473 indicate this is a semipermanently coupled three-car unit, and the middle car is a powerless trailer. The Standard fleet grew to 950 units in the decades after 1914. [NYCTA]

The main difference from the older IRT model was that instead of having doors in the end vestibules, the new car had three sets of twin doors spaced along the side of the car, dispensing entirely with vestibules. The doors were opened and closed by an electro-pneumatic system operated by a conductor from the center of the car. Later, in January 1921, the BRT perfected a system that allowed a single conductor to operate all the doors on an eight-car train.

The new BRT car, without a real name but known throughout the years simply as the "Standard," was longer than IRT equipment, measuring 67 feet as opposed to the IRT's 51 feet. The extra space allowed more seats per car. As a result, also, of the greater width in the Triborough Subway plans that the BRT inherited, the Standard was 10 feet wide, whereas IRT cars were but 8 feet, 9 inches wide.[5]

To rally press and public support for its new design, the BRT unveiled a full-sized wooden mock-up of the car on September 24, 1913. The next day the PSC gave the OK to order the car in quantity.

When the first Standards arrived from American Car and Foundry in 1914, beautifully painted in dark brown with a black roof, they were tested along sections of the Sea Beach line. On March 31, 1915, two eight-car trains made demonstration runs for a group of special visitors—the president and the engineering staff of archrival Interborough. The cars were everything the BRT said they would be, and more. Lavishly praised in industry journals, they promptly settled down to the task for which they were built. When the Standards first went to work for the BRT, Woodrow Wilson was president of the United States. Standards were still hauling passengers in New York when Richard Nixon entered the White House.

The new BRT steel cars first operated in revenue service in March 1915, when they replaced surface-type trolley cars that had been providing temporary shuttle service over the Sea Beach line between Eighty-sixth Street and New Utrecht Avenue. More of the new equipment went to work on Sunday, May 23, 1915, a full month before the inaugural of the first Dual Contract lines, when the amusement areas at Coney Island opened for the season. BRT trolley cars from all over Brooklyn converged on Sixty-second Street and the Sea Beach line. From Sixty-second Street, the Standards operated in nonstop express service directly to the old West End Depot in Coney Island.

The Standards should have been put to work on the Centre Street loop line as soon as they arrived on the property, but wooden cars continued to ply the Williamsburg Bridge until the Broadway el was upgraded to handle the heavier weight of all-steel equipment in 1916.

In contrast to the BRT's classy new cars, the Interborough's rolling stock design seemed to be stuck in a quite unprogressive rut from earliest days on into the roaring twenties. Passenger amenities were an area where the Interborough never earned especially high marks, for instance. Seating aboard its cars consisted of the unrelieved monotony of rattan-covered benches along the side walls of the cars with seated passengers facing each other directly across the center aisle. On the BRT Standard, by contrast, there were various combinations of seating arrangements more (but not completely) like a conventional railroad coach. To

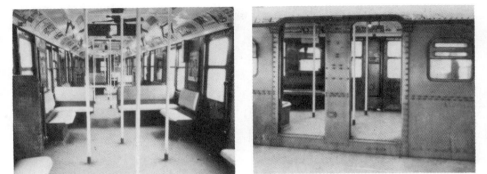

Left: Interior view of a BRT Standard. The use of three-two seating in a subway car is unusual. [NYCTA] *Right:* On a train of Standards, the conductor worked in the middle of a car; door controls were located in the wide space between the two center doors. During crowded rush hours, it took some doing for the conductor to move from one side of the car to the other as required by either outside or center island platforms. [NYCTA]

inform passengers where its trains were going, the railway used not the roller curtain destination signs then common in the street railway industry (and used on the BRT Standard) but crude metal plates with routes and destinations stenciled on them.

Interborough rolling stock did go through an appropriate evolution, though, from the first cars of 1904 until the last of the cars needed to open the Dual Contract lines were delivered in 1925. One key distinction between cars built before 1915 and those built afterward was the designation of the earlier cars as "high voltage" and the later as "low voltage." All drew the same 600 volts of direct current from the third rail, but the newer vehicles employed a substantially lower current—32 volts—for the operation of the motor controller and the multiple-unit apparatus. Low voltage soon became a standard feature on all U.S. rapid transit equipment. It eliminated the danger of feeding a lethal charge of 600 volts through the motorman's control station and allowed other technical improvements as well. With a typical New York urge for brevity, high-voltage cars were called "Hi-V's" and low-voltage cars "Lo-V's." (The BRT Standard was a low-voltage car, incidentally.)

The IRT was also instrumental in developing the "anticlimber," a device that prevents cars from telescoping into one another in a rear-end collision. A mishap on the Westchester Avenue viaduct on December 4, 1907, vividly demonstrated the value of the invention. Cars equipped with the knuckled, wraparound apparatus merely butted against each other with minimal damage, whereas two cars without the anticlimber were seriously damaged by telescoping. In another improvement, the Interborough replaced the original Van Dorn couplers of its early cars, essentially manually operated devices, with an advanced automatic model, a design the BRT adopted for its steel cars and that remained standard in New York until 1971. (And was re-adopted in 1983.)

Through 1925, more than 2,500 descendants of the 1903 experimentals, *August Belmont* and *John B. McDonald*, had been delivered. The original Composites were retired from subway service in 1916. As early as 1906, a tunnel fire demonstrated that they were less flame resistant than originally claimed, and their inability to withstand even minor collisions made them far less desirable cars than their all-steel running mates. At the order of the Public Service Com-

Interior view of a classic Interborough subway car. Notice the overhead fans, a metal-plate sign box on the left to keep passengers informed, and end-to-end advertising signs. [NYCTA]

mission, they were exiled to the IRT's Bronx and Manhattan elevated lines to serve out their days, some remaining in passenger service until after World War II. They remained as good looking a car as they ever were, but their distinctive appearance was seriously altered when progress dictated that they too have automatic sliding doors cut into their sides. A fish-bellied side brace was installed to compensate for structural weakness because of the newly inserted door.

There are those subway enthusiasts who see Interborough equipment as a many-splendored thing and look upon the slight differences between series of cars the way stamp collectors cherish watermark variations. A knowledgeable student of the IRT, for instance, usually could distinguish a train of 1905 model cars from the 1925 version merely by the sound of the motors running at speed. One of the most artful objects ever used in the subway was a large brass controller handle supplied as standard equipment on early Interborough rolling stock. To the dedicated connoisseur of subway accoutrements, this handsome object compares to the controllers on later cars as a Rembrandt painting to an amateur's daub.

The destiny that was in store for the Dual Contracts, however, was not decided in the conference rooms of the Public Service Commission or the executive offices of the two traction companies. It was shaped in Europe, where an Austrian archduke was assassinated by a Serbian terrorist, and in the sea lanes off Ireland where the Cunard Line's express mailboat R.M.S. *Lusitania* was torpedoed on May 7, 1915. The *Lusitania* went down just six weeks before the BRT and IRT began service over the first Dual Contracts lines. On February 26, 1917, with work in progress all over New York on various segments of the Dual System, President Wilson asked Congress for authority to arm U.S. merchant ships. On April 6, the United States declared war on Germany. World War I would irreversibly alter the nation's economic posture and produce conditions that were unforeseeable on March 18, 1913, when the Dual Contracts were signed.[6]

7

THE MALBONE STREET WRECK

PRIOR TO THE CONSTRUCTION OF THE Dual Contract systems, the BRT's Brighton Beach line was one of several older routes that operated into downtown Brooklyn over the rails of the Fulton Street el. The line also cut across the center of residential Brooklyn, serving growing communities in the Flatbush area, and eventually reached the Atlantic seashore resorts of Sheepshead Bay, Brighton Beach, and Coney Island. The Brighton line terminated in Coney Island at the Culver Depot, a long-gone transit palace where el trains and trolley cars congregated and that followers of electric traction often regard with the same kind of nostalgic affection burlesque enthusiasts have for the original Minsky's. On one end of the line, the Brighton was a typical city el; on the other end, like many other BRT lines that had evolved from steam-powered suburban railroads of the nineteenth century, it was a country-style interurban. It ran at ground level through rural areas to the beachfront, where wealthy New Yorkers of an older era indulged themselves at racetracks and exclusive seaside hotels. The same beachfront would entertain a later generation with the more egalitarian pleasures of a boardwalk, public beaches, and amusement parks. The change was very much due to the arrival of the various railways . . . and their later amalgamation into the BRT.

The Brighton line began life in 1878—on Monday, July 1, 1878, to be precise—and was called the Brooklyn, Flatbush & Coney Island Railroad. Its first train steamed away from the line's in-town terminal near Prospect Park at 5:00 P.M. on inaugural day hauled by a locomotive that bore the name *John A. Lott*. "Bunting fluttered gayly from the burnished machine," noted a reporter assigned to the first run by the *Brooklyn Eagle*, and the train puffed along through tunnels, under boulevards, and through cuts "so deep that nothing but the sky was visible." Fourteen minutes after getting underway, the train achieved its destination of Brighton Beach and the Brighton Beach Hotel, an establishment that was

The Brighton Beach line over the years. *Top:* A steam shovel takes big bites out of Flatbush real estate as the BRT upgrades the Brighton line to four-track alignment as part of the Dual Subway Systems. [Robert L. Presbrey collection] *Center:* Heading for Manhattan, and eventually Astoria, a Brighton express rolls through the open-cut right-of-way in Flatbush, circa 1956. [Author] *Bottom:* A ten-car train of contemporary R-68 units operating as the D train heads for Manhattan in 1987. Save one's being on the local track and the other on the express, the 1956 and the 1987 trains are in exactly the same spot. [Author]

owned by the railway company and whose economic future would presumably be assured by the construction of the new line.

Soon afterward, the Brighton line was extended north to Franklin and Atlantic avenues, where connection could be made with the Long Island Rail Road. After becoming part of the BRT system, it was extended two additional blocks to the north and connected with the Fulton Street el in 1896; three years later, in 1899, its operations were electrified. By this time, though, the Brighton line was no longer a small railroad catering primarily to seasonal hotel patrons. It was a major league mass transit line carrying thousands of daily passengers to their jobs in downtown Brooklyn and in Manhattan, where Brighton trains eventually terminated after crossing the East River over the Brooklyn Bridge.[1]

The Dual Contracts recognized the Brighton line's important role and proposed to upgrade its access to the employment centers of both Brooklyn and Manhattan. In lieu of operation over the Fulton Street el, the Brighton was to operate into a new subway that would connect with the Fourth Avenue line at the DeKalb Avenue–Gold Street junction and then continue over the Manhattan Bridge or through the Montague Street tunnel and give Brighton passengers access to both the BRT's Broadway line and the Centre Street loop. South of a point near Prospect Park and a station at Flatbush Avenue and Malbone Street, the old Brighton alignment would be retained. An earlier two-track and largely surface line had been improved by the Dual Contracts, and large segments had been upgraded by the BRT itself as early as 1907 under a grade-elimination project. Costs of this pre–Dual Contracts effort were shared by the company and the city. The BRT had pioneered a construction technique called "open-cut" on the Brighton line, in which tracks are placed in an open-air, concrete-lined depression or trench 15 to 20 feet deep. An open cut was far less costly than a subway, avoiding the unsightliness and noise of standard el construction while keeping the trains as inconspicuous in the neighborhood as possible.

The Brighton line featured a variety of construction styles. The open cut extended from the subway-el junction at Malbone Street all the way to Foster Avenue. From there to Sheepshead Bay, the line ran on a 15-foot-high earthen embankment and, from Sheepshead Bay to Coney Island, on a standard steel elevated structure—one of the few instances in all of New York where such an installation boasted four tracks. With the exception of the large, new Stillwell Avenue terminal in Coney Island, opened in May 1919 as a replacement for the Culver and West End depots, the southern portion of the Brighton line looks the same today as it did in 1918. It is easily the most distinctive rapid transit route in the whole city, and even the whole world, according to some partisans.

The Brighton line once provided one of the city's most pleasant experiences on an otherwise unpleasant hot summer day. Imagine the sensation as a Coney Island-bound Brighton local slows to take the curve into the Brighton Beach station and a fresh breeze off the ocean wafts in the windows and washes out the heat of the city with cool and salty air. Steel dust, traction motors, and uncomfortable passengers combine to underscore the oppressive heat of the day as the Brighton line approaches the ocean southbound at just the correct angle

A later-day view on the Brighton Beach line at the point where trains leave the below-ground open cut and ascend to an elevated earthen embankment right-of-way en route to Coney Island. Equipment shown here is a train of stainless steel R-32 units built in 1965 by the Budd Company. [NYCTA]

to capture any onshore breeze. Today air-conditioned trains have canceled this bonus.

The linkup between the upgraded old Brighton line and DeKalb Avenue was among the last Dual Contracts items to be built. In fact, the Fourth Avenue line was in service for more than a year before bids were finally advertised in September 1916. Therefore, in October 1918, most of the Brighton line south of Malbone Street had been brought up to Dual Contracts standards. However, because the subway link was unfinished, the line's only access to the business district of downtown Brooklyn and Manhattan remained the rickety structure of the Fulton Street el. The el was too lightly constructed for the new all-steel Standards, and Brighton service was provided with older wooden elevated equipment.

In that October, construction was well along on the subway connection, the junction already in place adjacent to the Prospect Park station, where the subway line and the Fulton Street spur would join.

At 5:00 P.M. on October 31, 1918, as the world took heart from rumors out of London that Kaiser Wilhelm had abdicated, the telephone rang in the BRT's Brooklyn headquarters. On the other end of the line was a man the company had once fired but who was now the mayor of the City of New York, John Francis Hylan—"Red Mike" as some called him, but never to his face. In 1897, as an engineer on the BRT's Lexington Avenue el when that line operated steam engines, Hylan had been discharged unceremoniously by a company supervisor for allegedly operating his train in a reckless manner. Hylan's message on All Hallow's Eve in 1918 brought no joy to his former employers. He told company officials that motormen on all subway and elevated lines had voted to go out on strike at 5:00 A.M. the next morning, November 1.[2]

The reasons for the walkout are instructive. Earlier in the year, the BRT had

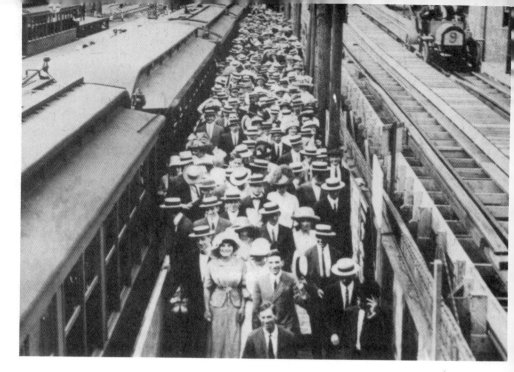

Culver Depot, circa 1910. Open platform elevated trains on both the Brighton and Culver lines bring swarms of Brooklynites to Coney Island for a day at the seashore. Straw hats are quite the style for the young men; boys off to the right are already enjoying themselves aboard one of the many amusement rides. (Author's collection)

fired twenty-nine motormen, and a subsequent hearing held by the War Labor Board, a federal panel, had determined that a key, and perhaps the sole, reason for the dismissals was the fact the men had joined the Brotherhood of Locomotive Engineers, a labor organization attempting to organize the BRT, but mere membership in which the traction company regarded as cause for dismissal. The War Labor Board's recommendation that the men be rehired with back pay was not binding, however, and the BRT refused to be moved by its line of reasoning. After all efforts at mediation and compromise failed, the brotherhood called upon its members and supporters to walk off the job on November 1, 1918.

In the days of private ownership, work stoppages were not infrequent. To keep trains rolling, dispatchers, supervisors, and other available personnel were hastily given rudimentary instruction in train operation. Thus, service of sorts was maintained the next morning, although the company and the union gave out different statistics on the impact of the walkout.

A twenty-three-year-old BRT dispatcher, Edward Luciano, put in a full day's work through midafternoon of that Friday, the first day of the month that would see the end of the war in Europe. But instead of heading home as usual after his shift, he was given a rush-hour assignment to pilot a Culver line train to Park Row on the Manhattan side of the Brooklyn Bridge and then back to Brooklyn over the Brighton Beach line. As was later brought out, Luciano was hardly the best choice on November 1 for the demanding assignment of operating a crowded electric train, let alone during the stressful circumstances of a work stoppage. He had recently returned to his job after a bout with the influenza that had taken so many thousands of American lives that year. More important, he and his wife had suffered the tragic loss of one of their children just a few days before, another victim of the dreaded plague.

Luciano's inbound run was uneventful. The return trip left the vaulted train shed on the Manhattan side of the Brooklyn Bridge at 6:14 P.M., the height of the evening rush hour. A wooden sign was hanging from the front platform of the lead car that read "Brighton Beach Only." After passing through the Sands Street station on the Brooklyn side of the bridge, Luciano's train took the cutoff near Tillary Street that led to the Fulton Street line and picked up additional homeward-bound passengers at various stations just beyond the Borough Hall area . . . Court Street, Boerum Place, Elm Place. When the train reached the junction between the Fulton Street el and the Brighton line at Franklin Avenue, the dispatcher-turned-motorman accepted an incorrectly set switch and signal and was proceeding out the Fulton Street line toward East New York before the mistake was realized. The error was understandable; with schedules thrown off by the strike, the towerman at Franklin and Fulton could not always be sure which train was supposed to be going where. Besides, Luciano's train was showing no marker lights, and the novice at the controls was totally unfamiliar with the Brighton route. He had never operated a train over the line, and the totality of his experience as a motorman, on any line, was but a few hours. The train returned to Franklin Avenue; after some switching, it was rerouted over its proper course.[3]

Between Franklin-Fulton and Malbone Street, the run was downhill; Coney Island-bound trains had to negotiate a sharp S curve at the base of this grade, enter a short tunnel, and cross over the still-incomplete subway that was later to run to DeKalb Avenue. The speed limit for this curve was 6 miles per hour.

Later, Luciano claimed that the air brakes failed on the downhill grade. Whatever the cause, the train gathered more and more speed as it approached Malbone Street and soon was out of control. The motorman later estimated his speed at 30 mph. A naval officer traveling as a passenger claimed that 70 mph was more like it!

As the first of the five cars, open platform el car No. 726, swung into the curve at the mouth of the tunnel, it derailed. The second car, motorless trailer No. 80, also derailed as it followed the lead car into the tunnel, and so did the third car, another trailer, No. 100. Behind these were two more motor cars, No. 725 and No. 1064. Both of these stayed on the tracks.[4]

The damage was to Cars No. 80 and No. 100 as they slammed into the concrete tunnel wall, and this is where the fatal injuries were the greatest. Car No. 80 had one of its sides and its roof torn away, and No. 100 was, for all intents and purposes, totally destroyed. It was the worst disaster ever to befall the New York subways or any other U.S. transit line. The death toll that night was 93 — 92 passengers and one of the BRT guards who was working aboard the train.[5]

Police and fire department rescue crews were forced to work at close quarters because the cars came to rest just inside the short tunnel under Malbone Street. As word spread through Brooklyn of the accident on the Brighton line, concerned families waited for news of their loved ones. Many waited in vain; few families in Flatbush were spared contact with the disaster—a cousin, a neighbor,

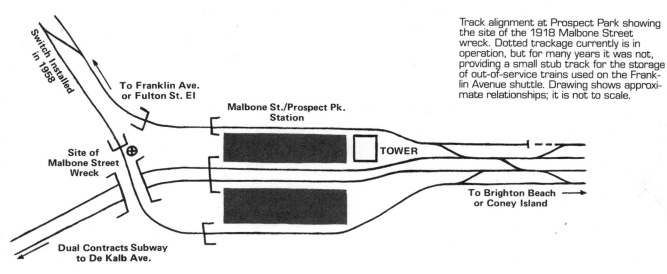

Track alignment at Prospect Park showing the site of the 1918 Malbone Street wreck. Dotted trackage currently is in operation, but for many years it was not, providing a small stub track for the storage of out-of-service trains used on the Franklin Avenue shuttle. Drawing shows approximate relationships; it is not to scale.

an in-law, a friend.

Charles Ebbets, Jr., son of the owner of the Brooklyn Dodgers, feared at first that his father was aboard the train. After receiving news that he was not, Ebbets opened nearby Ebbets Field as an aid station for the least seriously injured victims. Most of the seriously injured passengers were taken to Kings County Hospital, about a mile away.

November 2, 1918, the day after the fatal Malbone Street wreck. The curve off to the right is the one the train failed to negotiate. Marks can be seen on the center wall where wooden el cars slammed into the concrete. [Robert L. Presbrey collection]

Here are the remains of BRT el car No. 100, an unmotorized trailer unit totally destroyed in the accident, the worst ever to befall the New York subways. [Robert L. Presbrey collection]

This is the other unmotorized trailer car in the fatal Brighton Beach train that was involved in the Malbone Street wreck, car No. 80. It is shown here in the BRT's Thirty-sixth Street yard, where it was taken after being released by the Police Department. [Author's collection]

PLAYING POLITICS

In the late evening hours on November 1, 1918, Mayor Hylan, then in the first of eight frantic years as New York's chief executive, arrived at the crash scene to begin the official investigation. Hylan, more than any previous mayor, vocally advocated full municipal ownership and operation of the subways. He thought the Dual Contracts were a terrible mistake and never passed up an opportunity to mount an attack against what he called the "traction interests."

The mayor held that BRT management was criminally at fault in allowing untrained motormen to operate trains, and he instructed Kings County District Attorney Harry E. Lewis—who was initially inclined to place all the blame on motorman Luciano—to proceed at once against the higher-ups. Hylan even took advantage of a little-used clause in the city charter, and on the day after the accident, he assumed the role of "committing magistrate" and began to hear evidence on the case in the Flatbush court on Snyder Avenue. The hanging judge had come to town!

Hylan's foes—and the man had them in numbers—cried that the mayor was using a municipal tragedy to further his own political ends. But Hylan was hardly the only New York politician whose postaccident conduct may seem questionable by the standards of a later day. A statewide election was near, and the president of the New York City Board of Aldermen, Tammany Hall's Alfred E. Smith, was contending on the Democratic ticket for the position of state governor against incumbent Republican Charles Whitman. The day after the accident, November 2, 1918, Smith's people ran an obviously hastily prepared full-page ad in the *Brooklyn Eagle* calling on the borough's voters to turn out Governor Whitman because he supposedly had played politics with his appointments to the state's Public Service Commission. Smith's ad made no direct mention of the previous day's tragedy, but the Public Service Commission was an agency whose principal identity for people in Brooklyn was as the regulator of mass transit companies. "Brooklyn Tragedy Reflex Seen in Flatbush Swing to Democratic Candidates," headlined the *Eagle* after election day, an election day that saw Al Smith defeat Whitman for governor. (It was also the first statewide election in New York in which the electorate was not all male, a condition that wouldn't pertain at the national level for several more years.)

The trials dragged on for years after the Malbone Street wreck. Luciano was acquitted on a manslaughter charge on April 4, 1919.[6] Prosecution of five BRT officials continued through 1920 and included a change of venue for the various trials to Mineola. No convictions were ever obtained; hung juries, acquittals, and dismissals were the only results. And as to the accident itself that claimed ninety-seven souls on the evening of November 1, 1918, why not hear this editorial assessment from the *Eagle* over a year after the tragedy: "It is evident enough that if the regular motormen had not struck no inexperienced men would have been on the job. It is evident, also, that there is no moral obligation resting on a railroad management to concede the most absurd demands a union can make for fear of a strike." Presumably these include even such "absurd demands" as recommendations made by the federal War Labor Board.[7]

Less than two years after the wreck, on August 1, 1920, the tunnel connection to DeKalb Avenue opened for traffic, and steel cars began operating over the Brighton line. The spur to Fulton Street was turned into a shuttle operation at the same time but using wooden el-type cars. In July 1927, the wooden cars were replaced by steel cars. Signal techniques were also developed for electrically monitoring the speed of downhill trains. Should they exceed a prescribed limit, the brakes are applied automatically. Today, such a signal system protects every downgrade on the system. In 1958, a new switch was installed so that Franklin Avenue shuttle trains no longer had to negotiate the sharp S curve.[8]

The accident of November 1, 1918, left such a strong impression that the name *Malbone Street* could not survive. Today the street is known as Empire Boulevard.

TROUBLE FOR BRT

For reasons that went far beyond the Malbone Street wreck, the BRT entered receivership on the last day of 1918. Judge Julius M. Mayer granted the petition of a creditor, the Westinghouse Electric Company, terminating BRT's private status. Lindley M. Garrison, a former U.S. secretary of war, was appointed BRT receiver. Last-minute efforts to save the company failed. And thus, in the year of the Malbone Street wreck, the end of the war in Europe, a worldwide epidemic of influenza, and the murder of Czar Nicholas and his family in Russia, came also the end of the Brooklyn Rapid Transit Company. Conjunctive with Garrison's appointment, BRT President Timothy S. Williams offered his resignation. Williams, who had presided over the company as chief officer since 1911 and in other executive positions before that, was the man principally responsible for preparing the once-disorganized transit property for entry into the Dual Contracts in 1913.

Receivership ended in 1923 when the BRT was reorganized as the Brooklyn-Manhattan Transit Corporation (BMT), and the BMT went on to fulfill the promise that was once the BRT. But this 1918 receivership brings into focus a drastic change in fiscal conditions for the operators of the New York subways. In 1913, when the Dual Contracts were signed, subway profits were thought to be both lucrative and automatic. By 1918, urban traction companies were in precarious financial straits, throughout the rest of the country as well as in New York. The Malbone Street wreck took place at a few minutes before 7:00 P.M. Friday, November 1, 1918. Earlier that day, a conference was held in New York by the American Electric Railway Association, a professional group of street railway and rapid transit operators from across the country. (The BRT's top man, Colonel Timothy Williams, was in attendance despite the fact his railway was then being struck by the Brotherhood of Locomotive Engineers.) But this was no seltzer-

During World War I, the city's subway system relied on women workers to fill in for men who had gone off to war. Here, one woman explains the working of the automatic coupler on a BRT Standard to another, perhaps a new recruit. (Library of Congress)

bottle-in-the-eye-let's-have-fun-in-the-big-city convention. It was a serious and even somber meeting at which the delegates passed a motion to urge their various corporate members to divest themselves of their interests and sell their assets to the public sector, since the financial plight of urban transport providers was quite grim and had little hope of reversing itself.

Two compelling factors contributed to the BRT's receivership in 1918 and to the IRT's narrow escape from a similar fate in 1921. First, the national economy was hurting from an inflationary turn brought on largely by the press of wartime spending. Second, the Dual Contracts specified that the subway fare remain at five cents for the life of the contracts—forty-nine years. At the time the contracts were signed, both the BRT and the IRT welcomed this provision, seeing it as protection against demands that the subway fare be *lowered*! In 1913, that seemed a more probable threat than inflation.

And inflation took its toll. In 1914, the BRT paid about $14,000 for its first Standard cars. By 1920, the same cars cost nearly $40,000 apiece. The war also caused extended delays in building the 1913 network of lines, and every delay meant steeper construction costs as inflation accelerated. January 1, 1917, was the target date specified in 1913 for the completion of all Dual Contracts lines. When that date arrived, only minor additions beyond the routes opened in June 1915 were ready for traffic. Often, a section of line was finished and apparently awaiting service, but it would not be tied in with the rest of the system. Interest payments had to be met on such a line's construction bonds, despite the fact the line was producing no income.

The companies lobbied for corrective legislation amending the Dual Contracts to raise the fare, but such proposals only gave Hylan the kind of ammunition he needed to go to war against private interests' running subways in the first place. His major argument was that the preferential system was a raid on the public treasury. He was not moved by the fact the lines were losing money hand-over-fist despite the preferentials. In the face of such operating deficits, Hylan stood resolutely as the white knight defender of the nickel ride.

Subways were a major campaign theme in the 1921 mayoral and 1922 guber-natorial elections, in which Hylan was reelected and Al Smith defeated the incumbent Republican, Nathan L. Miller. For Smith, it was a return to the state's chief executive post; he had failed in a bid for reelection in 1920 when Miller rode into office on Warren Harding's coattails. But since the governor served only a two-year term, Smith was back in Albany in January 1923. He continued to serve for a total of four terms up through his unsuccessful run for the White House in 1928 and was as popular a governor as the state ever had.

In 1921, during his term in office, Miller had secured legislation creating an agency called the Transit Commission, another in a long and continuing series of state agencies that exercised broad control over city transit matters. This group, however, had a special mandate: to inquire into the possibility of some kind—any kind—of unification of the city's subways. Hylan, of course, had an easy answer for the commission: he advocated driving out the BMT and IRT and letting the city assume total control of the lines. In a speech from the steps of City Hall in 1921, when he accepted his party's nomination for a second mayoral term, he demanded that "the private operators turn the subways back to the city for municipal operation at a five-cent fare."

HYLAN VERSUS TRANSIT COMMISSION

The Transit Commission, hardly ready to confiscate the subways as Hylan would have preferred, began to explore less severe alternatives, and the mayor began to view the new agency as his mortal foe. What is of overriding interest here, though, is that both Hylan and the commission, despite their strong differences, were in agreement that the Dual Contracts were in need of radical repair.

In 1921, only seven years after the contracts were signed and with most of the lines completed and in service, it became apparent that the two traction companies could not realize the more optimistic benefits of the pact. The city's population had grown to more than 5½ million by 1920. Thus, even the extensive system of transit lines built under the Dual Contracts failed to meet the day-to-day requirements of the city's subway riders. More subway lines—or "transit relief" in the common phrase of the day—were clearly needed.

Hylan waged incessant political warfare against both the "interests" and Miller's Transit Commission. In 1925, he leveled a serious accusation against one of the commission's three members, Leroy T. Harkness, by insinuating that he was showing improper deference to his law partner, Judge Abel E. Blackman, a director of the Interborough. He accused the two members of the state bar of "actually fraternizing in private." To support this claim, he presented the fact that Harkness's name appeared on their office door in smaller letters than Blackman's, the assumption being that Harkness, the member of the Transit Commission, was subservient to the more powerful Blackman, who was a member of the board of directors of the hated Interborough, a company that Harkness was supposed to be regulating.

Hylan's assertion overlooked a small point. By the mid-1920s, the Transit Commission was entitled to name one director to the board of each company, the BMT and the IRT, and Blackman was the commission's man on the IRT. Blackman's position on the Interborough's board, in other words, was part of the commission's overall strategy in controlling the traction company, not a conflict of interest with his law partner, Harkness.

But Hylan never tired, and his passions never cooled. The man was convinced that it was wrong for private interests to run public subways, and he never passed up a chance to get in a left jab.

Al Smith made abolition of the Transit Commission a campaign pledge in 1922, and, in 1923, a bill was filed to strip the agency of its authority over city transit matters. Smith and Hylan did not enjoy a cordial relationship. Hylan was a product of the Brooklyn Democratic organization of John H. McCooey, and Smith was a loyal son of Manhattan's Tammany Hall. In 1917, the two men were contenders for the Democratic nomination for mayor. But when William Randolph Hearst let it be known he would not support Tammany and Smith, to avoid a primary fight the Manhattan and Brooklyn Democrats agreed to join forces behind Hylan, a man whom Hearst found much to his liking and also a man who had demonstrated an ability to win votes in a recent judicial election. Smith ran instead for president of the Board of Aldermen, and there was no love lost between him and Hylan.

But the differences between Smith and Hylan were largely personal and not based on issues. Any state Democrat in the 1920s could be expected to side with Hylan in transit matters, at least in broad substance. While running for governor in 1918, Smith had called for full public operation of both the BRT and the IRT, and in 1922 abolition of the Transit Commission, which was staffed by Miller's Republican appointees, was considered part of the Democrat's drive for increased "home rule" for New York City. Furthermore, the upper crust of industry, including the transit industry, was not the constituency a Democratic candidate felt obliged to cultivate. It was Red Mike's ferocious style and flamboyant oratory, rather than his formal positions on issues, that put him in a class apart, a class apart even from his own party.

In 1923, Smith's measure to abolish the commission was soundly defeated.

The Republican-dominated state legislature was not about to turn control of the subways over to a bunch of city Democrats. But even as the proposal was going down to defeat, a new man was making his first appearance in the continuing drama of the New York subways. Up in Albany, the bill was in the charge of the minority leader of the state senate, songwriter-turned-politician James J. Walker, the man who would succeed Hylan as mayor of New York in 1926.

This interesting sequence of photos was prepared by the Interborough in the 1930s to illustrate the role of the motorman in operating a train. *Top left:* With his air handle in his right hand, a motorman steps aboard IRT car No. 5560, a 1925-built unit turned out by the American Car and Foundry Company. The front vestibule was used as a motorman's cab on early IRT equipment. *Top center:* Ready to go! The motorman's right hand is on the brake valve, and his left is on the controller. The little handle to the left of the controller is the reverse key, a device that allows the train to operate forward or backward. *Top right:* A close-up of the motorman's hand on the controller. In the middle of the controller handle is a button that the motorman must depress while operating the train. Should he relax his grip and allow the button to pop up, the train would be thrown into an automatic emergency stop, the dead man's control, so-called. *Left:* Under way! Lanterns at the top of the car are marker lights. The motorman sets them at some established combination of red, green, white, or yellow so that passengers waiting for the train will know its route and destination as it enters the station. The two lanterns at floor level show two white lights at the head end and two white at the rear. Operating trains in revenue service with open end doors is no longer permitted. [All photos, NYCTA]

8

THE NEW MUNICIPAL SUBWAY

ON A RAINY SUNDAY IN AUGUST 1922, the year before Governor Smith's bill to abolish the Transit Commission was defeated, Mayor Hylan had an important announcement to make. Actually, he didn't make the announcement himself because he was on vacation at the racing meet in upstate Saratoga Springs. (Everybody who was anybody in New York spent August at the races in Saratoga Springs!) It was John F. Sinnott, who professionally served as the mayor's secretary, and personally was his son-in-law, who called reporters to City Hall that afternoon of August 27. On the same day, the rain washed out a St. Louis Browns baseball game with the Yankees, as well as a scheduled contest between Brooklyn and the Pittsburgh Pirates at Ebbets Field. The BRT, then in the depths of receivership and anxious to save a few dollars whenever it could, tried to take advantage of the poor weather and canceled the usual schedule of summer Sunday express trains to Coney Island. But rain or no rain, 100,000 people journeyed to the beach and amusement area. The impossible conditions on city-bound BRT trains that evening brought the company unfavorable front-page publicity in next morning's papers. The IRT also made Monday morning news when its uptown Manhattan service was disrupted for a spell on Sunday evening by a power failure.

The misfortunes of the traction companies were only a prelude to the big transit news for Monday, August 28, 1922. Reporters at City Hall for Sinnott's Sunday press conference had the real news: of a vast $600 million plan for a totally new municipally owned and operated transit system, a system that would tap areas in desperate need of transit relief. Until this time, transit investment in the original subway, plus the cost of the Dual Contracts lines, amounted to about $360 million. This was just half the projected cost of Hylan's new super-system, although this comparison fails to allow for inflated dollar values. Red Mike figured that a municipally run operation, even with the strictures imposed on city borrowing by the constitutional debt limit, could be completed in fifteen years.

Perhaps the most startling feature of the proposal was its plan to take away two of the private companies' most important lines: the BRT's Fourth Avenue route in Brooklyn and the IRT's West Side line in Manhattan. The technical term for this kind of seizure was *recapture*, and, oddly, the Dual Contracts themselves made it all quite legal and proper and, what's more, possible. With or without the approval of the companies, the city had the right to buy back certain Dual System lines from the BRT and IRT at a nominal cost, amounting to little more than a repayment of the company's invested capital. Recapture also meant the private operators could no longer run trains over the lines in question. Without the important trunk lines coveted by Hylan, both transit systems would soon wither and die as private operations, unable to maintain ordinary service and hopelessly outclassed by the new municipal subway. George McAneny, the former Manhattan Borough president and Dual Contracts negotiator and then a member of the Transit Commission, labeled the mayor's plan a political ploy that was "ludicrous in the extreme."

The defeat of Smith's bill in 1923 dashed Hylan's chances of getting a fast start on his grandiose plan, but it gave him a priceless issue to take to the public. He assailed his opponents in speeches, letters to newspapers, and talks over the new municipal radio station, WNYC.

Hylan was able to bring greater pressure against the BMT since three important BMT Dual Contracts projects had yet to be built, and the company was starting to feel the pinch for lack of them. Hylan not only promised they would never be built but that the city would never again put up money for construction of any privately run subway.

The three projects were the completion of the Centre Street loop from the station under the Municipal Building to a tie-in with the Montague Street tunnel, the construction of the final segment of the Fourteenth Street–Eastern line, and the construction of modern subway repair shops at Coney Island. The first project was expected to ease the heavy traffic on all Southern Division BMT operations (since the lack of this connection forced the Manhattan Bridge routes to operate far below their designed capacity) and created a stringent bottleneck at the DeKalb Avenue–Gold Street interlocking plant in Brooklyn.

The two-track Fourteenth Street line was especially urgent, for East New York had no direct service to midtown Manhattan. Passengers had to ride over the Williamsburg Bridge to Canal Street on the Centre Street loop and there transfer to Broadway trains and backtrack uptown. Canal Street's narrow platforms were becoming so crowded that many BMT officials felt that a major disaster there could happen at any time.

The Fourteenth Street line, Manhattan to the Montrose Avenue station in Brooklyn, did open in 1924, but the critical linkup with the rest of the Eastern Division at East New York was delayed by Hylan. The line was in partial operation only, separated from the rest of the BMT network. It carried only a handful of passengers and offered no relief for the press of traffic at East New York.

The BMT used an offbeat method to get subway cars into this isolated line. Twenty new Standard cars were hauled over the Long Island Rail Road to its Bushwick Yards, towed by truck along a temporary street track, and then eased down an inclined ramp into the subway.

One reason this vital linkup was delayed was that the 1913 contract called for it to be elevated between Montrose Avenue and East New York. Citizens of the Bushwick area objected, and community pressures forced the city and the BRT to plan instead for a subway. It was this delay that allowed Hylan to get into the picture; the full line did not begin running until July 1928, well into Walker's administration.

The BRT's main repair shops for elevated equipment were at Thirty-ninth Street, between Second and Third Avenues in South Brooklyn. The shop building, once the property of a BRT predecessor, the South Brooklyn Railroad and Terminal Company, had insufficient facilities to maintain the company's steadily increasing fleet of steel subway cars. (This main shop is sometimes confused with a near-by inspection and storage facility for el cars on Thirty-sixth Street and Fifth Avenue.) The original fleet of Standards had swelled to 950 cars by 1924, and the company needed a new maintenance and storage facility. Plans called for it to be built in Coney Island, but the Hylan administration refused to appropriate funds for the project, despite the fact that the Dual Contracts agreement legally bound the city to finance the project through completion. It, too, was finished only after Walker became mayor.

During the Hylan era, the BMT and the IRT had more to cope with than their feud with Red Mike. Riding statistics continued to soar. In its first full year of service, the original Interborough subway carried 106 million passengers. In 1923, ridership was slightly less than 715 million passengers on the expanded lines of both companies. As an economic move, automatic turnstiles were installed by the Dual Contract partners in 1921, equipment today so totally identified with the New York subways that it is difficult to imagine a time without them.

Turnstiles made economic sense in at least two ways. Prior to the deployment

Prior to 1921, passengers purchased tickets from what would today be a change booth and deposited them in a chopping box, operated by a uniformed guard. Turnstiles automated the "ticket choppers," as the men were popularly called, out of business. Despite the use of slugs now and then by artful dodgers, the turnstiles functioned smoothly and became standard equipment. Traffic through these Interborough units was two-way—out as well as in. [NYCTA]

of turnstiles, the standard procedure called for passengers to purchase a small pasteboard ticket at what today would be the change booth and deposit that ticket in a chopping box as they passed into the station interior and onto the platform. The chopping boxes had to be manned, so turnstiles allowed this labor expense to be avoided; and turnstiles, although not perfect in this regard, were far better able to detect and reject the use of slugs and other invalid coins than were the guards on the chopping boxes able to see and catch every artful dodger who tried to substitute worthless paper for authentic subway tickets.

In June the following year, 1922, the two New York subway operators adopted color schemes to be used on signs, entrance kiosks, and illuminated globes atop the kiosks. The IRT used blue and white. The BRT, and later the BMT, used green and white, with a dash of red from time to time. The colors were not applied to rolling stock, however, which continued to be painted in muted tones of brown, dark green, and black.

On the afternoon of June 25, 1923, the newly reorganized BMT was hit with a tragic accident. A Fifth Avenue el train out of the Sixty-fifth Street terminal in Bay Ridge derailed at the intersection of Fifth and Flatbush avenues in Brooklyn. Two cars—Nos. 913 and 919—left the track, fell off the elevated structure, and came to rest hanging between the tracks and the street. Eight passengers died; many were injured.

BRT trains had had some bad luck at this location over the years. On January 24, 1900, at 7:05 P.M., a five-car train from Bay Ridge caught fire just a few blocks from the 1923 crash scene. There were no injuries, but plenty of action that sounds, in retrospect, like the filming of a "Keystone Kops" comedy. Firemen began to direct hoses on the flaming lead car, No. 258, and were promptly sent sprawling when their streams hit the still-energized third rail. A substantial crowd attending a Knights of Columbus fair at the Thirteenth Regiment Armory poured into the street to watch, and a *New York World* reporter noted that "the mid-air blaze gave to them and to many thousand others one of those delightful experiences that diversify life in Brooklyn Borough."

Following reorganization in 1923, the Brooklyn-Manhattan Transit Corporation quickly became a strong and robust company. Hylan continued to claim that the reorganizaton failed to take proper regard of the city's interest in the bankrupt BRT, that a healthy BMT was secured only by double-dealing at municipal expense. One of the officers of the new corporation was Gerhard M. Dahl, an executive experienced in municipal transportation after serving as street railway commissioner in Cleveland. He also had an extensive background in finance. Dahl was able to meet Hylan on equal terms in a domain that today might be called "media politics," and he managed to argue the new BMT's case forcefully in a series of letters, pamphlets, and position papers.[1] As Hylan's second term was coming to an end, the press seemed to be picking up the BMT's line of reasoning, and it fell behind the company in its efforts to secure construction of the delayed links in its Dual Contract network. In these debates, the BMT was in an unusual position: it could cite its own poor performance to support its own arguments but lay the blame for that performance on the Dual Contract elements Hylan appeared to be continually delaying. Hylan kept shouting all the louder; the Hearst papers remained on his side to the very end.

BMT UNVEILS A NOVEL PIECE OF EQUIPMENT

In November 1924, superintendent of equipment for the BMT, William Gove, whose name is linked with all the finely designed rolling stock produced by the line, unveiled plans for a most unusual piece of equipment, a "Triplex," consisting of three car-body sections permanently joined to form an articulated unit 137 feet long. (Articulation means that a single set of wheels does the work of two. Instead of each section riding on its own wheels, or trucks, the center section shares its trucks with the sections ahead and behind.) The pilot models arrived in 1925 from the Bessemer Works of the Pressed Steel Car Company near Pittsburgh, and on August 31, the press took an inaugural ride from the BMT's City Hall station up to Fifty-seventh Street and back. The Triplex was a comfortable, quiet, and pleasant subway unit that did yeoman service on the BMT's Southern Division for forty years. Some devotees of the Triplex will claim in the face of all opposition that it is the finest piece of railway rolling stock *ever* produced.

An early and rare view of the BMT's articulated Triplex units, shown on the express tracks of the Sea Beach line. The front end treatment on the early models was changed in later production runs, and initial units such as No. 6002 here were altered to conform to the new design. [Author's collection]

Out of the Sixtieth Street tunnel adjacent to the Queensboro Bridge, whose outline rises in the background mist, a train of BMT D units maneuvers into the Queens Plaza station. Abandoned trackage to the left was used by Second Avenue el trains that once operated over the East River span. [Author]

The cars, also known as D units, included such novel features as illuminated signs on either end of the train and illuminated line and destination signs inside the car. If the end sign was illuminated in white light, the train was operating via the Montague Street tunnel; if the end sign glowed green, the train was operating via the Manhattan Bridge. Some New Yorkers rode these cars to work for as long as thirty years without ever knowing the meaning of the BMT's carefully worked out symbols.

An order for sixty-seven additional Triplex units was placed after the pilots proved out, and all were in service by the end of 1927. Four Triplex units were the service equivalent of a train of eight Standard cars, and because of the economies of the articulation design, the BMT was able to buy a more modern car than the Standard for less money. The Triplex was heavy. An unloaded train of eight Standard cars grossed about 760,000 pounds, and four Triplex units tipped the scales at 832,000 pounds. Eventually, still more units were ordered. By the end of 1928, the fleet totaled 121 units carrying the numbers 6000 through 6120.

The BMT rebuilt some older el equipment in 1925. Under a Public Service Commission directive to replace some of its aging elevated cars—motorized leftovers from the steam era—the company instead rebuilt some eighty open platform el cars into closed platform vehicles and permanently coupled them into three-car units for service on the Fulton Street line. These cars became known as the C units. Although noisy and downright ugly, the C's were structurally and mechanically sound. They improved Fulton Street service markedly with minimum cash outlay.

Interior view of a BMT Triplex showing woven cane rattan seats and illuminated route and destination signs. Notice the passageway into the next compartment of the three-section articulated unit. [NYCTA]

New rolling stock was secondary, however, to the principal transit news of the second Hylan term: the mayor's plans for a new municipal subway. In 1924, Senator James Walker again cosponsored legislation to abolish the Transit Commission and give Hylan a green light to proceed with his plans. A companion measure was also filed to alter the city's debt structure and permit additional subway borrowing. Both bills met with determined opposition, but a compromise was at least worked out that kept the Transit Commission in existence, with regulative powers over existing lines. A new Board of Transportation, appointed by the mayor, was then established to monitor Hylan's proposed municipal system.

The compromise passed the legislature in April 1924. The legislation included a passage stipulating that any new municipal subway would be held to a five-cent fare for its initial three years. After that time, the fare would have to be adjusted upward to cover operating expenses and meet construction and equipment debts. Republicans were proud of themselves. They not only had saved the Transit Commission but had directly challenged Hylan to keep his many promises. Democrats, including the mayor, were disgruntled because the Transit Commission had not been abolished and were disturbed even more over the legislature's refusal to take any action on raising the debt limit. Some felt they

The BMT's first attempt at rebuilding open platform el cars into more modern units resulted in the C units. Their venerable lineage easily discernible, they rocked and swayed along Brooklyn elevated trackage well into the 1950s. This train is on the Fulton Street el. [NYCTA]

had received but "half a loaf"; Hylan cried aloud that it was more like "a few crumbs."

Essentially, this legislation safeguarded the existing systems and kept them under the watchful eye of the commission but allowed Hylan to proceed with his own plans. The legislation pointedly excluded Hylan's 1923 goal of recapturing key BMT and IRT routes for inclusion in a municipal subway. Hylan could build his new city-run subway, but it would have to coexist with, not absorb, the private lines. There were very few legislators in Albany who did not feel this 1924 compromise was a very temporary arrangement. It hardly seemed possible that long-term stability for mass transit in New York could be achieved with three different subway systems, one municipally operated and two profit-seeking, but hardly profit-achieving, private ventures.

Transit unification, an important topic in many influential quarters even before Hylan received the authority to build the city's third subway system, was discussed with an increased sense of urgency as Hylan's new municipal subway began to take shape. By 1924, the Transit Commission had formulated its own unification plans. They envisioned, roughly, a purchase by the city of both BMT and IRT interests. "Purchase" in this case did not mean a simple cash transaction but a complex exchange of private and municipal bonds. The plans allowed the commission to show, on paper at least, that such a city takeover would free large blocks of frozen credits, allowing new subway lines to be built to tie in with the existing networks. According to the commission, a city takeover of the BMT and IRT—coupled with a major expansion program—would cost less than the construction of a third subway system.

The commission's unification plans remained a distant goal, however, as Hylan turned to the actual construction of his municipal subway. All city spending was held in check, and rigid priorities were established so that as much credit as possible could be earmarked for subway bonds.

THE BOARD OF TRANSPORTATION

In July 1924, a new three-man Board of Transportation was sworn in. John E. Delaney, a former commissioner of the state Public Service Commission, served as its chief officer. Delaney immediately met with George McAneny to discuss the mutual jurisdiction of the two rival transit bodies. This must have been a delicate and touchy session in view of the kind of open warfare that had prevailed between Hylan and the commission. McAneny's statement to the press afterward was measured: "In a case like this where authority and its commensurate responsibility are not always specifically defined in all their details, there is likely to be a 'twilight zone' of more or less doubt."

On December 9, 1924, the Board of Transportation adopted a basic route plan for the new system. It differed only slightly from the plan Hylan had announced in August 1922 and included Manhattan trunk lines on both Sixth and Eighth avenues, a line to Washington Heights, a cross-Brooklyn line, and several other connections. One of the original Manhattan els, the Sixth Avenue line, would be replaced by the new subway, and soon removal of the els became a popular goal in New York, for by 1925 the Manhattan els had been running for half a century and their useful days were commonly felt to be just about over.

Two days before this plan was revealed, on December 7, 1924, Governor Al Smith named Justice John V. McAvoy to conduct a "summary investigation" of what the governor described as the "intolerable" conditions prevailing on the subways. Charges and countercharges flowed from Hylan, the Transit Commission, and the two companies. Now there was still another party to the disputes, the new Hylan-appointed Board of Transportation. While all these groups railed at each other, the full Dual Contracts system remained incomplete, needed lines had yet to be constructed, and conditions on the subways themselves were crowded. Major General John F. O'Ryan, a member of the Transit Commission, harked back to wartime for an appropriate comparison: "Had I treated German prisoners during the war as passengers on the transit lines are here being treated, I would have been court-martialed."

The McAvoy commission heard testimony during December and January. Its findings, as reported to Governor Smith, were highly critical of Hylan, while generally praising the work of the Transit Commission. Former governor Miller's original appointees had by this time been replaced by Smith's own, and it is not unreasonable to see the McAvoy investigation as part of an effort to sandbag Hylan as the 1925 election drew near.

Although the Hearst papers continued to support the mayor, neither Smith nor the Tammany organization would accommodate Hylan for a third term. But because Red Mike was eager to stay in City Hall, a primary fight broke out for the Democratic nomination. In September 1925, Jimmy Walker, Tammany's man, dealt Hylan a crushing defeat. Walker carried all five boroughs including Hylan's own Brooklyn, where he outpolled the incumbent by 5,000 votes. It could easily be speculated that all 5,000 were BMT riders!

Hylan was at a disadvantage in his fight with Walker because his pet issue was effectively neutralized. He was unable to call Walker a tool of the hated interests. The senator's track record on transit was, if anything, better than Hylan's. Walker had always been a defender of the five-cent fare, and it was Walker who twice sponsored the legislation that allowed Hylan to begin work on the municipal subway. After polishing off Hylan, Walker then went on to defeat Republican Frank Waterman (of the fountain pen Watermans) in the November general election.

Not long before his defeat, Hylan enacted what may well have been his most triumphant performance. On Saturday, March 14, 1925, wielding a silver-plated shovel, he broke ground for his "baby," a municipal subway system, at the intersection of St. Nicholas Avenue and West 123d Street. Orating to a crowd of some 2,000 onlookers at Hancock Square in Washington Heights, Hylan laced into the "railroad corporations," the Transit Commission, and traction sympathizers generally. Vintage Hylan verbiage again excoriated the "million dollar traction conspiracy" perpetrated by his enemies. But this time the mayor was able to conclude on a victorious note. The ceremonial event of the day "means the beginning of the emancipation of the people of the City of New York from the serfdom inflicted upon them by the most powerful financial and traction dictatorship ever encountered."

On Thursday, April 3, 1925—Calvin Coolidge in the White House, Jack Dempsey the heavyweight champion of the world, and the Scopes trial about to become a nationwide sensation—the Rosoff Subway Construction Company put a steam shovel to work at St. Nicholas Avenue and West 128th Street. The new municipal subway was under way.[2]

Pressure to halt construction of the third system—and to expand instead the two earlier networks—intensified after Walker took office. The BMT had long been interested in the Washington Heights route, for instance. (There is still a short stretch of tunnel north of the BMT station at Fifty-seventh Street and Seventh Avenue that was built in 1919 with such a linkup in mind.) But in early 1927, the Walker administration entered a contract for a tunnel under the East River at Fifty-third Street. Completion of this route made anything but a new independent system impractical.

The question of whether the new line should be built to the smaller IRT dimensions or the larger measurements the BMT inherited from the Triborough System was resolved in favor of BMT specifications. This decision was particularly significant because in recent years the BMT and the Independent system have been merged and integrated into virtually a single system, while the IRT remains unto itself.

Work on the new subway proceeded slowly. Before any city-operated train could run in the new system, additional lines had to be authorized and their contracts drafted. In Brooklyn, it was proposed that the BMT's Culver line be recaptured so that the municipal subway might reach all the way from the Bronx to Coney Island. Also in Brooklyn, a new line out Fulton Street to East New York doomed the BMT's Fulton Street el. Even before the Dual Contracts were signed, there were proposals to tear down the western end of this elevated line and replace it with a subway. After 1913, a more modest plan emerged to upgrade the Fulton Street el to handle steel subway equipment and connect the line with the BRT subway at DeKalb Avenue. Following the Dual Contracts, large segments of the el were actually upgraded, and the many tunnels at DeKalb Avenue were designed to permit the construction of a ramp to the Fulton Street line. The plan, known as the Ashland Place connection, likely would have been completed had not a John Francis Hylan sat in City Hall for eight years. Now, a new four-track municipal subway would replace the Fulton Street el, and even rebuilt sections of the line would be torn down.

Regular operation on the first leg of the municipal subway began on Saturday, September 10, 1932, when the Eighth Avenue line opened from Washington Heights to Hudson Terminal in downtown Manhattan. The inaugural was unusual; there were no festivities, no speeches, no first train. Instead, at 12:01 A.M., all stations along the line opened simultaneously. Full schedules had actu-

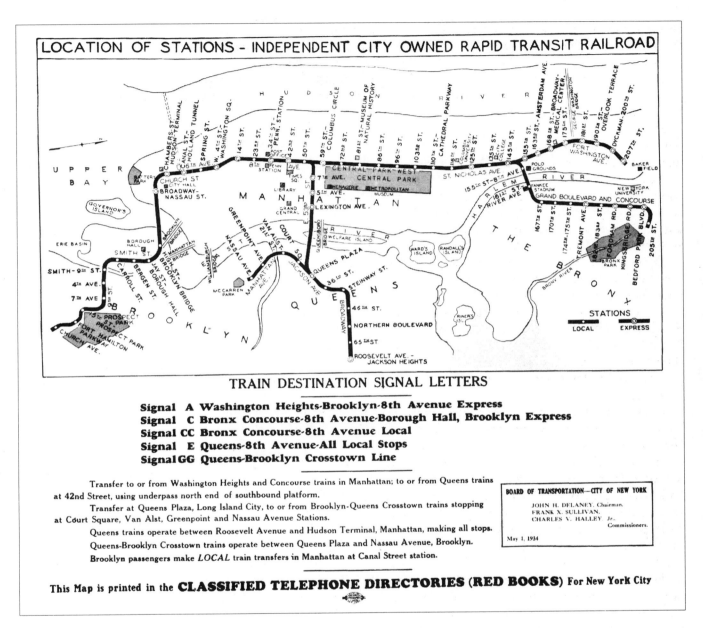

LOCATION OF STATIONS - INDEPENDENT CITY OWNED RAPID TRANSIT RAILROAD

TRAIN DESTINATION SIGNAL LETTERS

Signal A Washington Heights-Brooklyn-8th Avenue Express
Signal C Bronx Concourse-8th Avenue-Borough Hall, Brooklyn Express
Signal CC Bronx Concourse-8th Avenue Local
Signal E Queens-8th Avenue-All Local Stops
Signal GG Queens-Brooklyn Crosstown Line

Transfer to or from Washington Heights and Concourse trains in Manhattan; to or from Queens trains at 42nd Street, using underpass north end of southbound platform.

Transfer at Queens Plaza, Long Island City, to or from Brooklyn-Queens Crosstown trains stopping at Court Square, Van Alst, Greenpoint and Nassau Avenue Stations.

Queens trains operate between Roosevelt Avenue and Hudson Terminal, Manhattan, making all stops.

Queens-Brooklyn Crosstown trains operate between Queens Plaza and Nassau Avenue, Brooklyn.

Brooklyn passengers make *LOCAL* train transfers in Manhattan at Canal Street station.

BOARD OF TRANSPORTATION—CITY OF NEW YORK

JOHN H. DELANEY, Chairman.
FRANK X. SULLIVAN.
CHARLES V. HALLEY Jr.,
Commissioners.

May 1, 1934

This Map is printed in the **CLASSIFIED TELEPHONE DIRECTORIES (RED BOOKS)** For New York City

Like the Interborough, the new Independent Subway System printed its maps with north at the right. This map shows the extent of the system in May 1934. Of two planned Manhattan trunklines, only one is in service, that under Eighth Avenue. This priority of construction perhaps explains why New Yorkers tended to call the whole Independent System the "Eighth Avenue Subway" for many years. [Author's collection] ally been in effect since the previous Wednesday to get the line in shape for opening day. Not everyone was fully prepared to begin service, however. Many conductors put in several days' work in uniform jackets with sleeves merely basted on; the tailor was one contractor who failed to complete his task on time.

The lack of fanfare in 1932 contrasted sharply with the gala festivities that had marked the beginning of Interborough service in 1904. Another difference between 1904 and 1932 is worthy of mention. When passengers first boarded the Independent Subway, as the new system was called, there were no advertisements on the walls, owing to a delay in getting them installed. But soon enough, the stations and cars were festooned with blurbs for chewing gum, soap powder, funeral parlors, and the latest movies, though not for beer or hard liquor—prohibition was in full swing. Ironically, passengers felt the line looked naked and incomplete without ads. In 1904, passengers had raised quite a hoot and a holler that the ads desecrated the subway.[3]

Twelve hours after the new subway opened for business, the Italian liner *Conte Grande* backed slowly away from its pier at the foot of West Fifty-seventh Street and steamed down the Hudson River and out to sea, bound for Gibraltar, Naples, and Genoa. Aboard was James Walker, now *ex*-mayor of New York. He had tendered his resignation to New York Governor Franklin D. Roosevelt several days earlier after his administration's credibility and public confidence had been utterly destroyed through a series of dramatic public investigations. He was going to Europe to rest and regain his health and his strength. Walker returned to the United States in a few weeks, only to be hounded by creditors. Broken in spirit, he sailed once again on the *Conte Grande* in November, this time accompanied by Betty Compton, the woman he had courted for so long—a true voyage into exile from his beloved New York.[4]

During Walker's six years as mayor, the bitterness and hostility of the Hylan era faded, even if Walker's formal policies on transit matters were not all *that* different from those of his predecessor. But there clearly were different levels of emphasis between the two men, even if their positions were similar. Transit simply wasn't the passion with Walker that it had been with Hylan, for instance.

That times were changing could be seen as early as March 22, 1926, when the Walker administration celebrated the opening of its first new subway line. It was a minor addition to the city's network: the extension of the Interborough's Queens line a mere quarter-mile from Grand Central to a station adjacent to the New York Public Library on Fifth Avenue. But its inauguration was celebrated with gusto and included movies at the nearby Hippodrome on into the night. The press saw the festivities as evidence that past transit difficulties had "seemingly ended with the advent of the new administration." Walker himself had sounded the same theme when he took the oath of office. "This administration will not seek to glorify itself at the expense of delay in this most essential necessity. More transit facilities must be provided without any kind of political or personal interference," he said.

The new Independent subway ran almost exclusively below ground. Here a test train emerges from the subway onto a 4-track viaduct that will enable service to vault across the famed Gowanus Canal in South Brooklyn. [Author's collection]

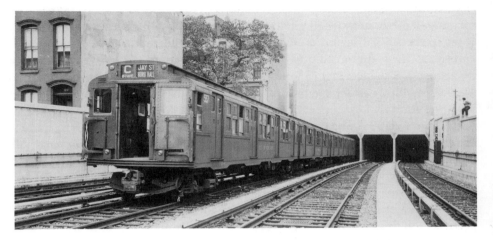

TROUBLE, TROUBLE, AND THE FIVE-CENT FARE

Of course, the mere fact that the transit companies could expect civil behavior from the new mayor of the city was not enough to solve all their problems. While the BMT settled down to business, thankfully free of Red Mike, the Interborough was left to capture a few unpleasant headlines. It suffered a massive strike in July 1926, a near-classic study out of the turbulent middle years of the American labor movement. The Interborough was unwilling to grant its workers the right to bargain through anything save an ineffectual company union, and management had the muscle to get its way. The IRT obtained an injunction in the state supreme court restraining the Consolidated Railroad Workers of Greater New York from "inducing" anyone to join its organization, and offered $100 to any employee who supplied information leading to the arrest and conviction of anyone violating the order. Six years later, when the new municipal subway was doing large-scale hiring, men who had been fired by the IRT for taking part in the 1926 strike were accorded preferential treatment. Rival BMT was no more progressive in labor relations than the Interborough. It, too, actively discouraged independent unions. For example, in 1920, each employee found in the November issue of the company magazine, the *BRT Monthly*, a pledge that the employee would not join a particular union trying to organize a membership drive at the time. All were expected to sign the pledge card and return it to the company. Elsewhere in the magazine, among the news items about picnics and the softball leagues, were pithy quotations equating trade unionism with bolshevism.

In addition to suffering from labor unrest, the IRT was feeling the pinch of the five-cent fare, and it began to push for a higher tariff. Unable to get relief through the legislative process, company attorneys were told to take the matter to court. Like many theological, political, and matrimonial matters, the argument turned on a very tenuous distinction between two seemingly identical terms.

In 1907, the state Public Service Commission had been established with statutory power to set subway fares. IRT lawyers argued that this authority, later delegated to the 1922 Transit Commission, was itself sufficient to override the Dual Contracts' five-cent fare stipulation. But the PSC would only have authority to override the Dual Contracts fare requirement because these were signed *after* the PSC itself was established. Contract One, the original subway, and Contract Two, the Brooklyn extension of the Interborough, were signed in 1900 and in 1902, and their terms could not be put aside by PSC edict. Because these earlier contracts also specified a five-cent fare for the term of the contract, the IRT case centered on whether the Dual Contracts fare of five cents was a new and different obligation from the five-cent fare stipulation of Contracts One and Two.

The IRT won an initial victory before the U.S. Statutory Court in May 1928, and the Walker administration was faulted for not raising effective objection against even the assumption of federal jurisdiction. Eighteen months after the court action, Walker was up for reelection. The IRT victory brought out the wolves calling for Walker's hide, and from the dark and depressing past came the thundering sound of John Francis Hylan, who finally was able to charge that Walker was "soft on the interests."

But Beau James was entitled to a miracle. He got it when the U.S. Supreme Court, in an unexpected opinion delivered by Associate Justice James Clark McReynolds, ruled that the statutory court order was "improvident and beyond the discretion of the court." The IRT lost its case, the five-cent fare remained in effect, and the thorny problem of whether five cents is really five cents remained unanswered. On the crest of this victory, Walker rode into a second term as mayor.

The Interborough faced costs of more than a million dollars from its unsuccessful action. The line had been so confident of victory that it had even minted tokens that would have been used when the fare was raised to seven or eight cents. But the taxpayers of the City of New York, in effect, wound up footing the bill because the IRT charged up all the costs to operating expenses, the first category of cash outflow under the Dual Contracts.

The amount of subway fare had been a highly emotional issue from the beginning. Back in 1906, the BRT charged a double fare on el trains to and from Coney Island.[5] Justice (and later mayor) William J. Gaynor ruled in August that the company could not collect the double tariff, but the BRT would not be dissuaded. It hired a corps of 250 special policemen, or "heavyweight inspectors" in the words of the *Times*—and "goons" in anybody else's language—to enforce the company's double-fare policy. On Sunday, August 12, disturbances broke out at the various points in Brooklyn where the extra fare was collected. More than 1,000 men, women, and children were ejected from company trains and trolleys, including Brooklyn Borough president Bird S. Coler, a man who not unsurprisingly became a firm advocate of municipal operation of subways and els. An entire car full of passengers unwilling to pay the extra nickel was uncoupled from a Coney Island-bound train and left on an isolated siding. A young girl's body was found floating in Coney Island creek, and it was suggested her death was caused by the enthusiasm of the "heavyweight inspectors." In the middle of this overheated atmosphere, a BRT lawyer suggested that the line had the clear right to kill anyone who refused to pay the extra fare!

Even after winning the IRT case, Walker faced a potential time bomb on subway fares: the legal requirement that after three years of operation, the Independent must charge a fare that would meet all expenses. To avoid the absurdity of the new municipal line's charging a higher fare than the BMT and the IRT, Walker pushed ahead with plans for full subway unification. Samuel Untermyer, who was retained by the Transit Commission as special counsel, worked out a plan for the city to assume complete title to the private lines for $400 million. One of Walker's quiet aims in unification was the elimination of open trading in traction securities. For despite the annual operating deficits of the two companies, their complex schemes of financing and indebtedness made it possible for investors to earn dollars on BMT and IRT stocks and bonds. Unification, as envisioned in the Untermyer plan, would end this speculation, Walker felt.

But unification proved to be an even more drawn-out business than the negotiation of the Dual Contracts. If the formation of the Transit Commission in 1921 is considered the first step in the process, then unification took nineteen years to accomplish!

In 1932, the year the Independent opened, the Interborough entered receivership. Immediately, speculation began as to whether receivership would aid or hinder unification. One possibility, strongly urged by Untermyer, was that the courts could move to dissolve the IRT's 999-year lease on the four elevated lines, the pact Belmont engineered in 1902. Although the IRT subways turned a small

Classic IRT. Car 5214 was built for the Interborough by Pullman in 1917 as the company expanded its fleet to meet new Dual Contract responsibilities. Note "fishbelly" under the center door, a design feature to ensure proper body strength in the car at the point of the doorway. [Author's collection]

profit, the antiquated els more than ate up this net and prevented the company from achieving a sound fiscal position. In addition, the els had no long-range role to play in New York's transit picture. However, before the els could be eliminated, the claims of the original Manhattan Railway bondholders would have to be satisfied.

Thus, by the mid-1930s the Interborough was in dire straits, and the els were living on borrowed time. Meanwhile, the Independent subway was being opened piecemeal, unification was in the wind, and the BMT, although receptive to the general idea of unification, was enjoying, at least operationally, perhaps its finest hour.

Forty years after the Independent opened for service, a yard full of R-4 units awaits the call to rush hour service on the CC line. Addition of sealed-beam headlamps is the principal external change in these cars over the years. [Tom Nelligan]

9

THE ROAD TOWARD UNIFICATION

IN 1934 FIORELLO LA GUARDIA WALKED into City Hall as the standard-bearer of a "fusion" administration. The former Republican congressman was not a representative of a conventional political party but a crusader for reform that transcended traditional party lines and drew support from both Republicans and Democrats. After several years of investigations into the Walker administration, New York was ready for new solutions to its problems.

Despite the oppressive Great Depression, New Yorkers, during the decade before World War II, indulged in a variety of pursuits. The 102-story Empire State Building was completed in May 1931; price, $41 million. The skyscraper was built by a syndicate headed by former governor Al Smith and instantly became a source of considerable civic pride, its observation tower a potent tourist attraction, though not foreseen as the site of "King Kong's last stand." There was the transatlantic speed competition being waged season after season by two fine ocean liners, French Line's *Normandie* and Cunard's *Queen Mary*, to beguile New Yorkers after 1935. The vessels would tie up at the city's new deep-water piers on the Hudson River north of West Forty-third Street, each arrival dutifully covered by photographers from New York's two popular tabloids, the *News* and the *Mirror*. In June 1937, a major American legend had its beginnings when Joe Louis, a young boxer from Detroit, knocked out James J. Braddock to become heavyweight champion of the world. Adjacent to the 161st Street station of the IRT's Lexington-Jerome line, other sporting legends flourished throughout the 1930s. There in Yankee Stadium, teams led by Babe Ruth and Lou Gehrig rewrote the American League record book.[1] It was a time for debates on isolationism and rearmament; it was a time when the zeppelin seemed the harbinger of things to come; it was a time when everyone had a theory on the mysterious disappearance of Judge Joseph F. Crater in New York on the sixth

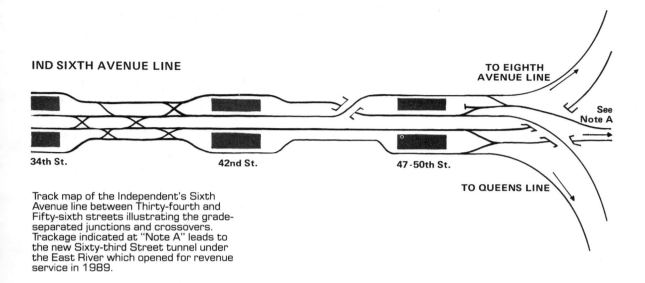

IND SIXTH AVENUE LINE

TO EIGHTH
AVENUE LINE

See
Note A

34th St.   42nd St.   47-50th St.

TO QUEENS LINE

Track map of the Independent's Sixth
Avenue line between Thirty-fourth and
Fifty-sixth streets illustrating the grade-
separated junctions and crossovers.
Trackage indicated at "Note A" leads to
the new Sixty-third Street tunnel under
the East River which opened for revenue
service in 1989.

day of August 1930; and it was a time when the best-known telephone number
in town was "PEnnsylvania 6-5000," the title of a popular Glen Miller tune.

Through the La Guardia years, the Independent continued to expand. The
last major trunk link to be placed in service was the Sixth Avenue route in Manhattan, on which the first revenue train ran on December 15, 1940. But certain
segments of the new system were delayed until after World War II.

Originally, the Sixth Avenue subway was planned to take over the existing
Hudson & Manhattan (H&M) subway tunnel under Sixth Avenue south of West
Thirty-third Street for local service; a new two-track tunnel was to be constructed
for express service. This plan was later abandoned because the H&M was built
to IRT-size clearances, and the cost of refitting the tunnels to handle 10-foot
wide cars would have been prohibitive. So the H&M was not ousted from its
tunnel; indeed, it was given a completely new terminal at Thirty-third Street
and Sixth, and the Independent built a right-of-way for itself around and under
the old tunnel. Only a two-track line opened in 1940, however; proposed express
tracks were not constructed for another quarter-century.

FEATURES OF THE INDEPENDENT

Compared to the BMT and IRT, the new municipal subway was an engineering
marvel. Its stations were built to generous dimensions with color-coded tile
on station walls to help passengers identify their stops with ease. The spacing
of stations was worked out by precise formula.

From time immemorial, New Yorkers have had a positive addiction for riding express trains, much to the chagrin of transit planners. Local trains regularly carry large numbers of passengers only as far as the next express stop, where everyone gets off to catch the express. Independent engineers attempted to induce local riders to stay aboard their trains right through to final destinations. To this end, the number of local-only stations in the central business district of Manhattan, the area below Fifty-seventh Street, was held to a bare minimum—three out of twenty. The major express line down from the Bronx under Eighth Avenue and Central Park West had no express stops at all between 125th Street and Columbus Circle. The reason: local passengers boarding trains below 125th Street would see no advantage in changing to an express. There isn't, and they haven't.

Sharp curves force subway trains to operate at inefficiently slow speeds, so the new municipal lines were built with wide, high-speed curves. Costly "flying junctions" were constructed so trains could proceed on diverging routes with minimum delay. In general, the physical plant of the new system was a glistening and shiny showpiece of a subway—a far cry from the older systems, which were starting to show not only their age but the incremental character of their construction.

Thanks to its well-built roadbed and efficient signal system, the Independent subway featured a passenger capacity of 90,160 per hour per track. The comparable BMT statistic was 73,680, and the IRT rate was 59,400.[2]

Several other features of the Independent are of interest. The older lines generally operated on conventional railroad-style roadbeds—rails spiked to cross-ties sitting in stone ballast. The new system largely adopted a technique previously used only in stations. Ties were not imbedded in ballast but in indentations in the concrete flooring. Full-length ties were not used, but rather "half-ties" were placed under each rail, with a drainage ditch between them. This arrangement has more than once saved a life because a person falling in front of an approaching train has sufficient room in the ditch to lie flat and allow the train to pass over. The technical rationale for the ties-set-in-concrete method was that it resulted in a more secure roadbed, free from the frequent distortions of ordinary ballast and ties.

At two spots, one in Astoria and the other in Flatbush, the Independent tried something different. Express tracks at these points diverged from the right-of-way used by locals, took a shortcut along the "third leg" of an imaginary triangle, and arrived at a common terminal over a shorter route. The Independent also pushed three more two-track tunnels under the East River, raising the number of transit river crossings of that river to thirteen.[3]

Rolling stock for the new subway was nice, but utilitarian, equipment. The cars measured 60 feet, 6 inches long, 10 feet wide, and a shade over 12 feet high. (Presumably by accident and not design, the end-to-end length of the new subway cars equaled, to the inch, the distance between home plate and the pitcher's mound on a baseball diamond.)[4] Each car was able to accommodate 282

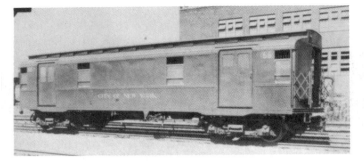

Who says all IND cars look alike? The system's fleet of basic passenger cars may have had little variety, but there were always cars like No. 66, one of two revenue collection vehicles added to the roster in 1939, to add a little spice. Shorter than a conventional car and with fewer windows, No. 66 was designated an R-8a unit and was built by the Saint Louis Car Company. [Author's collection]

passengers, though only 60 could be seated. Each weighed 80,000 pounds and cost the city $38,000. Among other innovations, they featured left-handed screw threads in the emergency lighting system to thwart bulb snatchers. The regular light bulbs, officials presumed, would always be burning, and their heat alone would be ample defense against larceny. But the emergency system, which is battery powered and designed to take over during power outages, needed added protection because its bulbs were always cool. The new cars borrowed an idea from the BMT Triplex: end signs to identify the route of the train and its destination. But whereas the BMT used numbers to designate its various lines, the Independent adopted a letter code, a notation that jazz musician Billy Strayhorn found so fascinating one day when he was in an especially creative mood.

The original IND letter code was a masterpiece of symmetry, as well as an inspiration for a jazz artist. Trains came into Manhattan from the north over one of three different branch lines, and they navigated their way through the city's business districts over either of two trunk lines, one under Eighth Avenue and the other under Sixth Avenue. That makes six possible combinations, and each was given its own letter designation; a single character represented express service and a double character a local. The A train was actually the Eighth Avenue express off the Washington Heights branch; the BB train was the Sixth Avenue local out of Washington Heights; the E train was the Eighth Avenue express that originated on the Queens branch, and so forth.[5] The "orphan" of the system, the GG train, was a local on a line that wasn't built for express service; it connected Forest Hills in Queens with South Brooklyn via Greenpoint and Williamsburg, and to this day it is the only major subway line ever built in the city that doesn't serve Manhattan. (The old designation, GG, has become a more prosaic G under a new system of train identification recently adopted.)

The first cars were ordered under contract R-1, and the cars have since been known by this contract number. In fact, the R Series has been continued into modern times on the New York subways; the most recent subway cars, for instance, are R-68 units, delivery of which began in 1987.

The cars ordered for the Independent subway in the 1930s—1,703 of them, designated R-1 through R-9—offered swift acceleration and generous speed capabilities, but they were not as comfortable or as quiet as the BMT Standard, nor were they any match for the Triplex. Comparisons may be unfair, however, because few who made them were without bias, including BMT men who had

Fresh and shiny after being delivered to the new Independent Subway System by the American Car and Foundry Company, two R-1 units are eased off a barge in the Harlem River at the 207th Street Yard in upper Manhattan. Cars ran tests on the BMT in 1931 before the Eighth Avenue line opened in 1932. [NYCTA]

a chance to operate some of the new units. They were put in service on the Sea Beach line in July 1931 for tests. Independent cars could run on BMT rails, of course, because both the BMT and the municipal lines were built to the same general specifications—in effect, the old "big railroad" dimensions of the original Triborough Subway System. (Well, one slight qualification is in order. Once it became apparent during the negotiations of the Dual Contracts that the Public Service Commission's desire to attract a conventional railroad to operate into and connect with the new city subway would not reach fruition, tunnel diameter and curve radius specifications were eased up a bit. The BRT/BMT-IND lines have broader clearances than the older IRT, but they are not quite so generous as was originally specified for the Triborough System.)

This is the Bergen Street station in Brooklyn on the new Independent Subway System. A train of R-1 units is running tests. [NYCTA]

The "city cars," as they were called by the BMT during their trial operation on the Sea Beach, were returned to the Independent in November 1931, a line still ten months away from inaugurating service.

STILLWELL AVENUE

The Transit Authority's current Stillwell Avenue terminal in Coney Island
is built on the site of the Brooklyn
Rapid Transit Company's old West
End Depot, and it's located but a
single, albeit long, block from the
beachfront . . . which is to say the
Atlantic Ocean. The terminal itself is
an eight-track, four-platform facility
built on a poured-concrete elevated
structure and is the southern termi-
nus of four important subway routes.
Today, the lines are identified by letter code: N, D, F, and B. But most
Brooklynites still use older terminology, and the routes are more commonly called, respectively, the Sea
Beach, the Brighton, the Culver, and
the West End.

Summer 1987: A train of R-68 units operating on the Brighton line pulls into Stillwell
Avenue terminal. [Author]

Summer 1955: A train of R units operating on the IND D train leaves track 6 of the Stillwell Avenue on a run to the Bronx. Standards off to the left are operating in Brighton local
service. [Author]

Trains approach Stillwell Avenue
from two different directions: Brighton and Culver trains run parallel to
the ocean and enter the terminal
from the south after making a
90-degree turn, and Sea Beach and
West End trains come in from the
north. Deadhead moves to nearby
yards and shops also use this northern approach.

There have been but minor changes to the place since it opened in
1919 as a Dual Contract–financed
replacement for both the West End
Depot and the Culver Depot, the latter formerly located near the site of
today's West Eighth Street station
on the Brighton and Culver lines [see
map]. Platforms were extended to
handle ten-car trains; an original
two-track bridge across Coney Island Creek was supplemented by a

second to ease a bottleneck there; tracks are now identified by number, where they used to be lettered; track 7 is currently stub ended, where it once provided an alternate connection to the Culver line; and today all trains serving the terminal use steel subway cars—no more wooden elevated equipment.

Maybe the biggest changes to the Stillwell Avenue Terminal over the years involve not its subway services but the feeder surface lines that provide connections for passengers. Today, they are prosaic motor buses —B-36/Surf Avenue and B-74/Mermaid Avenue. Not too many years ago, they were streetcars, and they gave the terminal a touch of panache that it now lacks. Trolleys from Surf Avenue looped into the street level of the terminal during its early days, and through the late 1940s, today's Mermaid Avenue bus was the Norton's Point trolley, and it climbed an incline and deposited passengers at subway train level just beyond the bumper posts of tracks 7 and 8.

Stillwell Avenue Terminal is still a pretty terrific place, though.

Looking to the north in 1972, a train of R-32 units moves up the incline into the Stillwell Avenue terminal. [Tom Nelligan]

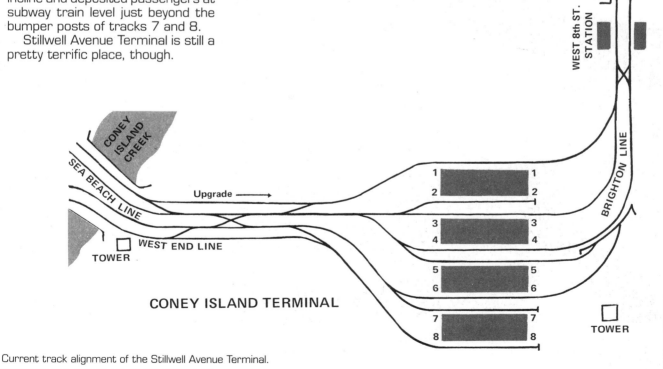

Current track alignment of the Stillwell Avenue Terminal.

The Independent Subway System. *Top left:* A photographer posed a train of new R-1 units in the Jay Street station in Brooklyn on January 31, 1933. [NYCTA] *Top right:* It's early 1972, and a train of veteran R units pauses at the Columbus Circle station on a northbound run as the CC train. [Nelligan] *Bottom left:* Passengers were kept informed with roll signs showing both terminals—lighted in the operating direction—and a large line sign displaying the letter code of the route. [Author]

MEANWHILE, BACK ON THE BMT

During the 1930s, the BMT completed its long-delayed Dual Contracts links. The Nassau Street line in Manhattan was opened with fitting ceremony on May 29, 1931, when Mayor Walker rode into the new Broad Street station aboard a freshly scrubbed Triplex. The line was the last of the network of transit lines mandated by the Dual Contracts of 1913.

The Nassau Street line linked the station under the Municipal Building—by then known as the Chambers Street station—and the Montague Street tunnel. It had been difficult and expensive to build because it had to thread its way through a highly congested district under a narrow street, dodging three older subway lines in the process. The present BMT station at Fulton and Nassau streets, with its puzzling complex of passageways, is testimony to why this line,

A Brighton train approaches the Stillwell Avenue terminal in Coney Island in 1954. Lower level tracks on this double-deck elevated structure host Culver line trains. [Author]

which is less than a mile long, carried a price tag of $10 million. Once the Nassau Street line opened for traffic, the Centre Street loop subway was finally complete. Ironically, the first venture in underground transit for the BRT was in 1908 when the company began to run el trains over the Williamsburg Bridge and into the north end of the Centre Street loop.[6] Since 1931, the loop has generally been known as the Nassau Street loop. The two stations that were opened in 1931 were finished off in the same style of color-coded tile work that was used on the Independent.

The BMT opened its maintenance facility in Coney Island during Walker's administration, thereby cementing a long relationship between the Brooklyn traction company and the seaside resort. Before the turn of the century, Brooklyn transit lines had converged on Coney Island. By building the principal repair facilities of the system within a mile of the ocean, the company retained its historic identity with the area.

The BMT's Stillwell Avenue terminal, which replaced the older Culver Depot and the West End Depot in 1919 and is served by four different subway lines, stands but a stone's throw from the ocean in the middle of the Coney Island amusement area. The eight-track Stillwell Avenue facility—replete with popcorn and saltwater taffy stands—is today perhaps the busiest rail passenger terminal in the country, with almost a thousand departures and arrivals daily.[7]

In the 1930s, the BMT again earned high marks for equipment development. In 1934, the company took delivery of two radical pieces of rolling stock. One was built by Pullman-Standard and equipped with Westinghouse electrical components; the other was turned out by the Budd Company of Philadelphia, with electrical gear by General Electric. Both the Budd train and its Pullman running mate were five-unit articulateds designed to be sufficiently light in weight to operate on elevated lines where standard steel subway cars were prohibited. The Budd unit met this challenge by using stainless steel for its body shell, and the Pullman product was built of aluminum. The Budd train was unofficially called *Zephyr* because it resembled the Budd-built *Zephyr* streamliners of the Chicago, Burlington & Quincy Railroad. The Pullman train, with its two-tone green color scheme, was dubbed the *Green Hornet*, after a popular radio character of the day. Both units measured 170 feet in overall length, roughly the equivalent

The BMT looks into lightweight equipment. *Top:* One of two experimental five-unit articulated trains built in 1934. This stainless-steel vehicle was turned out by the Budd Company; the other experimental was a product of Pullman-Standard. [Author's collection] *Below:* The first of twenty-five production models based on the two 1934 experimentals was No. 7004, shown here in 1936 at the Rockaway Parkway station of the BMT Canarsie line. Units spent most of their service life in Canarsie line service. [NYCTA]

of two-and-a-half Standard cars. Their newly designed mechanical and electrical gear gave them swift acceleration rates.

These experimentals were put through a series of convincing demonstrations on the Fulton Street el. They featured modern and comfortable appointments, which the riding public found quite pleasant. Both were equipped with indirect lighting, quite the vogue at the time, and the *Green Hornet* had a system of chimes that sounded when the doors were operated. The Budd train had a relatively long service life, running chiefly on the Franklin Avenue shuttle when its demonstration days were over. It was not scrapped until 1959 and ran as late as 1954. But the *Green Hornet*'s aluminum body was just what the scrap drive needed, and in 1942 it "went to war." The government's requisition of the train was done with such secrecy that many BMT workers had no idea what happened to the unit. Only a postwar announcement by Mayor La Guardia's office dispelled some imaginative rumors. One romantic tale had the train running through a secretly built tunnel under the English Channel ferrying counterspies into France and bringing rescued bomber crews back to England!

The major innovation pioneered by the two new trains was operational. Their metal construction fitted them to run in the subway; their light weight allowed them to run on els. Previously, only lightweight wooden cars could navigate the older els. Steel subway equipment was too heavy for such lines, and the law prohibited wooden equipment from carrying passengers underground.

All of this raises an interesting point—more semantics than engineering—the difference between a genuine el and a rapid transit line that happens to be built on an elevated structure. In the late 1960s, for instance, the Myrtle Avenue el was referred to as the city's "last el." Yet a score or more of avenues all over town had—and still have—extensive overhead transit lines, operating on what certainly *look* like els.

In New York, a bona fide el is best described as an elevated line dating back to presubway days that is not operated as an extension of the underground system. The distinction quickly loses clarity, though, because New Yorkers tend to call any elevated line an el, even those built as subway extensions during the Dual Contracts program. Then too, many of these Dual Contracts elevated lines were rebuilt from older, genuine els. To confuse matters more, on some of these rebuilt elevated lines, wooden el trains and steel subway trains operated in joint service.

Despite the eminent demise of the downtown segments of the Fifth Avenue complex and the Fulton Street line—routes no longer needed with the opening

A Manhattan-bound train made up of two five-section articulated units rolls into the Broadway Junction station on the Fourteenth Street–Canarsie line. This busy spot in East New York is where the Broadway, Jamaica, Fulton Street, and Fourteenth Street–Canarsie lines intersected. Of the four, only the Fulton Street line no longer operates. [NYCTA]

of the municipal subway—the BMT felt there was ample call for equipment such as the Budd train and the *Green Hornet*. The Myrtle Avenue el, for example, seemed to have a definite future, and the Transit Commission, which had a hand in the experiments, was anxious to work up a design for lightweight equipment on the chance that the Manhattan els might somehow be given a reprieve and thus need new rolling stock.

The BMT soon ordered a fleet of production-model units with specifications similar to the two experimentals. Twenty-five of the five-section articulateds, called multisection cars, were delivered in 1936. They provided base service on the Fourteenth Street line for a number of years and capitalized on their lightweight design by operating out to Richmond Hill over a section of the Fulton Street el where orthodox steel subway cars could never run. The "multis" became a nonstandard item on the subway roster once the elevated lines were phased out after World War II. They were scrapped in 1960.

GOOD-BY, SIXTH AVENUE, EL; HELLO, WORLD'S FAIR

The IRT was not in sound health through the 1930s. It performed its daily tasks; nevertheless, the line could not shake off receivership. It was definitely a poor sister of BMT and the spanking-new Independent. In anticipation of the forth-coming municipal subway for the same route, IRT's Sixth Avenue el departed the New York scene on December 4, 1938. Through a deal that was heavily criticized later, its steelwork was sold as scrap to interests in Japan. The IRT did manage to design and order a new subway car for service on the Flushing line out to the 1939–1940 World's Fair, the line's first new equipment since 1925. Although it was the first IRT car without end vestibules, it was not an outstanding vehicle because it was designed to mate with some of the line's

Only once did the Interborough order rolling stock that differed essentially from the body style the company adopted in 1902. That was a fifty-car order for service to the 1939–1940 World's Fair. Here, five of the new units are shown at the plant of the Saint Louis Car Company prior to shipment. [General Steel Industries—St. Louis]

The new Independent subway operated a seasonal service to the 1939–1940 World's Fair in Flushing Meadow over a right-of-way that is today the Van Wyck Expressway. Here, a four-car train heads away from the fairgrounds. Soon, it will be adjacent to a platform at the Kew Gardens station on the Queens line of the new system. [NYCTA]

oldest equipment. The "World's Fair cars" followed the Interborough tradition of old-fashioned metal plates for car interior route and destination signs, years after cloth roller signs had become standard practice in the traction industry. They did have illuminated roll signs on the car ends, however.

Although built to the IRT's narrower specifications, the Flushing and Astoria lines were operated jointly by the BMT and IRT as specified in the Dual Contracts. The BMT could not, of course, use its 10-foot wide steel subway cars on these lines. It instead maintained its half of the service with open platform elevated-type cars, built in 1907, which were compatible with IRT standards. As the World's Fair approached, the BMT was in a quandary about equipment. It could not justify the expense of newly designing a car that could be used only on the Flushing and Astoria routes. Yet it was not content to use outdated el equipment in blue-ribbon World's Fair service. The dilemma was solved by rebuilding older open platform el cars—at the Coney Island shops—into closed vehicles that became known as the Q units. (The Q stood for Queens.) These typically sound BMT products were designed under the supervision of William Gove, a man whose name deserves to be enshrined in the very highest ranks of an electric railway hall of fame, were one to be established. Painted in World's Fair colors of blue and orange, the cars were as snappy looking a fleet of transit vehicles as ever hauled passengers in New York. The Q units would also go on to chalk up many additional distinctions over their remaining thirty years of service, as will be seen.

Like the private companies, the new Independent also operated to the 1939–1940 World's Fair. Trains from the Queens line ran through the Kew Gardens storage yards, then into the fairgrounds over a specially built line that was torn up after the fair closed. Today, this right-of-way forms part of the Van Wyck Expressway.

A final note of interest about the Independent subway is that although its original financing scheme was developed during the municipal administration of John Hylan, before it was completed it was able to secure federal funding from the administration of Franklin Roosevelt. The Public Works Administration provided over $25 million to assist in the construction of 18 miles of the new system.[8]

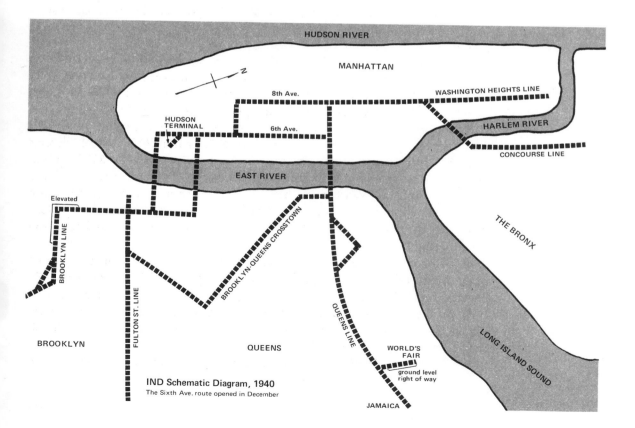

IND Schematic Diagram, 1940
The Sixth Ave. route opened in December

10

UNIFICATION: THE BOARD OF TRANSPORTATION

THERE IS A RECURRING PATTERN IN THE STORY of the New York subways: each decade appears to have been dominated by a single theme. In the century's first decade, the prime item was the building of the city's first subway. From 1910 through 1920, the Dual Contracts provided the focus of interest. In the 1920s, it was Hylan's drive for a municipal subway. During the thirties, the theme was unification.

The fiscal picture in the 1930s was especially cloudy. Thus, money problems served as the principal spur toward unification. From the time the Dual Contracts lines were in full operation—officially 1919 for the IRT, 1920 for the BRT, though several links in both systems were incomplete—through the La Guardia years, the city collected only $19 million from the IRT to service its Dual Contracts debt. No money was ever received from the BRT or the BMT. To avoid default on its Dual Contracts bonds, the city had been forced to divert $183 million from general revenues over this period. Theoretically, turnstile receipts were to have been the source of this money and the city should have been free from any liability. Because of a general deterioration of the Dual Contracts vision, money had to be raised from other sources since the notes were backed by the city's credit.

As each of the two subway operators slid into receivership during this period, some degree of unification appeared to be highly desirable. Moreover, while the city juggled its accounts to raise an unanticipated $183 million, the two traction firms were able to post profits, in varying years, amounting to some $91 million. Such revelations naturally provided fuel for arguments on behalf of total public operation of the subways.

Although early talk of unification did not necessarily envision complete public

It's 1957. The evening rush hour is winding down, and weather forecasters are saying the light snow that's falling could intensify during the night. Brighton locals are backed up on the elevated approach to the Stillwell Avenue terminal as the BMT Division adjusts its schedules and assignments to conform with the lesser demands of the post–rush hour period. [Author]

operation of the subway system, gradually it became obvious that such was the only plausible alternative. Substitution of low-interest, tax-exempt, municipal bonds for the outstanding BMT and IRT private notes, coupled with the replacement of three operating agencies by one, were felt to be the central features of any workable unification plan.

Another item bearing on unification and subway finances was that after reaching slightly over 2 billion annual riders in 1930, the number of passengers using the subway began to fall off in 1931—a full year before the Independent opened for business.

Samuel Untermyer's final unification plan never cleared the Board of Estimate; therefore, La Guardia felt a fresh start was needed. The mayor appointed Adolph Berle and Judge Samuel Seabury to deal with the transit companies. In 1935, both the BMT and IRT signed "memoranda of understanding" for transit unification under municipal ownership according to what became known as the Seabury-Berle plan.

After protracted deliberations, the Transit Commission rejected the plan in the spring of 1937. Many suspected the Democratic members of the commission were anxious to embarrass La Guardia, who may have been elected as a fusion candidate but who remained a Republican through and through. Thundered the mayor: "The Transit Commission has been stalling on this problem for sixteen years at a cost to the public of 16 million dollars in salaries." Whatever the reason, the commission's action served to cool enthusiasm for transit unification on all fronts for more than a year. But in May 1938, transit conditions were still critical, and La Guardia and the Transit Commission decided to ignore past differences and work together for unification. An amendment passed by the legislature was ratified by the state's voters in November 1938. This exempted $315 million from the city's debt ceiling. With funds thus earmarked for buying out BMT and IRT, negotiators were able to approach their task with enthusiasm.

THE OLD ORDER PASSETH

Full and final unification was achieved in 1940. On Saturday, June 1, with the British Expeditionary Force being hastily evacuated from Dunkerque, a ceremony was held at City Hall. Some $175 million in 3 percent municipal bonds was given to the BMT in exchange for the company's tangible assets. The previous evening, as part of a separate but concurrent deal, service was terminated on the downtown portion of the BMT Fulton Street el and on the entire Fifth Avenue line. These structures were then purchased by the city for removal. Money to buy the el lines—a transaction apart from the $175 million—was principally raised by assessing property owners along the el routes for the betterment that their removal would bring about.

The final Fulton Street el train left Park Row for the trip over the Brooklyn Bridge shortly after 11 P.M. on Friday, May 31, with Mayor La Guardia aboard. As it pulled out of each stop in Brooklyn for the last time, the station lights were extinguished in a moving gesture to dramatize the passing of an old order. The outer leg of the Fulton Street line, from East New York to Richmond Hill, remained in service, as did the tracks on the Brooklyn Bridge, which were used by the BMT's Myrtle Avenue el.

The next night, another ceremony was held. Seventy-one-year-old Joseph McCann, who was retiring as a BMT motorman, commanded a train of BMT Standards from the Fifty-seventh Street Manhattan terminal to the Times Square station. When he arrived, McCann and the BMT had made their last run. The platform was awash with dignitaries and reporters, because at exactly 12:01 A.M. on Sunday, June 2, 1940, the Brooklyn-Manhattan Transit Corporation formally, officially, and irrevocably surrendered its properties to the city as specified in the terms of the agreement signed at City Hall several hours before. BMT president William S. Menden spoke first and presented La Guardia with the keys, as it were, to the system. It was fitting that Menden be the corporate officer who presided at the line's obsequies. Years earlier as a young and promising engineer heading up the BRT's design section, it was Menden who helped perfect plans for the Standard subway car. If anything typified the BRT and the BMT, it was this fine piece of equipment.

La Guardia turned to John Delaney, whose Board of Transportation now controlled the BMT, and said, "I hereby entrust these properties and the safety of millions of passengers to you. I know you will do a good job."

Delaney then appointed La Guardia a motorman—with badge No. 1—and ordered His Honor to take out the train McCann had just brought in from Fifty-seventh Street. As flashbulbs exploded, the mayor donned a motorman's jacket and hat, took hold of a special set of chrome-plated control handles, and posed for a picture in the cab of a freshly painted train. When it came time to run the first city-operated subway train on what had just become the BMT Division of the city's Board of Transportation, La Guardia deferred to a regular motorman.

A week and a half later, on Wednesday, June 12, 1940, ceremonies were again held at City Hall. Backed by an issue of $151 million in municipal obligations, the properties of the IRT were purchased by the city. Thomas E. Murray, the Interborough's receiver, gave the mayor the company's copy of Contract Number Three, the IRT's Dual System Pact, a contract that would soon cease to be the operating mandate for the system. Present at City Hall for the ceremony were former mayor Jimmy Walker and former Brooklyn Borough president Bird S. Coler, a man who had been elected to that post many years earlier on a platform calling for full municipal ownership and operation of the city's rail transit systems.

The next day, June 13, 1940, saw important things happen. At the Brooklyn Navy Yard, where the battleship U.S.S. *Arizona* was launched in 1915 on the same day the BRT ran its first subway train over the Manhattan Bridge, another man o' war, the U.S.S. *North Carolina*, slid down the ways in preparation for hostilities yet to come. In France, Nazi troops marched into Paris. ("I remember every detail; the Germans wore gray, you wore blue," a movie actor would shortly say.) And at 12:01 A.M. in New York on that same day, the Interborough Rapid Transit Company quietly became the IRT Division of the Board of Transportation of the City of New York.[1] As in the sale of the BMT, most of the Second Avenue el and all of the Ninth were abandoned and their structures deeded over to the city for dismantling. Of the original four elevated lines, only the Third Avenue line remained in full operation. It survived for another fifteen years. Its abandonment was not sought in 1940 on the theory that the el would be needed until a proposed Second Avenue subway was completed.

Labor difficulties almost derailed the whole unification process. By 1940, Mike Quill had emerged as the prime spokesman for the transit workers; his Transport Workers Union (TWU) enjoyed union shop status with both the BMT and the IRT. Quill himself had become a colorful and controversial character on the New York scene in the late 1930s, and his distinctive Irish brogue was often heard on the airwaves. He was called "Red Mike"—again, the nickname appears in the subway saga!—but not because of the color of his hair. Quill was a vocal apologist for all manner of left-wing political causes, regularly espoused pro-Soviet sentiments, and carried a Communist party card. His appearance before Congressman Martin Dies's House Committee on Un-American Activities in May 1940, for example, was a tumultuous scene that resulted in his ejection from the hearing room. Quill also had a magnificent forum at his disposal—he called it his "soapbox"—for, until the 1939 election put him out of office, Michael J. Quill was a bona fide member of the potent New York City Council.[2]

Although La Guardia had been an early ally of Quill, he saw subway unification as a means of breaking Mike's hold on BMT and IRT. Consequently, the mayor suggested that after unification, the 13,000 BMT and 15,000 IRT employees who would be absorbed into the civil service system thenceforth work under an open shop policy.

Quill would have none of this. "We won our freedom through the closed shop," he maintained, "and we aren't going to give it up." With an ominous strike threatened, John L. Lewis, president of TWU's parent organization, the CIO, was engaged to mediate the dispute between Mike and the mayor. "Mediate" he did. The closed shop was retained, and shortly after unification, the TWU expanded into the ranks of the Independent.

REPRIEVE FOR THE NICKEL RIDE

Unification brought few immediate or visible results. The Independent System became known as the IND Division of the larger complex. Another experimental train the BMT had ordered from the Clark Railway Equipment Corporation was delivered to the Board of Transportation in late 1940.[3] However, the three divisions in general retained their preunification character and identity until well into the postwar period. The war itself brought a swinging increase in riders, taxing the system to its utmost, reversing the downward trend in patronage that had begun during the Depression. And for the first time since World War I, the five-cent fare was not in danger.

One capital improvement was the purchase of a 4-mile segment of a former electrified railway in the Bronx, the New York, Westchester & Boston. This was a suburban line that ran from the east bank of the Harlem River to Port Chester and White Plains. (Despite its name, the line never came within 150 miles of Boston.) In December 1937, the entire line was abandoned, a victim of the Depression, increased automobile travel, and its own lack of a mid-Manhattan terminal. (In postwar years, when Westchester County became a genuine boom territory, NY, W&B was sorely missed.)[4]

On May 1, 1940, the city assumed title to the old right-of-way that was located within city limits. Shuttle service was instituted on May 15, 1941, using refurbished open-gate el cars. In the mid-1950s, the line was tied into the IRT subway network and is now known as the Dyre Avenue line. Something of an oddity is that when the service was initially taken over by the city in 1941, although it *looked* like a component of the IRT Division, it was administered as part of the IND and operated by IND personnel.

But it was the war that affected other desirable developments. Even minor construction projects, such as the completion of a few IND routes that were only months away from being finished, had to sit idle until after VJ Day. What did happen during the war, though, were a couple of interesting abandonments. The final leg of the Second Avenue el, which ran from South Ferry to East Fifty-ninth Street and then over the Queensboro Bridge to Queens Plaza, was phased out in 1941. The BMT's Myrtle Avenue el, damaged by fire, was cut back from Park Row in Manhattan to Jay Street and Myrtle Avenue in Brooklyn. These

In 1972, a Lexington Avenue express heads for Dyre Avenue along a right-of-way that once belonged to the ill-fated New York, Westchester & Boston Railway. [Tom Nelligan]

are the only times rapid transit crossings of the East River were ever eliminated. Removal of IRT tracks from the Queensboro Bridge served to isolate the Flushing and Astoria lines from the rest of the IRT; the BMT's Coney Island shops then became the major site for repairing the equipment of these two IRT lines.

Brooklyn Bridge el service had been electrified since 1896 when the original cable cars were supplemented by electric equipment. With the cutback to Jay Street, the famous old Sands Street station at the Brooklyn end of the bridge passed from the scene. In the days before the Brooklyn els were electrified, Sands Street served as a union depot for steam-powered trains of several companies from all over the western end of Long Island.

Thus transit unification was established as war broke out over Europe. Two companies, long on heritage if short in years, had participated as best they could through forty years of tremendous growth and development in New York City. Although unification under municipal aegis eventually became an economic necessity, the very construction and operation of subway lines in New York in the first quarter of the twentieth century would not have been possible without the Dual Contracts partners. Their status as profit-seeking corporations was a liability in 1940; it had been salvation in 1913.

The distinctive shape of a BMT D unit is apparent in this 1954 view, though the swirling snow masks other details. This is the Brighton Beach line near the Avenue M station. The buildings to the left were once motion picture studios of the Vitagraph Corporation, where many famous films of the silent era were made. Today, the facility is a television studio. [Author]

Interior view of a new R-10 unit. Cars differed from prewar IND R units in several
respects, including fluorescent lighting for
passenger convenience. [NYCTA]

11

ENTER THE TA

THE END OF WORLD WAR II SAW A RETURN of the many chronic transit maladies that had been obscured by the extraordinary press of wartime traffic. Inflationary pressures finally doomed the nickel ride, for instance. On July 1, 1947, the Board of Transportation raised the tariff to ten cents, the first increase since the day the subway opened in 1904. With this doubling of the fare, many additional free transfer points were established among the three divisions. Wherever practical, barriers were torn down so passengers could pass unhindered among BMT, IRT, and IND. "IRT sheep mingled today with BMT goats," quipped the *Daily News.*

Rolling stock was in short supply all over the sprawling system at war's end. The first cars purchased after the 1940 unification that can truly be said to have been designed for service on either the BMT or the IND were ordered in 1946. Designated the R-10 units, 400 of them were turned out by American Car and Foundry in 1948 and 1949. These vehicles were built to the same external dimensions as the prewar IND cars, but they featured a more modern-looking interior design, as well as improved propulsion and electrical equipment. The R-10 was equipped with four motors per car, not two as had previously been the standard, and this has been the norm for New York subway cars ever since.

The basic body and interior design of the R-10 was executed by IND engineers on a prototype car before the full order was delivered. A prewar R-7A unit that had been badly damaged in an accident became the test bed for the new design. This car, No. 1575, served for many years. But because the four-motor R-10s could not run in multiple unit with the two-motor prewar cars and since mechanically and electrically No. 1575 remained an R-7A, many unsuspecting traction buffs were surprised to find what *looked* like an R-10 running in a train of older units.

An R-10 unit showing a later paint scheme used on this interesting fleet. The initial assignment of the R-10s was the IND A train. [NYCTA]

Each R-10 cost more than $77,000, a barometer of the way rapid transit expenses were reflecting postwar economic conditions. The newcomers were assigned to the IND A line, where they not only remained for many years but became essentially identified with that route and service. Their arrival allowed the transfer of some older R-1 cars to help ease shortages on the BMT; their usual assignment there was the Fourth Avenue local.

A scaled-down version of the R-10 was ordered at the same time for the narrower confines of the IRT, and for the first time, the city's original subway system was operating a fleet of cars that looked very much like the newest cars operating elsewhere in the city. They were shorter and narrower, of course, but the IRT's R-12s and R-14s were otherwise look-alikes of the R-10 units running on the A train. (One quick way to tell the difference is that IRT units featured three sets of doors along each side, while BMT-IND cars had four, a distinction that has prevailed on all new cars ordered over the past forty years.)

Here, in 1972, four 1948-era R-12 units approach the Gun Hill Road station in the Bronx over the final section of the Third Avenue el to remain in active service. [Tom Nelligan]

The R-15 was a small fleet of cars built by American Car and Foundry in 1950 for service on the IRT Flushing line. The "turtle-back" roof profile was a new feature on New York subway cars. The small circular device extending out from the car is an early radio antenna. [NYCTA]

A different-looking car, the R-15, was also ordered for IRT service after the war. Like the R-12s and R-14s, the R-15s were assigned to the Flushing line. They featured a rounded "turtle-back" roof and a new ventilation system; their overall design and profile was destined to become the new standard for New York City subway cars for another twenty years.

All the new postwar IRT cars were assigned solely to the Flushing line and not to the basic Manhattan-Bronx routes of the old Interborough. The reason was that the Broadway–Seventh Avenue line north of Times Square and the Lexington Avenue line south of Grand Central—the original Contract One route—were oriented around the vestibuled body style of August Belmont's basic car design. The R-12s, R-14s, and R-15s lacked end vestibules, had a different door arrangement, and could not travel the older routes unless considerable reengineering work was done along the right-of-way. Platform gap fillers, for instance, installed at several stations built on curves, would not function at all with cars of a different design.

A dramatic service improvement took place in fall 1949 when the Dual Contracts arrangement of joint BMT-IRT service on the Flushing and Astoria lines was eliminated. The Flushing line with its new cars became the exclusive responsibility of the IRT, while the Astoria route had its platforms shaved back to take care of operation as an extension of the BMT's regular subway service. Routes through the eight-track Queens Plaza station were consolidated, and half the sprawling structure was torn down.

The Q units, designed for BMT service to the 1939–1940 World's Fair, became surplus property. Because they had been rebuilt in 1938, they were too valuable to scrap at a time when equipment was at a premium. They were trans-

Near the site of today's Lincoln Center, trains of both the Ninth and Sixth Avenue els operate in this view from the mid-1930s. The two els operated on a joint structure (over Ninth Avenue) north of West Fifty-third Street. [NYCTA]

ferred to the Third Avenue el. However, they proved to be too heavy for service there. Although the Qs were originally el cars themselves, rebuilding had upped their tonnage to more than the spindly el could handle. The solution? Discard the Q's BMT trucks and remount their bodies on lighter running gear made available when the old IRT Composites were retired. Thus equipped, the final series of cars designed for BMT began running on the last Manhattan Railway elevated line. One observation must be added: even with lighter trucks, the Qs were still heavyweight units authorized to carry passengers only while running on the center, or express, track of the three-track Third Avenue el. They had to deadhead in one direction and operated only during rush hour. Base service on the Third Avenue line was provided by a fleet of so-called multiple-unit door control (MUDC) cars — standard el cars whose open platforms had been hastily enclosed and equipped with remote-controlled sliding doors. During the Hylan era, bitter court battles had been waged between the Interborough and the city as each side tried to get the other party to foot the million-dollar bill for improvements.

The Third Avenue el was gradually reduced in size during the postwar years. Finally, on May 12, 1955, the line ran its last train, and the colorful history of the Manhattan els came to an end.

Of course, a few qualifications are necessary in any absolute statement about New York transit matters! A 6-mile leg of the Third Avenue el of the Bronx survived until 1973, and a miniscule segment of the Ninth Avenue el actually survived longer than the Manhattan portion of the Third Avenue el. When the Ninth Avenue el was abandoned in 1940, a section less than a mile long, from

On a gloomy day in 1954 with its demise just about a year away, a train of MUDC cars on the Third Avenue el heads out of Chatham Square station en route to Gun Hill Road in the Bronx. (Author)

155th Street and the Harlem River to a junction with the Jerome Avenue line in the Bronx, remained in service. This shuttle served the Polo Grounds and the New York Central's Putnam Division terminal at Sedgewick Avenue. After the New York Giants moved to San Francisco following the 1957 season and the railroad gave up passenger service on the "Put" in 1958, the shuttle was phased out. It was not around, unfortunately, when the New York Mets came into existence in 1962 and made the Polo Grounds their home for two baseball seasons.[1] (The Mets' permanent home, Shea Stadium, is served directly by the IRT Flushing Line. Bill Shea, after whom the stadium is named and who was instrumental in returning National League baseball to New York in 1962 after it had departed in 1957, served for a time as a board member of the Metropolitan Transportation Authority.)

POSTWAR SUBWAY AILMENTS

In the immediate postwar years, the Board of Transportation was simply not working out as an effective instrument of subway governance. Master plans were forever, it seemed, being issued; construction of new high-speed lines was always in the news. But daily straphangers could not appreciate reading about a glorious subway future when they were stalled in a cold and dirty train and delayed by some unexplained mechanical failure. Even the more modest goals envisioned by proponents of subway unification in 1940 were largely unachieved by 1950, and the Board of Transportation was overseeing three subway divisions that were unified more in name than in actuality. Meanwhile, increasing numbers of riders took advantage of the highways built after the war for travel to and from work in private automobiles. As a result, subway service and conditions began to deteriorate in the late 1940s. Labor relations went from bad to worse; the annual operating deficit of the system continued to soar (despite the 1947 fare increase); lack of money resulted in a backlog of deferred maintenance. With only insufficient and undependable equipment available, service became deplorable.

The attempted solution to the city's postwar transit ills was a new operating agency, the New York City Transit Authority (TA). Created by state legislation, the TA assumed jurisdiction on June 15, 1953, and remained in sole charge until March 1, 1968, when it was absorbed into the larger and more comprehensive Metropolitan Transportation Authority (MTA).

Essentially, the TA was responsible only for the operation of the still city-owned transit plant. Income and outgo of cash had to be balanced, although the new agency was not responsible for securing funds for capital improvements such as new line construction and the purchase of subway cars. Such improvements were to be financed by other monies, chiefly municipal bonds, which were exempt from the city's constitutional borrowing limit. (An important although unspectacular piece of legislation was passed in 1962, an amendment to the State Public Authorities Act, which permitted the TA to sell its own revenue bonds, up to $92 million worth, for the purchase of new rolling stock.)

At the heart of the power structure of the Transit Authority was an unsalaried five-man board. Two members were appointed by the governor and two by the mayor. Together, these four members chose the fifth. The entire board then selected its own chairman. In 1955, a three-man salaried panel replaced the original five-man board.

When the TA assumed control, political hay was pitched in every possible direction as spokesmen for the downtrodden arose to defend the ten-cent fare—for an agency bound by law to avoid deficit operations would inevitably have to raise the fare to at least fifteen cents. On July 25, 1953, that is precisely what happened, and a small brass turnstile token became the new medium of exchange. A problem arose after the token fare was instituted: a German coin, worth but a few pennies, as well as several kinds of play money available in any dime store, could actuate the turnstiles. After the TA increased the sensitivity of its mechanical coin collectors—at least, it *claimed* to have done so—the problem subsided. One man profited from the new fare, Manhattan Borough president Robert F. Wagner, Jr. Entering the 1953 Democratic primary race for mayor, Wagner adopted the slogan, "New York deserves more than a token mayor." On January 1, 1954, he was sworn in as the city's chief executive.

Much of the TA's early success—and there was quite a bit of it—must be

When the IND was extended to Coney Island over the former BMT Culver line, Stillwell Avenue terminal saw some strange bedfellows. Here, a BMT Standard on the Brighton local lays over between runs as a train of R units arrives from the Bronx on the IND's D line. [Author]

attributed to work begun by the old Board of Transportation. At noontime on a rainy Saturday, October 30, 1954, a train of IND prewar R units operating on the D train out of the Bronx emerged from a tunnel portal in the middle of Brooklyn's McDonald Avenue. It ran all the way to Stillwell Avenue Terminal over tracks that until that morning were the BMT's Culver line. Thus, sixteen months into the TA era, John Hylan's goal of through service from the Bronx to Coney Island was fulfilled, although unification made recapture of the BMT by the IND unnecessary. The BMT Division simply ceased operations on the Culver between Coney Island and Ditmas Avenue. BMT trains continued to operate on a small, elevated remnant of the Culver between Ditmas and a connection with the West End at Ninth Avenue. In 1975, even this 1.1-mile leg was abandoned outright. (John Hylan was hardly the only person who ever thought of eventual subway service from the northern reaches of the Bronx to Coney Island. John McDonald, the contractor who built the Interborough's Contract One and Contract Two lines, also felt such service would evolve in time. He said it would be the city's version of a "Cape-to-Cairo railway" when it happened.)

IND cars used on the Culver line had been confined to underground tunnel routes for their entire previous service life, except for a short viaduct over Brooklyn's Gowanus Canal and two summers of service to the 1939–1940 World's Fair. When faced with the outdoor adversities of rain and snow on the Culver's elevated structure, they had to be equipped with a device never before needed—windshield wipers on the motorman's cab.

Thirteen months later, on December 1, 1955, a tunnel was opened in Long Island City connecting the BMT's Sixtieth Street tube under the East River and the IND Queens Plaza station, permitting BMT trains to operate over the IND to Forest Hills. For the first time, the compatible rolling stock of the two divisions shared common trackage. Trains of BMT Standards began running on John Hylan's municipal subway, intermixed with trains of IND R units running on the GG service.

THE CITY BUYS PART OF A RAILROAD

A major transit extension was mapped out by the TA in the late 1950s when the city acquired title to the Long Island Rail Road's (LIRR) Rockaway line. A long trestle over Jamaica Bay on this route often caught fire. After an especially destructive blaze on May 8, 1950, the hard-pressed and bankrupt commuter railroad was thankful to negotiate the line's sale. On June 11, 1953, for $8.5 million, the City of New York bought itself a railroad. Extensive rebuilding included sand fills in lieu of the fire-prone trestles. On June 28, 1956, subway service was extended to the Rockaways. The new line stretched more than 11 miles, making it one of the longest chunks of new subway ever to open for service at one time. The line's price tag—purchase price plus rebuilding—was $56 million. Perhaps the most startling feature of the Rockaway line was that it opened for business precisely on its target date, a first for a New York transit line.[2]

The double fare charged on the Rockaway line was a departure from long-standing practice. Not since the days prior to the Dual Contracts, when BRT trains to Coney Island required a double fare, had more than a single payment been necessary on the subway. The double fare lasted from 1956 until 1975, when it was lifted with the introduction of the fifty-cent subway fare.

Before IND trains could begin service across Jamaica Bay, however, several other improvements and connections were necessary. In 1948, the IND Fulton Street line was extended from East New York to Euclid Avenue. This was one

A train of new R-16 units made the inaugural trip over the new Rockaway line on June 28, 1956. [NYCTA]

of those segments of the original Independent System that was almost finished before construction had to be halted during the war. It was an eye-opener when service began: all stations along the new segment featured fluorescent lighting, unique at the time but now expanded to the entire New York City subway system.

But even a terminal at Euclid Avenue was some distance away from being able to connect with the LIRR Rockaway line. Thus, in 1956, the IND was expanded once again. This time a ramp was constructed so trains could continue beyond Euclid Avenue and gain access to the structure of the BMT's Fulton Street el. This was the second invasion of BMT territory by the IND, and once again with the arrival of IND trains, BMT service was eliminated.

The eastern end of the Fulton Street el, where the IND trains now operate, had been built to heavy-duty standards at the time of the Dual Contracts on the assumption the BMT's whole Fulton Street line would one day be upgraded and funneled into the DeKalb Avenue–Gold Street junction through the Ashland Place connection. But the Ashland Place connection was never built, and the Fulton Street el was largely abandoned before the war (actually those sections of it under which the new IND Fulton Street subway had been built were abandoned). The eastern end of the el remained, and it was over its rebuilt easternmost portion that the IND was extended in 1956. Before the arrival of the IND, this rebuilt section of el could be reached only over an older and lightly constructed segment of the Fulton Street el. Consequently, it was served by BMT C-type el cars and the 1936 BMT multisection articulated units.

The eastern end of the Fulton Street el that became part of the IND System in 1956 crosses the LIRR's Rockaway line, and after a connecting ramp was built at Liberty Avenue near Woodhaven Boulevard, subway trains began operating to stations with such breezy names as Wavecrest, Seaside, and Rockaway Park.

An important historical footnote must be mentioned when one talks about the novelty of subway service across Jamaica Bay. Long before IND trains began to run over the line—fifty-eight years before, as a matter of fact—the BRT and the LIRR were operating a joint service between points on the former's elevated network and the Rockaways over this same line. The joint service lasted from 1898 until 1917; structural evidence of the two connecting ramps where trains descended from BRT elevated lines to join the LIRR at grade can still be seen. One connection was at Chestnut Street on the Broadway-Brooklyn el, and the other was off the Fifth Avenue line at Flatbush and Atlantic avenues, the site of the railroad's Brooklyn terminal today.

The Rockaway line enabled the TA to provide direct subway service to one of New York's racetracks, Aqueduct Park, the first station after trains descend from the structure of the Fulton Street el, and special express service is provided in season for "improvers of the breed." An oddity of the Rockaway line is that it appeared, in 1956, to be an expansion and extension of the IND Division. In actuality it was supervised and operated for a time as the TA's *fourth* subway division. Through trains from Manhattan to Rockaway, for example, changed crews at Euclid Avenue in a manner not unlike a railroad division point in the middle of Kansas or Nebraska.

What surely must be considered the TA's most important expansion was completed on November 26, 1967, when the Chrystie Street connection opened. This project affected service on nearly every BMT and IND line in the city. Indeed, following the service changes brought about by Chrystie Street, the separate identities of the BMT and IND divisions—and the Rockaway Division—vanished.

The connection itself is but a short tunnel in downtown Manhattan, but it allows BMT trains off the Manhattan Bridge to operate into the IND's Sixth Avenue trunk line, a route that was upgraded from two- to four-track capacity as part of the same project. BMT trains from the Williamsburg Bridge were also given access to the Sixth Avenue line, and a rebuilding of the BMT's complex DeKalb Avenue-Gold Street interlocking plant in 1958 greatly increased the capacity of the Manhattan Bridge and improved operational flexibility.

The first twenty-four hours of business on the Chrystie Street link were chaotic. With the new line came new schedules and operating practices, and it often seemed that no two TA employees were following the same timetable. Every trip that day was an adventure into the unknown. Not even the motormen knew for sure where any train would wind up. The newspapers were filled with stories of misplaced persons who found themselves on the Grand Concourse when they were trying to get to Kew Gardens and in Coney Island when they were headed for Harlem.

In essence, the Chrystie Street connection completed the unification process that was begun in 1940. Following November 1967, the TA even tried to discourage public reference to the BMT, IRT, and IND. The former IRT lines were to be called the A Division, and the joint BMT-IND routes constituted the B Division. Happily, the effort was a failure, and the more traditional nomenclature has been allowed to resurface.

Trains on the combined BMT-IND network are now identified by letter code, essentially an expansion of the original IND notation; the IRT uses a number system. In more recent years, a color code has been developed to work in conjunction with the letters and numbers to identify the routes and lines. The newest subway cars have abandoned destination signs on the head end. In their place is a huge letter or number code, brightly illuminated in the color of the route on which the train is operating.

This new system of subway identification took a heavy toll from the BMT's colorful and historic names and destinations. Many claim the integration effectively absorbed the BMT into the IND. Such old titles as Sea Beach express and West End local are no longer in official use, and trains that once bore the name Brighton express now read "D-Avenue of the Americas Express" on their roll signs. But just as New Yorkers stubbornly resist calling Sixth Avenue by the name it has officially borne since the La Guardia years, people in Brooklyn still use the old BMT titles.

THE "TA LOOK" UNDER THE SIDEWALKS OF NEW YORK

By the late 1960s, the TA had moved forward and turned what had been three separate subway systems into a smoothly functioning unit. Nowhere was the TA's work more evident than in the subway cars. Prior to the TA takeover, there was no long-range car replacement policy. Many IRT units had been in daily service for fifty years, and in 1955 the oldest of the BMT Standards celebrated their fortieth anniversary.

In 1953, the TA ordered its first rolling stock — 200 BMT-IND cars designated the R-16 units. They were assigned to the BMT's Broadway-Brooklyn line, freeing other rolling stock for the opening of the Rockaway line, as well as several routes operating without enough equipment. Prior to 1954, the BMT was forced to rely on units such as old el cars to serve outlying stations on the Culver and West End lines during rush hour because of the shortage of steel subway cars. Trains from Manhattan terminated at places such as Bay Parkway and Kings Highway, and older wooden cars ran in shuttle service beyond to Coney Island, a picturesque though inefficient arrangement.

The first R-16, painted in a glossy coat of olive green paint and bearing the number 6400, arrived from the American Car and Foundry Company on October 21, 1954, just in time to participate in a low-key ceremony marking the fiftieth anniversary of the New York subways. The newcomer was displayed on the lower level of the City Hall BMT station together with an IRT car that had been in operation for half a century, No. 3453, one of the first all-steel Gibbs cars.

As an indication of how costs were soaring, the R-16 units cost the TA $121,441.11 each. Basic R-1 exterior dimensions again were followed. However, the total weight of each car was 85,000 pounds, two and one-half tons heavier than the prewar R units. The R-16s returned to large and legible roll signs on the sides of the cars. The immediate postwar cars featured small roll signs positioned at the roof lines of the cars, an arrangement that drew a good deal of criticism.

Because the TA couldn't order new equipment fast enough, it also purchased thirty cars from the Staten Island Rapid Transit in 1954, after it had abandoned a portion of its passenger service. The units were reasonably similar in looks to the BMT Standard — except for end vestibules, IRT style — and they are the only second-hand cars ever to run in the New York subway. Twenty-five were motor cars that ran for several years; the other five were trailers that never saw passenger service for the TA.

In 1954, the Transit Authority began to turn its attention to the IRT. The old line had not been so thoroughly attended to since the days of August Belmont and Frank Hedley! Between 1954 and 1962, 2,510 cars were ordered. Together with the 350 units purchased in 1946 and 1947, these cars replaced the entire Interborough fleet. Cars that had been ordered over a period of twenty-five years

After being reconditioned at Coney Island shops, two ex–Staten Island Rapid Transit cars are ready for service on the BMT Culver line. Note the similarities in the roof line and general profile between this design and the BMT Standard. [Author]

(1903–1925), were replaced in eight. In addition to acquiring new rolling stock, the TA devoted considerable energy—and cash—to upgrading and replacing the IRT's aging signal system, extending the length of local platforms on the original 1904 route, and improving the electrical power distribution system that feeds current to the third rail. The whole IRT improvement program cost over $500 million, considerably more than the cost of constructing the IRT in the first place.

An interesting operational change was implemented as part of this whole IRT improvement package. From earliest days, the service pattern on the West Side IRT called for both express trains and locals to run on both of the two branches that split at Ninety-sixth Street. But this system caused frequent delays because fully half the trains passing through the Ninety-sixth Street station were forced to change tracks over a set of crossover switches where the two branch lines separated.[3]

One way to solve the problem would have been the construction of a major underground junction to eliminate the at-grade crossovers. This was quickly ruled out because of its excessive cost. Instead, TA engineers calculated that the improved running times that the new rolling stock would bring justified a far simpler solution: make all trains to and from one branch locals south of Ninety-sixth Street and all trains off the other branch expresses. Thus, no trains would have to perform a cross-over maneuver at Ninety-sixth Street, and service patterns would be less subject to disruption. And it worked—thanks to a new signal system that helps move trains along more efficiently and a fleet of new cars with much better acceleration and braking rates than the old-timers they replaced.

The IRT's replacement cars were ordered under eight different contract numbers between R-17 and R-36. They were look-alike units with the exception of the R-36 cars, ordered in a blue and white color scheme for service to the

A minor point in keeping the system functioning smoothly is a way of informing train operators where they must stop a train of a given length. It won't do to have a train's last two cars back in the tunnel when the conductor opens the doors. The system is simple. Numerals are spaced out along the platform to indicate the stopping point for a train of that many cars. Problems sometimes develop during transition periods, as on the BMT when the 67-foot Standard was being replaced by new 60-foot R units. This photograph shows a solution: the circular "5" is the old BMT notation; the "R-6" indication shows where a train of six of the newer cars should be stopped. [Author]

1964–1965 World's Fair at Flushing Meadow—the same site as the 1939–1940 fair. In 1958, the R-26 units introduced a feature that would become standard on new car orders for a dozen years: every two cars were semipermanently coupled into a two-car set, an arrangement generally known in the transit industry as a "married pair." Because the two cars share a common motor-generator set and compressor unit, cost and weight reductions are significant. The R-26 and R-28 units are coupled into married pairs using a conventional TA-style automatic coupler; R-29 and later married pair units are more permanently joined with a nonautomatic drawbar. One slight deviation from the married pair concept was that forty of the R-33 units came as single cars. They were painted in the same livery as the World's Fair R-36 fleet and made possible the operation of eleven-car trains on the Flushing line—one of the few services on the entire TA system ever to exceed ten-car train lengths. (A train of ten 60-foot cars on the BMT or IND was, nonetheless, longer than an eleven-car train of IRT 51 footers.)[4]

Before this new rolling stock could be phased into regular IRT service, certain station platforms had to be altered. At such locations as Union Square and South Ferry, mechanical gap fillers that moved out to meet the open doors of stopped trains were positioned according to the door locations of a standard pre–World War I Interborough car. They were modified—part of the $500 million project—to mate with the new R units. At some stations, the entire platform was moved to eliminate the need for the gap fillers. Prior to 1953, a hapless Board of Transportation spokesman ventured the opinion that because of these platform irregularities, the IRT would "never be able to operate new cars."

A noble experiment—air-conditioning—was tried in 1956 on a train of new R-17 units. It failed. As a result, the TA began to feel air-conditioning was an impossible dream for subway trains. This view, however, overlooked the fact that the Hudson Tubes had an entire fleet of cars proving just the opposite.

FAREWELL TO THE STANDARDS

Then in the 1960s, before anyone could really get used to the idea, the final BMT Standards came due for retirement. The TA had more than 200 Standards rebuilt in the late 1950s, but even the rebuilds failed to see the dawn of the 1970s. In late summer of 1969, the lines of the former Brooklyn Rapid Transit Company were moving their usual numbers of people, but the famous and durable subway car that had so long been identified with the BRT and the BMT was no longer in on the action. The newer Triplex units had been retired even earlier, the last of these heavyweights having been withdrawn in 1965 before the opening of the Chrystie Street connection. Suddenly many people realized how the years were passing as still another link with the days of their youth vanished from the scene. "It was bad enough when the Dodgers moved to Los Angeles," one Flatbush native remarked, "but Brooklyn isn't Brooklyn without the old BMT cars."

Between 1953 and 1968, the Transit Authority signed orders for 1,950 subway cars for the IND and BMT. Together with the new IRT cars, the TA had thus equipped the entire Dual Contracts network of subway lines with second-generation equipment. When R-42 units began to arrive in 1969, the TA started to phase out the R-1 cars that had opened service on the Independent subway in 1932.

In 1963, the TA contracted with the Budd Company for 600 BMT-IND cars. It was the largest single order ever placed for passenger equipment with a U.S. car builder to that time. Budd proposed to finish off the R-32 units in stainless steel. (Prior to 1963, standard TA rolling stock was sheathed in a low-alloy, high-tensile steel exterior.) The Budd "Brightliners," as they were called when new, were not only more pleasant to look at, but they also impressed TA engineers with the weight reductions of stainless steel. In subsequent invitations for bids,

In the spring of 1969, the final BMT Standards were serving out their days on the Fourteenth Street–Canarsie line. But here comes the future: a train of new R-42 units recently assigned to the line and shown here in the yard adjacent to the Rockaway Parkway station. By year's end, several milestones will be reached: people will walk on the moon, the once-lowly Mets will be world baseball champs, and the BRT/BMT Standard will be gone. [Author]

the TA formulated a cost-reduction factor that potential builders could subtract from their quoted price to make allowance for the reduced power costs of a lighter-weight car. Budd, however, won the R-32 contract without such a factor.

The Budd Company was back after several years' absence from the New York subway scene. Budd's first subway train had been the prewar BMT experimental. Then, a postwar ten-car experimental—the R-11 units—had been ordered by the Board of Transportation, but a further order for production model cars never materialized.

The arrival of the new R-32s was celebrated in unusual fashion. On Wednesday, September 9, 1964, a first run was staged for the press, TA brass, and officials of the car builder. But the route was not along TA trackage. Instead, the special ran out of New York Central Railroad's Mott Haven Yard, down the Park Avenue tunnel, and into Grand Central Terminal, where the train was met by a twenty-piece band, on Track 37. The standard TA overriding third-rail shoes were adapted so the train could draw current from Grand Central Terminal's codeveloped underriding type of third rail. A New York Central engineman and a TA motorman rode in the cab.

The R-32 units, as well as subsequent stainless steel equipment, are indeed bright and shiny compared with older subway cars and have retained much of their sparkle. The gritty exterior of the typical nonstainless steel vehicle has long defied color classification. A British journalist commented in the 1920s that the subway "carriages," as he called them, "seem to have adopted the protective colouration of all ground-burrowing animals." New TA cars through the late 1950s arrived on the property freshly enameled in green, red, or deep maroon. However, after only a few weeks service in the hostile environment of the underground tunnels, the difference between a red car and a green one could not be detected by the naked eye. If dust and dirt are sufficient to discolor totally the body of a car, they must be taking a heavy toll on the mechanical

When the TA took delivery of its first train of R-32 units from the Budd Company, a different kind of inaugural run was staged. Here on September 9, 1964, the inaugural special makes its way out of the Mott Haven yards of the New York Central Railroad for a special run into Grand Central Terminal. Both a TA motorman and an NYC engineman were in the cab. [NYCTA]

When delivered to the city for service on its new Independent Subway System in the 1930s, the new R units bore gold lettering on their sides that proclaimed "City of New York." After years of toil in the grimy environment of subway tunnels, the lettering became covered with dirt and grit. As the MTA's car cleaning programs got under way, the grit was removed, and the gold lettering reappeared, as in the car being scrubbed at left. The right view shows a train of R-32 units making its way through one of the new mechanical carwashers. [Both NYCTA]

and electrical systems of the vehicle, not to mention the pulmonary apparatus of passengers.

Not until the 1960s did the TA begin to install mechanical car-washing units at principal repair shops (the first was at the 207th Street Yards of the IND in June 1960), and experiments were conducted with soaps and detergents. As the prewar IND R units inched through the newly installed car washers, gold lettering reading "City of New York" that had been applied to their sides in the 1930s once again became visible after years of being covered over by dirt. (As luck would have it, no sooner had the TA moved its car-washing program into high gear than the scourge of spray-painted graffiti arrived. The investment in fancy mechanical car washers was largely obliterated by slobs apparently under compulsion to paint 6-foot high messages in vivid colors on TA rolling stock.)

Beginning with the R-40 order, built by St. Louis Car Company in 1968, New York finally adopted air-conditioning as standard equipment on its new subway cars, the TA's previous dogma notwithstanding! The R-40 also featured major design variations from the general car profile pioneered by the R-15 units in 1947. In place of a vertical bulkhead with line and destination signs over the end door, the R-40 had an angular shovel nose on a 15-degree slant, and a large illuminated letter code next to the end door, a design developed for the TA by Loewy/Snaith. The shovel-nose feature was not especially well received. It used up valuable interior car space, as capital a transit crime as there is, and the design also created safety problems for passengers passing from one car to another—there was nothing to hang onto to keep one's footing. Thus, brackets and chains had to be grafted onto the supposedly smooth front of the cars, seriously compromising the designer's purposes. The final cars in the order came with a new bulbous nose developed by the Sundberg-Ferar firm—*the* design for the foreseeable future.

The R-40s, however, did revive a design long out of favor on the subways: car sides that taper slightly toward the roof. The BMT's *Green Hornet* and the original Interborough Composites were the only prior cars with such a feature.

The TA's rolling stock policy places firm trust in comparatively heavyweight equipment. The use of stainless steel in the R-32 reduced weight per car to 70,000 pounds, compared with 80,000 pounds for a similar but nonstainless steel car. (By comparison, Boston's Massachusetts Bay Transportation Authority [MBTA] operates a subway car 4 feet longer than the R-32s but similar in width and height. Yet the Boston car weighs only 63,000 pounds.) Much, if not all, of the extra weight on TA rolling stock is accounted for by the trucks. Indeed, half the weight of a TA car is in its running gear! The standard product is a cast-steel equalized truck with outboard journal boxes and roller bearings. When Budd was negotiating the R-32 contract, its engineers tried to convince the TA of the merits of a more lightweight truck and recommended its own inboard Pioneer III design. A handful of cars actually came equipped with Pioneer III trucks for tests. But TA officials still believe heavyweight hardware means a more trouble-free car. Conventional trucks have since replaced the Pioneer IIIs, which are sitting unused in Coney Island shops.

Thus, the New York City Transit Authority passed the interval from 1953 to 1968. It obeyed its legislative mandate of meeting operating expenses out of revenues, and it also convinced city authorities of the urgent need to make

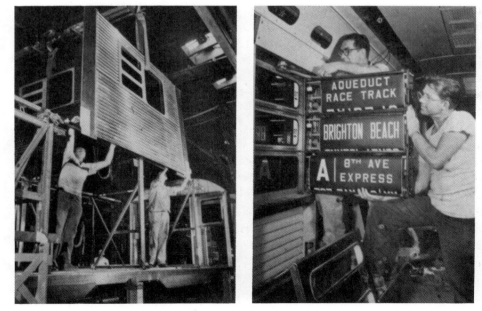

Assembling R-32 units at the Budd Company's Red Lion plant in Philadelphia, although the combination of signs displayed on the roller curtains is quite improbable. [NYCTA]

large-scale capital investments in the existing transit plant. In fact, one of the most controversial fiscal policies of the 1952–1968 TA was its diversion of the revenue raised in a $500 million 1951 bond issue to such improvement projects. When voters approved this expenditure, they presumed—and were told—that they were earmarking funds for totally new transit lines such as the long-discussed Second Avenue subway in Manhattan.

A realtor in Flatbush once sold a house to a young couple with a promise that the IRT subway would soon be extended out along Nostrand Avenue. That was in 1937. After the 1951 bond issue was approved in a referendum, the new subway was thought to be just months away. The young marrieds have meanwhile grown up and retired to Florida. The subway has yet to be built.

A train of new R-32 units poses for the "company photographer" under the sidewalks of New York. [NYCTA]

QUILL'S LAST HURRAH

John Vliet Lindsay was the mayor of New York for two hectic terms, from 1966 through 1973. Of the approximately 3,000 days he served as the city's chief executive, none matched the first thirteen!

Lindsay took over as mayor at 12:01 A.M. on January 1, 1966, and during his first *hour* of incumbency, he had to sit by helplessly as officials of the Transport Workers Union stormed angrily out of a bargaining session with the Transit Authority at the Hotel Americana. A paralyzing subway and bus line strike was under way, pending agreement on a new labor contract.

Local 100 of the TWU was under the command of Michael Joseph Quill, its president, by now a peppery 61 years old.

Most observers feel that it was the onset of the new administration that doomed the collective bargaining effort. Under the former mayor, Robert F. Wagner, accommodations were always reached—always at the last minute, it seemed, and always with a strike just hours away but reached nonetheless.

It's interesting to note that although the contract talks were nominally between the TWU and the Transit Authority, the municipal administration always played a key role. Under New York State law, the TA had to have a balanced budget. Since subway fare increases are never popular, it would be only the mayor—with access to the full city fiscal apparatus—who could "find" some last-minute cash to reach an accommodation with the union. And Wagner was extremely resourceful in this regard. On one occasion, he might agree to have the city absorb the cost of the TA's police force; at another time, he could arrange to have additional monies turned over to the TA in exchange for the cut-rate fares charged for students riding the subway to school.

Lindsay, who joined the negotiations in late December, spoke of lofty principles of collective bargaining and lectured Quill on his civic and moral responsibility. The strike became inevitable.

Quill and the union leadership were hauled off to jail, and when a settlement was finally reached after thirteen awful days in New York, most people felt that it was the union that emerged victorious. Furthermore, it was also generally felt that Lindsay, had he used different tactics, could have reached an agreement with Quill and company without the city's having to endure a thirteen-day strike.

While in jail, Quill suffered a heart attack and was rushed to Bellevue Hospital. He recovered, was released from custody after the strike, and seemed ready to resume command of his union. Indeed, he even appeared willing to patch up his differences with John Lindsay, a man he had deliberately referred to as "Mister Lind-sley" in the heated and angry days before the strike. But such was not to be. On January 28, 1966, Mike Quill passed away, and, four days later, 3,000 transport workers filed silently into St. Patrick's Cathedral to pay last respects to their leader. The flag of the Irish Republican Army draped his casket, and with the kind of touch Mike would have appreciated, his funeral took place while the city's hearse drivers were out on strike. The Teamsters authorized a union driver anyway for Quill's last ride.

Mike Quill has been one of the most colorful characters in the entire saga of the New York subways. To his credit, he was also a man who played the game fair and square. "If Mike gave you his word on something," a TA official later said, "you better believe he'd deliver."

Still, Quill will best be remembered as the shrill-voiced Irishman who, though he probably never heard of Marshall McLuhan, knew how to use the communications media like few others before or since. Just before his arrest at the start of the 1966 strike, he was asked if he would obey a court order directing his men to return to work. His reply was classic Mike Quill: "The judge can drop dead in his black robes, and we would not call off the strike."

PLEASE FOLLOW THE BOOK OF RULES

Like most other transit systems, the New York City Transit Authority publishes a book of rules. In addition to the version for employees, there is also a "book of rules" for passengers. Many of its dictates are ordinary enough but consider some of the forms of prohibited on-board behavior: entertaining passengers by singing, dancing, or playing a musical instrument; drinking, selling, or giving away alcoholic beverages; conducting a religious service; and riding on the roof of a subway car.
[Tom Nelligan]

The R-40 story. *Top:* As designed, the R-40 car represented a radical departure from earlier TA rolling stock. [NYCTA] *Center:* Early production model cars accurately represented the original design, except notice the first compromise: modest handrails on either side of the end door. [NYCTA] *Bottom:* It just didn't work! All kinds of railings and chains had to be grafted to the hapless R-40 to accommodate the design to the realities of the New York subways. For that matter, the final cars in the order came with a totally different end design. [Tom Nelligan]

The New York City subway system, circa 1988. The dotted line shows the route of the Second Avenue subway, currently on the back burner in the MTA's long-term plans.

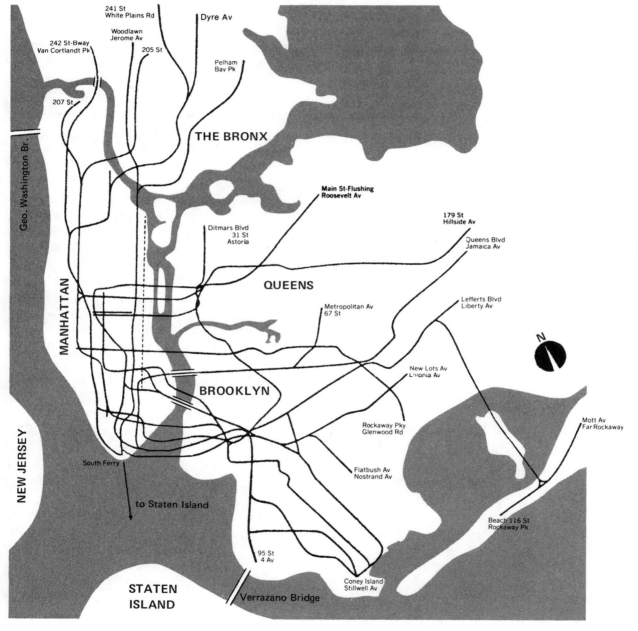

12

FROM TA TO M TO INFINITY

IN A MIDTOWN MANHATTAN OFFICE IN 1956, the chairman of the New York State Temporary Commission on Constitutional Reform had a long talk over coffee and doughnuts with the first deputy city administrator of Mayor Robert Wagner's administration. Thus did Nelson Rockefeller, then two years away from his first term as governor, meet Buffalo-born William J. Ronan, an academician with a doctorate from New York University in international law and diplomacy and a man destined to inherit the mantle of August Belmont a dozen years later. "I've been a Rockefeller Republican ever since," Ronan mused when recalling the meeting.

When Rockefeller went to Albany as the state's chief executive in 1958, he took Ronan along as his private secretary. In 1965, the state completed a deal to buy out the troubled Long Island Rail Road, and Ronan was placed in charge of the Metropolitan Commuter Transportation Authority (MCTA), the public agency formed to run the line.

But the MCTA was a short-lived enterprise. In November 1967, Rockefeller and Ronan were successful in securing voter approval of a $2.5 billion bond issue. As a result of accompanying legislation, the MCTA was transformed into the MTA (Metropolitan Transportation Authority), an agency of much greater scope and responsibility.

The MTA assumed control over a variety of existing public transport agencies on March 1, 1968, and was given a mandate to bring privately run commuter rail lines under its wing as well. Part of the $2.5 billion was to be used to buy railroad coaches and locomotives for the Penn Central, for instance. The new authority's twelve-county transportation district covers some 4,000 square miles and includes 12 million residents. Its principal responsibility, however, was and is the properties, routes, equipment, and good name of the New York City Transit Authority.[1]

The MTA coordinates metropolitan transportation matters from its mid-Manhattan headquarters and achieves unity amid diversity by a statutory requirement that makes the MTA chairman and ten other board members the chief officers of the component agencies as well. In addition to managing the TA, Ronan and his colleagues became the executives of record for the Triborough Bridge and Tunnel Authority, the state-owned Long Island Rail Road, and the TA's awkwardly named subsidiary, the Manhattan and Bronx Surface Transit Operating Authority (MaBSTOA, an acronym that New Yorkers actually *pronounce*). Over the years since its founding, additional agencies—such as the Staten Island Rapid Transit—have become part of the MTA complex. (One reason for placing the Triborough Bridge and Tunnel Authority under the MTA umbrella was to allow toll yields from its bridges and tunnels to help subsidize subway operations, and this has indeed happened. Curiously, this was a reversal of policy as discussed in the 1920s. Then it was proposed to raise subway fares by a penny or so to establish a fund so bonds for the planned Triborough Bridge could be retired without having to charge tolls on the facility.)

On February 28, 1968, two days before the MTA assumed power, the first phase of its long-range plan for New York—area transit improvements was unveiled. The initial program was scheduled to be completed within ten years (it wasn't!) and called for an expenditure of $2.5 billion. A portion of that amount would come from funds approved in the 1967 bond issue. The rest would be met with local and federal assistance. Of note was the fact that beginning in 1964, Washington had begun to make dollars available to urban areas for capital investment in mass transit facilities.

Many of the new transit lines envisioned by the MTA were routes that have been long discussed in New York, such as the Second Avenue subway, once a far-off gleam in the eye of Red Mike Hylan. Other plans, proposed in the light of shifting patterns in residential development, included a line into the Rosedale section of Queens to connect with both the BMT Jamaica Avenue line and the IND Queens Boulevard subway. The MTA had set its sights on what certainly appeared to be New York's most ambitious scheme for transit expansion since the Independent was begun.

With the creation of the MTA, the New York subways were provided with a management structure of contemporary design. Yet in the final years of the 1960s and early years of the 1970s, it was the personality of square-jawed, six-foot-two William Ronan—articulate, flamboyant, and frequently abrasive—that became the main issue on the subway scene. The eleven-member MTA board, for instance, supposedly was pieced together with many checks and balances. Yet few would deny that Ronan was in complete charge. A frequently heard cliché was that the MTA was a "wholly Ronan empire."

Ronan's early problems developed when the LIRR's highly vocal riders focused on him as the source of their discontent. Until new MTA-designed cars were in service and debugged, the Long Island managed to grab the adverse headlines and keep late-night television comedians well supplied with one-liners. But as conditions gradually improved on the former suburban railroad, the TA became a disaster area in its own right, and Ronan was again on center stage. "Ronan stinks" was the complete and entire text of a letter to the editor of the *Daily News* during one of numerous crises. A series of accidents, breakdowns, fires, and derailments, including a serious sideswipe crash on the IND Queens line in May 1970 that claimed two lives and injured seventy, effectively dramatized that the subway was not well. A newspaper account in late 1969 summarized matters: "The Transit Authority's performance record has plunged recently to its lowest level in decades."

The breakdown of subway performance during the early years of the MTA era can be attributed in part to the after-effects of a benefit the TWU won for its members in the 1968 contract, a pact negotiated before the MTA takeover. Essentially, it allowed a transit worker to retire under favorable terms after twenty years of service, a policy long in force for city police and fire department employees. The resultant loss of skilled workers was heavier than anticipated. In one key 4,000-man maintenance section, 1,400 trained workers retired during the first year of the contract, and new workers could not be trained quickly enough to take their place. Many observers regard the new retirement program as the leading cause of the deterioration in subway service since 1968.

A more speculative reason can be found in the always murky area of preserving the transit fare. In January 1970, subway patrons began coughing up thirty cents per ride. A new and larger token was distributed — 26 million of them — and the system's 3,047 turnstiles were adjusted to accept the new coin. Pressure to hold the line on fares was so strong that there was speculation in many city rooms that Ronan had ordered a cutback in routine maintenance in an effort to avoid the increase. Ronan, as a matter of fact, was willing to admit that the system suffered from deferred maintenance. But he insisted this was a condition the MTA inherited, not one it created.

A train of Saint Louis Car Company – built R-38 units running on the GG line pauses at the Smith – Ninth Street station in Brooklyn. Before various IND routes were extended onto ex-BMT elevated lines and except for temporary service to the 1939 – 1940 World's Fair, this was one of but two stations on the IND located out-of-doors.

With their final days not far off, a three-car train of BMT Q units heads toward the Bridge–Jay streets station on the Myrtle Avenue el. Originally open platform el cars, these cars were rebuilt into fully enclosed vehicles for service to the 1939–1940 World's Fair. [Author]

In July 1969, the MTA made official something that had been in the wind for months. Ironically, the announcement that Brooklyn's old Myrtle Avenue el was to be closed was reported in the newspapers on Sunday, July 29, the day humans first set foot on the surface of the moon. The Myrtle Avenue line was the city's last full-blooded, bona fide el. Originally a steam-powered BRT operation, it had been the last transit line in North America to operate wooden equipment. Actually, for more than half its route, the Myrtle Avenue el shared trackage with an elevated subway line. This portion of the trackage was built to heavy-duty standards at the time of the Dual Contracts and remains in service. But west of the intersection of Broadway and Myrtle Avenue, the line was still an unreconstructed elevated route, little changed from the days when steam engines hauled open-platform cars and passengers wore starched collars and derby hats.

Formal service on the thirty-five-block, eight-station stretch of line ended at 12:01 A.M. on Saturday, October 4, 1969. Later that day, several chartered trainloads of railway buffs toured the route and paid their last respects to the old el. The equipment the line operated during its final years were BMT's Q cars, rebuilt for the 1939–1940 World's Fair, transferred to the IRT's Third Avenue el after the war, and finally sent back to the BMT in the late 1950s. With the passing of the Qs, the last BMT-designed rolling stock departed from active service. Thus the small fleet of rebuilt el cars outlived the Standards and the Triplex units.

THE NEW ROUTES PROGRAM

But the MTA was more interested in the future than the past, and so the new agency quickly moved ahead with a program of capital development and expansion . . . new subway lines and major improvements to old ones. However ambitious and valid the expansion plans may originally have been, though, they never quite jelled. Maybe it's just as well.

Left: At Port Deposit, Maryland, a section of the MTA's Sixty-third Street tunnel slides down the ways into the Susquehanna River. *Right:* Under the care and protection of three Moran tugboats, the tunnel is seen in Lower New York Bay approaching the Verrazano-Narrows Bridge and the entrance to New York Harbor. [Both MTA photos] *Below:* The traditional fireboat welcome normally associated with newly arriving ocean liners was laid on for the tunnel, as here the *Firefighter* throws streams of water skyward. [Author's collection]

On October 27, 1972, sixty-eight years to the day after the opening of New York's first subway line in 1904, ground was broken for the Second Avenue subway. Governor Nelson Rockefeller, Mayor John Lindsay, U.S. Secretary of Transportation John Volpe, and Senator Jacob Javits were on hand at East 103d Street and Second Avenue for the ceremonial start of the new project. Not one of the political eminences was quite able to make a dent in the asphalt paving with his pick-ax, though, and a union worker with a power rig had to come forward to save the day. The symbolism was lost at the time but serves as a perfect metaphor for the whole project.

The Second Avenue subway was to be a north-south trunk line to serve many of the sections of Manhattan that were experiencing residential and commercial growth, essentially the Upper East Side. It would also connect with many of the system's existing lines from Brooklyn, the Bronx, and Queens. Two IRT lines in the Bronx, the Pelham and the Woodlawn-Jerome, were so identified. Since the Second Avenue line was designed to BMT-IND clearances, these IRT lines would require some adaptation before they could accommodate larger BMT-IND rolling stock.

Manhattan's earlier trunk line subways were largely concentrated on the West Side; four of the five are west of Fifth Avenue, and only one, the Lexington Avenue line, serves the booming East Side. An unusual feature of the Second Avenue line was that it was planned as a two-track line, not the four-track subway that had become the Manhattan standard. Engineers calculated that with the higher speeds made possible by newer trains and more modern signal systems, a two-track Second Avenue subway would provide more than enough carrying capacity.[2]

But it won't for a while. Three years after ground breaking, work on the Second Avenue subway was brought to a halt, and those sections of tunnel that were completed were sealed up to await some brighter day when the project might be reactivated.[3] A somewhat similar tale can be told about a planned East River tunnel from the foot of East Sixty-third Street in Manhattan to Queens, with a midriver stop at Roosevelt Island. Originally, it was to have linked up with the BMT Broadway line, the IND Sixth Avenue line, and the new Second Avenue line in Manhattan, but it has yet to achieve the promise its designers once claimed. That promise presumed the construction of a new "super-express" line across Queens to relieve overcrowded conditions on the existing IND Queens line, one of the busiest routes in the whole system. But the "super-express" never materialized. Work proceeded on the Sixty-third Street tunnel itself, but when completed in 1989 the line terminated at a station in Long Island City, with no link-up at all with any subway routes, new or old, serving residential sections of Queens. Newspapers and politicians dubbed it the "tunnel to nowhere."

What happened? Basically, the City of New York's monumental fiscal problems of the mid-1970s brought things to a halt. Although the MTA appears to be an independent agency and is often in the headlines concerning its direct fiscal dealings with Albany and Washington, it relies on the city treasury for tremen-

Manhattan's Fifth Avenue has never been served by any kind of rail operation: no horsecars, no cable cars, no els, no subways, no trolley cars . . . just horse-drawn omnibuses and then motor buses. But, look here: a bona fide IRT R-33 unit being hauled up the avenue aboard a flatbed truck! It was part of a parade to promote the 1964 – 1965 World's Fair, not the advent of a new transit operation. [NYCTA]

dous sums of money each year.[4] When those funds fell from their anticipated amounts, the MTA had to rethink its whole position. It pulled back from its new routes program and determined that a far more prudent course would be to funnel its limited resources into the full refurbishment of the existing system rather than spread those resources between building new lines *and* repairing old ones. On the assumption there's never anything new, this was much the same thing the TA did with the proceeds of the 1951 bond issue.

Under this new policy, modest plans have been drawn up to link the Sixty-third Street tunnel with the existing IND Queens line. A similar plan has been followed on a project in the Jamaica section of Queens, the Archer Avenue subway. Originally intended to funnel city subway trains onto portions of the Long Island Rail Road for direct service to places like St. Albans and Springfield Gardens, the Archer Avenue project was instead cut back to a terminal close by the LIRR's Jamaica Station that allows subway passengers — but not subway trains — to make their way onto the Long Island for continuing travel to points east.

Even so oriented, the Sixty-third Street tunnel will still stand as a monument to the MTA's faded dreams from 1969, for the subway will run on but one level of the tunnel, a tunnel whose full dimension includes a second lower level. Here, it was once planned to run LIRR trains en route to a new East Side terminal for that busy commuter line. Like the Second Avenue subway, this proposal has also been shelved.

It is wrong, though, to conclude that there is anything defeatist in the MTA's decision to see to the rehabilitation of the existing plant before seeking extension or expansion. True, there have been changing patterns of commercial and residential activity in New York, and a good case can be made for extending this subway line into a new area of housing a mile or so beyond its current terminal or building an entirely new line where one does not now exist but job sites or apartment houses do. And it is doubly ironic to recall the days of the Dual Contracts when the concept of subway construction in advance of need was a principal motivating force behind that magnificent municipal achievement.

But the subways, as well as the commuter railroads that are also the MTA's responsibility, are old and have suffered from much in the way of deferred maintenance over the years. The MTA is convinced that it must focus its resources on the hidden side of things—the tunnels, the bridges, the electrical systems, and the signals. So although it is possible to regret that the Second Avenue subway is not now carrying passengers up and down Manhattan, it is satisfying to realize that the MTA has made a major decision to invest its capital resources in a thorough refurbishment of the existing rail transit plant, both subway and commuter railroad.

SUBWAY PATRONAGE

The number of annual subway riders has seen fifty years of decline since the days of the Great Depression, save for the extraordinary press of traffic during the years of World War II. Wartime aside, the New York subway carried its record number of passengers in 1930, when slightly more than 2 billion passengers dropped their nickels in the turnstiles, and that was accomplished with but the BMT and the IRT in operation; the IND wouldn't carry its first passenger for another two years. Performance today is in the range of half that figure, although the TA has been successful of late in at least stabilizing patronage and even racking up short-term increases now and again.[5]

These statistics on patronage, however, can lead to misleading conclusions. What can be misleading is this: although the system has lost large numbers of riders in the face of an equally impressive growth in population throughout the metropolitan area, the subway's performance in carrying workers to their jobs in the business districts of Manhattan remains more constant than not. In common with other mass transit trends throughout the country, the loss in patronage has been largely among riders other than people heading to and from work during rush hours. An old IRT hand from the 1930s might look at today's annual patronage figures and think the Interborough was playing a lesser role in the city's economy than it did years ago. And he'd be right. But if that same

This circa 1965 photo at Grand Central on the IRT Flushing line was taken at midday, as evidenced by the empty platforms. During rush hour, this line operates on an intense 90-second headway, and platforms are always crowded. [NYCTA]

old hand were to visit Grand Central Station on the Lexington Avenue line at 5:15 P.M. on a weekday, he'd feel quite at home. It would look as busy as ever. (It is also important to note that fifty years ago, the basic workday in the United States was five and a half days, not five, and that alone has to be part of any explanation of patronage trends.)

One hardly incidental impact of this phenomenon—called *peaking* by transit planners and operators—is economic: the cost of maintaining and operating a transit system is driven by the equipment and the facilities and the employees needed at the peak hours of service. That these resources remain idle, or underutilized, for twenty of the day's twenty-four hours underscores why private companies have fled from the transit scene and left the responsibility to the public sector, where corporate standards of efficiency and return on investment need not apply.

Another by-product of the city's monetary problems was yet another subway fare increase on September 1, 1975. At that time, the tariff rose to fifty cents. To forestall the hoarding of tokens, the TA announced that a different-sized token would be issued for the new fare. Then at the last minute, it was revealed that, no, there would not be a new token, merely an increase in the price of existing tokens on the effective date.

The big change that the MTA did make in its token happened in 1986, when all the old tokens were recalled and a new issue put in circulation. To help guard against an alarming increase in the use of fraudulent tokens, the new token contains a steel center piece that the turnstiles were adjusted to recognize magnetically. Use of a token lacking this new feature not only fails to gain one admission to the subway; it also constitutes evidence of an attempt to defraud and can result in the issuance of a summons.

As to the rate of fare, it has continued to go up. The cost of a token was raised to sixty cents in 1980, seventy-five cents in 1981, ninety cents in 1984, an even dollar in 1986, a dollar fifteen in 1990, and a dollar and a quarter in 1992. Various half-fare options are available for elderly and handicapped individuals at times other than the rush hour, and there is even serious talk heard of adopting a variable rate of fare on the subways for everyone in the future, so that lengthy trips would cost more than short ones, various multiple-ride discounts could be considered, and possibly there could be variations in fare depending on time of day. The availability of new electronic fare-collection equipment will make such things possible, although subway executives in New York have a healthy skepticism about the durability of such hardware and are proceeding slowly until they are convinced their current system of tokens and turnstiles is ready to go the way of the tickets and chopper boxes of yesteryear.

Despite all increases in fare, though, extensive public subsidies are necessary to meet ordinary operating expenses. This, too, is a by-product of the fact that equipment and personnel levels are dictated by peak-hour needs but fares are no longer collected from off-peak riders in the same proportion they were many years ago. Just a little over 50 percent of routine operating expenses comes from money paid by passengers; the rest must be supplied by subsidies from various levels of government.[6]

Although the TA and many of the area's commuter railroads are under common MTA guardianship and somewhat more closely coordinated than in the past, there are no plans to merge the services in any real sense. Overlapping union jurisdictions are often cited as one barrier to any kind of operational unification, plus the fact that a merged, say, TA and LIRR could well be subject to a full gambit of federal railroad regulation—such as each subway car being regarded as a "locomotive" and requiring periodic federal inspection as such—and this could prove costly. Rolling stock on the TA and the commuter railroads, though, is starting to look a bit similar. The TA's early MTA-designed equipment —the R-42, the R-44, and the R-46 cars—is outwardly not dissimilar from the LIRR's Metropolitan cars and came from the factory finished in the same stainless steel with blue trim. Even older equipment on both railroad and subway was at first painted in similar hues of gray and blue. New rolling stock on the ex–New York Central and ex–New Haven commuter lines out of Grand Central Terminal, also MTA responsibilities and now jointly called the Metro North Commuter Railroad, imitate LIRR stock.

Of course, things are never static; the original graphic and color standards the MTA adopted in the early 1970s are starting to change—and change in a direction that emphasizes diversity, not unity. Metro North has added touches of red to its original blue-gray livery; the LIRR has begun to strip its stainless steel cars of all blue trim to avoid the expense of repainting metal that doesn't have to be painted and has added yellow trim on car ends for visibility purposes; and the TA has also specified undecorated stainless steel on its most recent rolling stock. On a growing fleet of rebuilt cars, the TA has adopted a most attractive paint scheme: dark maroon body, silver roof, and black trim.

NEW CARS

In its design of new subway rolling stock, the MTA has followed a pattern that has certain parallels to what has happened in the area of new routes and other infrastructure investment: a policy that was originally focused on making major changes to the status quo has lately been reoriented around more basic goals. The MTA's first effort at buying new subway cars produced something that was less than a smashing success. Whether the fault for this should be placed at the feet of designers, manufacturers, or the TA's own maintenance crews is probably moot. But the fact is the first new cars designed under MTA auspices caused problems.

In 1970, when new equipment was needed to begin the replacement of the original IND rolling stock, some big changes were made. The overall dimensions of the prewar R units continued to govern car specifications for BMT-IND equipment through the 400-unit R-42 order in 1968—a vehicle 10 feet wide and 60 feet long. Then the R-44 was developed—"the most revolutionary subway car in fifty years," said a press release issued by the MTA. The rhetoric was correct.

The R-44 measures 75 feet in length, the longest subway cars ever built for New York service. The extra length means that eight cars do the work of ten 60-footers, which translates into significant savings in capital investment and long-term maintenance. Instead of married pairs of cars permanently coupled, the R-44s feature two different body styles that are not permanently, or even semipermanently, coupled. One has a full-width motorman's cab across a single end of the car, and the other has no cabs at all. In other words, one car is a single-ended control motor, and the other is a motorized trailer. In general practice, the cars are run in four-unit combinations—cab, trailer, trailer, cab.

The MTA ordered 300 R-44s from the St. Louis Car Division of General Steel Industries for TA service, plus an additional 52 to reequip the Staten Island Rapid Transit, which became an MTA, but not a TA, responsibility in July 1971.

The first four R-44s arrived on TA property in the fall of 1971. They made their debut for the press on October 5, smack in the middle of a heated, but

Saint Louis–built R-42 units show off the system's current standard treatment for the end of a subway car: a color-coded letter rather than marker lights or verbal messages. [NYCTA]

An eight-car train of new R-44 units runs speed tests on the Long Island Rail Road shortly after delivery. The 75 footers clocked a top speed of 83 mph during these trials. [Tom Nelligan]

unsuccessful, campaign to win electoral approval for yet another transportation bond issue—a $2.5 billion package to continue financing the MTA master plan.

The R-44s are not compatible with earlier TA equipment. They have a different kind of coupler, for instance, the first change in design since the Interborough replaced its original Van Dorn couplers in the century's first decade, and the new cars are capable of speeds up to 80 mph. The MTA intends to limit their actual speed to 70 mph, but even this performance will not be achieved until such new lines as the Second Avenue subway are ready for service. On existing lines, the R-44s will be limited to 50 mph, the speed of conventional subway trains.

St. Louis had only begun to deliver the R-44 order when the MTA announced that a 745-car fleet of similar equipment—the R-46s—had been ordered from Pullman-Standard. This $214 million purchase—two-thirds of it paid for by the federal government's Urban Mass Transportation Administration (UMTA)—re-

This is the South Chicago plant of Pullman-Standard, and it's 1975. R-46 unit No. 564 rides the transfer table while it and another unit near completion. Absence of blue striping on these cars at this stage of their manufacture makes them resemble later R-62 and R-68 units. [Author]

placed all of the remaining original R units from the IND and gave the subway an entire fleet of postwar cars. The final revenue trip using the old R units took place on March 31, 1977, and the order for the R-46s was the largest ever written for any kind of rail passenger cars in the United States. When the MTA agreed to alter its payment schedule to the manufacturer, the order was increased from 745 to 754 cars at no increase in cost.

New York had not ordered equipment from Pullman-Standard since 1940, when some R-9 units were purchased by the IND. However, Pullman-Standard's relationship with the MTA's predecessors dates back to the early 1880s when the firm turned out trailer coaches to be hauled behind steam engines on the Brooklyn els.[7]

In keeping with the novelty of the R-46, Pullman-Standard developed a unique way of delivering the cars from its south Chicago plant to New York. Previously, subway cars had been hauled in freight trains on their own wheels. The R-46s were lifted aboard flatcars at the factory and unloaded by crane when they reached Jersey City. Subway cars traveling as "passengers" on flatcars are not subject to the special handling restrictions—and costs—incurred when the cars are coupled into a freight train as part of its consist. What's more, railroad clearances require that subway cars running on their own wheels must have their third-rail shoe beams removed en route, to be reinstalled after delivery by TA crews. The R-46s arrived with all hardware in place.[8]

It is difficult to speak well of the R-44 or the R-46. All the trucks on the latter had to be replaced, for example, following complex litigation.[9] And so when it came time for yet more new rolling stock in the early 1980s, it was back to the drawing board. What emerged this time was a far less complex vehicle than the early MTA cars. The new couplers were not retained, for example, and the cars of the 1980s came equipped with the standard model that had served the city well since before the days of the Dual Contracts. Externally, the new cars looked quite like the R-44 and the R-46—and the R-42 as well, for that matter—but that's where the similarity stops. All of the new vehicles are single units with an operator's cab at each end. Two fleets were added to the roster in the mid-1980s: the R-62 for the IRT and the R-68 on the joint BMT-IND network.

The R-44 and the R-46 were built with automated operation in mind on the new routes the MTA was convinced it was soon going to be operating. The operator's station on these cars is something that resembles a console at "mission control." The operator sits before a display panel of fifteen or so lights, buttons, switches, and gauges and operates the train with a relatively inconspicuous handle to the right—one handle for both acceleration and braking. In the anticipated automated mode, this handle is locked in a single position, and the operator can devote complete attention to the buttons, switches, and gauges as the train operates with nary a hand being laid on. The operator's position in the R-44 and the R-46 is the closest one can find in the whole TA system to the general style and tone of such newer American rapid transit systems as found in Baltimore, Washington, and Miami.

Except for the experimental R—110A units, the newest equipment on the subway network once headed by August Belmont are these stainless steel R—62 units. Here, in July 1987, a ten-car train snakes off the Jerome Avenue elevated structure and into the Lexington Avenue subway. Aboard are thousands of disappointed New York Yankees fans whose team was defeated moments before by the visiting Boston Red Sox. The photographer's vantage point is inside Yankee Stadium, "the house that Ruth built." [Author]

But there's nothing about the R-62 and the R-68 that resembles automated rapid transit at all. These new vehicles provide operators with separate controls for power and brake such that George Morrison, the motor instructor who gave Mayor George McClellan his rudimentary lesson before His Honor took the city's first subway train out of the City Hall station in 1904, would be quite comfortable aboard an R-62 making its way around the same City Hall loop today. In fact, Morrison would probably have no difficulty at all running an R-62!

But if the R-62s and R-68s are a return to basics in a design sense, there is another way in which they are something that has never before happened in New York: they are the first TA passenger cars to be purchased from overseas suppliers. Like portable radios, polyester slacks, and catchers' gloves, offshore manufacturers have cut deeply into domestic production. When the MTA began to develop specifications for new rolling stock, U.S. manufacturers of rail transit cars had dwindled to but one, the Budd Company, and even it had become a wholly owned subsidiary of a firm in West Germany. It wasn't long after, for that matter, that even Budd called it quits, after changing its name for a few seasons to Transit America.

Action on the Brighton line. Two Brighton Beach—bound trains carry Brooklynites home on a pleasant Friday in the summer of 1987. On the express track is a graffiti-adorned train of R—32 units; the train whose headlamps are casting starlike patterns beneath the overpass is composed of new R—68 units. [Author]

ENDLESS CYCLES

If anything has emerged as a timeless and universal characterization of the New York subway, it is the endless search for some future salvation, some not-yet-realized resolution of its difficulties and cure for its ills. Plans are made, programs developed, goals established. But they never quite live up to their initial expectations, and a new cycle must begin.

William Barclay Parsons, the chief engineer on the city's original subway, put it well in an article he wrote for the *New York Times* to commemorate the twenty-fifth anniversary of the subway on October 27, 1929. (Two days later, the New York Stock Exchange experienced its infamous "black Tuesday.") Wrote Parsons: "As a matter of fact, New York was the first city in the world to develop a transit problem; since then it has never been without one, and it bids fair to retain one indefinitely."

It's always difficult to say where one stands at any given time, of course. The graffiti epidemic of the 1970s proved to be far more serious than anyone would have imagined or ever was willing to admit. It conveyed a sense that matters in the subways were totally out of control. Coupled with the onset of old age in various subsystems, a decidedly negative impression began to feed on itself. It is impossible to describe the feeling one received upon boarding a subway car whose every surface—interior and exterior—was covered with illegible scrawlings of several vintages. The sight of a subway train with several cars having inoperative lights but seated passengers struggling to read their newspapers by the minimum illumination provided by the emergency lighting was stark testi-

The scourge of graffiti that hit the New York subways in the mid-1970s has sometimes been seen as a form of genuine artistic expression. There are full-color "coffee table" books one can buy, for instance, that romanticize the "artists" and their work. The sad fact of the matter is, though, that when the cars were covered end to end with spray paint, the impression was that matters on the New York subways were totally out of control. Here is an example of what things looked like when the epidemic was at its peak. [Author]

mony to the legendary ability New Yorkers have of adapting to difficult circumstances when necessity dictates. Things were in very bad shape.

Perhaps most disheartening were the continually publicized programs designed to cure the graffiti disease, with no sense whatsoever if what was being proposed was going to work or if adequate resources were available for its effective execution. *Let's paint the cars white*, was the sum and substance of one ill-starred campaign that the newspapers reported as a serious and sensible effort. *Then we can get the graffiti off as soon as it's applied*. In the history of North America, only General Custer can claim he was ever given worse advice. And as to the assortment of chemicals, powders, and potions that were supposed to rid the fleet of the ravages of spray paint almost like magic, the less said the better.

The epidemic may now have run its course. And if so, it's thanks to hard work. Resources have been redirected within the vast TA bureaucracy, and virtually every subway terminal has a crew of people who inspect each train after each trip and get after anything awry. The new R-62s and R-68s, of course, have helped create a new atmosphere, but new cars alone, without adequate attention to good maintenance, are no answer. The graffiti artists were able to desecrate full trains of R-44s and R-46s before they ever carried a revenue passenger!

The full and complete rebuilding of some older rolling stock has been equally as important as purchasing new cars in the gradual improvement the subways seem to be showing in the late 1980s. Quantities of older R units have been shipped to out-of-town facilities for such work. Hornell, New York, 300 or more miles from Times Square, was once the home of the locomotive shops of the

This scene may look like a country interurban line in the Midwest, but it isn't; it's a TA subsidiary, the South Brooklyn Railway, a freight-hauling short line whose principal customer is the TA itself. The South Brooklyn is now dieselized, but as late as the mid-1950s, steeple cab motors such as No. 5 shown here could be found hauling trains along McDonald Avenue in Brooklyn. [NYCTA]

An air view of the TA's sprawling Coney Island yards and shops. The TA has two major repair and overhaul facilities, this one plus the 207th Street installation in upper Manhattan at the north end of the IND's Washington Heights line. Over a dozen other facilities perform lesser levels of maintenance and routine inspection of rolling stock and also provide tracks to store equipment when busy rush hour schedules are not in effect. [NYCTA]

This otherwise conventional contemporary photograph shows the downtown kiosks at the Wall Street station on the IRT line that runs down Broadway to Bowling Green. This was part of the Interborough's Contract Two line; the iron fence behind the kiosks protects the burial ground of Trinity Church, the resting place of Alexander Hamilton and Robert Fulton, among others. For a truly surprising before-and-after contrast, look back to page 34 and a 1906 photo of this same scene. Not much has changed, has it? [Author]

Erie Railroad, a line that gradually lost its identity in a series of mergers. A private company, now working under contract to the TA, has tapped the skilled labor in this small city and set up production lines for the rehabilitation work; the beneficiaries are passengers on the Lexington Avenue express and the Pelham local. The rebuilding includes the installation of air-conditioning equipment in cars that were not originally so equipped.

But progress and improvement are never absolute; the New York subways can continue to do their job day after day, but there will always be a new problem to address tomorrow. In 1904, people complained that the ventilation of the Contract One stations was poor and needed improvement. Highly indignant letters frequently appeared in the city's newspapers complaining about the quality of air in the underground stations.

Well, days have come and days have gone, and now most trains on the Contract One lines are air-conditioned, a welcome feature during the hot and humid weather that often grips New York each summer. Before the advent of air-conditioning, subway *stations* were generally a bit more comfortable than the streets above during a heat wave; it was crowded trains that were the problem during a hot day's journey. But now, with air-conditioned rolling stock exhausting heat into the tunnels, the stations have become the problem. Descending to platform level after several days of temperatures in the nineties can be . . . well, less pleasant than it used to be. Now the letters-to-the-editor columns of the city's newspapers feature all manner of complaints about . . . *the quality of air in the underground stations.* One can only wonder what August Belmont might have said about it all.

TAKE THE A TRAIN . . . TO PUEBLO, COLORADO?

In the early 1970s, the U.S. Department of Transportation initiated a program of urban transit grant assistance with some high-visibility experiments and demonstrations. A test track for rail transit vehicles of all types was established in the Colorado desert outside Pueblo.

R&D people who were pleased to get away from the grimy urban environment where subway trains normally run found the fresh Rocky Mountain air brought perils of its own. Rattlesnakes quickly learned that the shady side of the rails on the transit test track was quite to their liking, and visiting engineers had to take precautions not to disturb their repose. "I'll take rats in the tunnels anytime," a homesick urbanist said one day as a recalcitrant reptile was encouraged to remove itself to permit the installation of wayside detection equipment for an experiment in vehicle acceleration.

The first transit vehicle to operate at the Pueblo facility was an unusual two-car subway train. Dubbed the State-of-the-Art Car—SOAC is the inevitable acronym—it was a federally funded project managed by the Boeing-Vertol Company to demonstrate the latest technology in various subsystems of railcar design.

After leaving Pueblo, the two-car SOAC did something no other transit equipment ever did before, and perhaps never will again; it ran in revenue service on six transit systems in five different U.S. cities: New York, Boston, Cleveland, Chicago, and Philadelphia, in that order.

Other early visitors to Pueblo were two sets of TA rolling stock participating in still more federally funded experiments. R-32 units Nos. 3700 and 3701 were shipped to Torrance, California, from New York in 1972 to have experimental energy-storage flywheels installed. En route back east, they stopped off in Pueblo for initial testing before the full experiment got under way in New York. [The flywheels were eventually removed from the pair in 1976 when

Is there any more improbable a spot in all of the United States where one might expect to find a New York subway train than the Colorado desert outside Pueblo? Pikes Peak looms in the background in this scene at the U.S. Department of Transportation's test facility. [Author]

the experiment had run its course.]

The other Pueblo visitor from New York was a pair of new R-42 units, Nos. 4653 and 4765, and they remained at the test track for some time to help run a variety of tests and experiments. The sight of two typical New York City subway cars calmly sitting under the high desert sky of Colorado, with Pikes Peak looming in the background, was as improbable as . . . well, as improbable as Alfred Eli Beach one day thinking he could run passenger cars under the sidewalks of New York.

The first transit vehicles to operate at the Pueblo facility were these state-of-the-art cars, experimental vehicles that later ran in demonstration service in five U.S. cities. Their first stop was New York; this view in the summer of 1974 shows them operating in Boston. [Author]

Old and new. Above, a train of contemporary PATH rolling stock pauses at the 33rd Street station in Manhattan after completing a run from Journal Square. [Author] These modern cars replaced older equipment, below, designed by the Hudson & Manhattan R.R. for trans-Hudson service. [Port Authority of New York and New Jersey]

EPILOGUE: BUT THERE'S MORE . . .

OVERSHADOWED BY THE AWESOME DIMENSIONS of the New York City Transit Authority's electric railway operations are two other rapid transit lines that operate in New York City . . . entirely or in part. These are over and above the several commuter railroad services that also serve the region with electric-powered passenger trains.[1]

PORT AUTHORITY TRANS-HUDSON

The Port Authority Trans-Hudson (PATH) is an arm of the Port Authority of New York and New Jersey, the agency that is primarily known for being the owner and operator of, among others, the Lincoln Tunnel, the George Washington Bridge, La Guardia Field, the World Trade Center, and two Manhattan bus terminals for motor coaches bound for, and returning from, points far and near. PATH became a Port Authority, and thereby a public sector, responsibility in 1962 when the line's corporate existence as the Hudson & Manhattan Railroad came to an end after a long and painful bankruptcy. The Port pumped millions of dollars into the old railroad to rehabilitate its deteriorated plant and equipment, and when the last of the ferryboats that used to provide trans-Hudson connections for railroads with passenger depots on the west bank of the river were abandoned in 1967, the newly refurbished subway line became all the more vital for commuters heading for their Manhattan offices. The effort was successful, and under Port Authority auspices, PATH has become a premiere transit operation.

Of course, some would say it always was! PATH's predecessor, the old Hudson & Manhattan, was opened four years after the Interborough hauled its first passenger when William Gibbs McAdoo put together a group of financiers and revived an earlier failed effort to tunnel under the Hudson River and link Manhattan with New Jersey by rail. McAdoo was little bothered by the fact that underwater river tunnels with electrified rapid transit trains running through them was an idea then on the cutting edge of technological development, and he quietly proceeded to complete the unfinished tunnels, built another set downstream from the first, and opened the Hudson & Manhattan for its first cash-paying customers on February 25, 1908. The motorman on the H&M's inaugural run was the line's superintendent, E.M. Hedley, brother of Frank Hedley of IRT fame.

(McAdoo's enthusiasms knew few bounds. In later years he would serve as U.S. secretary of the treasury under President Woodrow Wilson, a man who also became McAdoo's father-in-law during their mutual stay in Washington;

In pre-PATH days, the H&M operated cars that were not totally unlike IRT equipment. Here, in 1954, a two-car train enters the Journal Square station in Jersey City. [Author]

be elected to the U.S. Senate from the state of California; and make two spirited runs for the Democratic presidential nomination, the only chieftain of a U.S. mass transit system ever to entertain such ambitions—at least so far.)[2]

The Hudson Tubes, as McAdoo's line was popularly called, connected a number of communities along the New Jersey side of the Hudson River, and the railroad depots located in them, with two Manhattan terminals. One was downtown at Cortlandt and Church streets close by the city's busy financial district, and the other was in midtown at Sixth Avenue and West Thirty-third Street. This latter line made its Manhattan landfall at the foot of Morton Street and the Hudson River, twisted inland to Sixth Avenue, and then continued north under that thoroughfare. McAdoo had plans to continue this Sixth Avenue line beyond its "temporary" terminal at West Thirty-third Street and tap the Grand Central area, and he also saw his H&M as a potential participant when the City of New York began to talk about building the subway lines that eventually became the Dual Contracts.

But such plans remained mere dreams. The configuration of the H&M circa 1915 pretty well defines the PATH system of today: twin Hudson River crossings; service to the old Delaware, Lackawanna & Western Railroad terminal in Hoboken (last of the New Jersey passenger depots and currently a busy place as part of New Jersey Transit's publicly operated commuter railroad network); and a line out across the Jersey Meadows to Newark. It is here that PATH passengers can transfer to still other New Jersey Transit commuter trains, Amtrak service to many points, and one of the area's better-kept rail transit secrets, New Jersey Transit's Newark subway, a 4-mile line that operates vintage PCC-type streetcars in what transit planners today like to call "light rail transit" service. Indeed,

The Newark subway was originally a conduit into that city for many streetcar lines radiating out from downtown, although there was one basic line, No. 7/City Subway, that operated solely on the reserved right-of-way. After World War II, the conventional streetcar lines were motorized one after another until only the basic No. 7 service was still operating trolley cars. By the early 1950s, its days also seemed numbered; its cars were getting old. But the City Subway in Newark has survived and is today a key link in the mass transit system operated by New Jersey Transit, a new public agency. Here, on an afternoon in December 1953, deck roof car No. 3259 heads toward downtown. Just behind it, one of the PCC cars recently purchased is being used to train motormen in the operation of the new rolling stock. [Author]

if the New York Giants and the New York Jets can play their home football games today in the New Jersey Meadowlands, a case can certainly be made for calling the Newark subway "New York's last trolley line."[3]

During H&M days, that line's operation from Cortlandt Street in downtown Manhattan through Jersey City and on to Newark was known as the joint service. West of Jersey City's Journal Square station, trains ran over special third rail–equipped tracks that actually belonged to the Pennsylvania Railroad (PRR), and both the H&M and the PRR owned compatible fleets of 48-foot multiple-unit cars that were used on the Cortlandt Street–Newark run. (Other fleets of "H&M-only" cars ran on all services save Newark.)

Under PATH auspices, there is no more joint service; the ex–PRR trackage is now reserved for PATH use only, and even the extra fare that once prevailed on the joint service beyond Journal Square has been eliminated in favor of a conventional flat fare rapid transit style of tariff. Given the billions of dollars in new commercial and residential development that is being pushed to completion along the New Jersey side of the Hudson River, it is a rather conservative prediction to suggest that the subway system opened in 1908 by William Gibbs McAdoo has its best years yet to come.[4]

Before the World Trade Center was built atop the lower Manhattan terminal for today's PATH service, H&M trains terminated at roughly the same place, but beneath an older edifice that was called Hudson Terminal. In this 1912 photograph, we see the entry gate passengers used when heading for Manhattan Transfer and a connecting train of the Pennsylvania R.R. [Author's collection]

STATEN ISLAND RAPID TRANSIT

If the PATH system remains relatively unknown because its trains visit New York City in the sheltered environment of its own deep-bore tunnels, the Staten Island Rapid Transit (SIRT) avoids the limelight while running in broad daylight but in the city's least populous and most removed borough, Staten Island. Today, the operation is called the Staten Island Rapid Transit Operating Authority (SIRTOA); it is an arm of the same Metropolitan Transportation Authority, the MTA, that is the NYCTA's parent body. Needless to say, such was not always the case.

Rail passenger service on Staten Island began in 1860. A line was built from Clifton, where the ferryboats from New York docked, across the long dimension of the pear-shaped island to Tottenville, a dozen or so miles away. Here there was a ferryboat connection across the Arthur Kill to Perth Amboy, New Jersey.

Over the years, the line's fortunes prospered and waned in relation to general economic conditions on Staten Island. By and by, the railway and the two ferry-

Midway between Saint George and Tottenville, two Staten Island Rapid Transit Operating Authority trains pass on the line's two-track main line. These cars are similar to the TA's R-44 units and were ordered from Saint Louis Car Company as an add-on to the R-44 contract. [Author]

Before new MTA rolling stock arrived in Staten Island, service was provided by a venerable fleet of 67-foot multiple-unit cars that bore striking resemblances to the BRT/BMT Standard. One obvious difference between the two was that the SIRT cars featured end vestibules, IRT style. But the Staten Island cars had harsher lines than the Brooklyn car; where the Standard had gentle curves, the SIRT design was angles and straight lines. [Author]

boat services were merged into a single corporate entity, and in 1884 the joint railway-ferry company began a long period of corporate relationship with the Baltimore & Ohio Railroad (B&O), a major east-west trunkline that saw in Staten Island a possible site for a large New York terminal. It was under this arrangement that the name Staten Island Rapid Transit was first used. *Rapid transit* today is synonymous with electrified rail passenger service. Its coinage in 1884 referred to a steam-powered service and is thought to be the first use of the now-popular term.

In 1905 the ferryboat service between Manhattan and Staten Island was taken over by the municipal government and has been operated by City Hall ever since. It likely marks the first major shift of an urban transport activity from the private sector to the public. The SIRT's other ferryboat service, the much shorter line between Tottenville and Perth Amboy, remained part of the railway until 1948, when it was spun off for another dozen or so years of independent operation. In 1963, this ferryboat service was abandoned outright.

Freed of responsibility for the Upper New York Bay ferry service, SIRT, with both financial and technical support from its parent corporation in Baltimore, turned its attention to the task of feeding passengers to the municipal ferry terminal at Saint George, not conveying them all the way to their jobs in Manhattan. In 1925, a major project was implemented to replace the line's steam-hauled passenger trains with new electric-powered trains; a hundred 67-foot multiple-unit cars were ordered from the Standard Steel Car Company.

The cars looked a lot like the BRT/BMT Standard. Indeed, while the whole

1925 electrification project was prompted by state legislation passed in 1923 requiring the elimination of steam engines in cities with a population of more than a million residents, there had always been talk of a tunnel under the Narrows one day that would permit through electrified rapid transit service over both the BRT/BMT and the SIRT. To this day, sharp-eyed observers can detect indications in the tunnel alignment south of the station at Fifty-ninth Street and Fourth Avenue in Brooklyn where such a line would have linked up with the BMT; this civil construction was completed a full decade before the SIRT invested in its own electric multiple-unit cars.

Clearly the SIRT cars were designed so they might comfortably navigate in BMT subway tunnels, and the Staten Island line acknowledges that it received significant technical assistance from the BMT during its electrification project. Something of a puzzlement, though, concerns whether the SIRT cars were designed to be able to operate in multiple unit with BMT equipment. It has often been claimed they were. In later years, when the SIRT sold a quantity of used equipment to the NYCTA for service on the BMT, it developed that they would not so operate, but compelling evidence that they were supposed to from the start is lacking.[5] A qualification is also needed to the assertion that the SIRT cars "looked like" the BMT Standard. In general size and shape, they did; but the SIRT cars were designed with IRT-style end vestibules, the absence of which on the Standard was one of its more important characteristics, and their angular lines were quite harsh compared to the subtle curves of the BRT/BMT car.

The SIRT eventually electrified three separate lines: the main line between Saint George and Tottenville, a branch off this route between Clifton and South Beach, and another line out of Saint George to Arlington. The first electric train to carry revenue passengers was a South Beach service on June 5, 1925, and the Saint George–Tottenville line joined the new order on July 1 of the same year.

After World War II, the SIRT began to suffer. Passenger service to both South Beach and Arlington was eliminated in 1953, and these lines were deelectrified. With this reduction in service, thirty surplus multiple-unit cars were sold to the NYCTA. Their principal assignment there was the Culver line, although they could also be found on the Brighton-Franklin shuttle with regularity and even on the West End from time to time. Coney Island shops took pride in the refurbishing project that was necessary to ready these cars for TA service, and they were turned out in an attractive burgundy and tan color scheme somewhat similar to the IRT R-14s. Route and destination signs were old metal plate apparatus taken from out-of-service elevated equipment.

Public subsidy of the SIRT's remaining service to Tottenville began in 1954, and in 1971 the line became a wholly public sector operation under the MTA umbrella. At first the B&O remained on Staten Island as the operator of freight service over SIRT lines, but in the massive corporate realignments that have lately redrawn the whole profile of American railroads, the B&O—now absorbed by the massive CSX Railroad—withdrew from Staten Island. The future of freight rail service in the borough of Richmond remains unclear.

One of SIRT's original fleet of electric multiple-unit cars sits in the terminal at Saint George. These vehicles were designed and purchased when the SIRT was owned by the B&O. [Author]

New equipment for the SIRTOA became an urgent MTA priority after 1971. To ease a severe car shortage, ex–LIRR equipment was lent to the line for a short time. But the permanent answer became a fleet of fifty-two new stainless steel multiple-unit cars that were built by the Saint Louis Car Company in 1972 and are virtual duplicates of the TA's own R-44 fleet. Indeed, they were ordered as an add-on to the R-44 contract.[6]

Thus equipped, the SIRT moves into its future. Interestingly, while it has always used rolling stock similar in size and dimension to that element of the city subway system that uses larger-size rolling stock, the BMT-IND network, the PATH system is a near duplicate of the smaller IRT in the size of its subway cars.

It is a fitting epilogue to the story of the better-known New York City subway and rapid transit network to spend a moment talking about these two smaller operations, PATH and SIRT. The table shown here presents some relevant data to contrast PATH with SIRT and both with the NYCTA.[7]

PATH, SIRT, and NYCTA: A Comparison

	PATH	SIRT	PATH & SIRT	NYCTA
Route miles	13.79	14.29	28.08	247.31
Stations	13	22	35	469
Rapid transit cars	342	64	406	6,108
Annual passengers, 1990 (millions)	56	6	62	1,028

APPENDIX A

PASSENGER EQUIPMENT ROSTER

IND R-1 unit. [NYCTA]

I: Equipment purchased by the Interborough Rapid Transit Corporation prior to the 1940 unification

CAR NUMBER	NAME OR DESIGNATION	BUILDER	DATE	NOTES
3340	*August Belmont*	Wason	1902	1
3341	*John B. McDonald*	Wason	1902	1
2000–2159	Composites	Wason, St. Louis & Jewett	1903	
3000–3339	Composites	Wason, St. Louis, Jewett & Stephenson	1903–4	
3342	First steel car	PRR	1903	
3344	*Mineola*	Wason	1904	1
3350–3649	Gibbs Hi-V	ACF	1904–5	2
3650–3699	Hi-V deck roof	ACF	1907–8	3
3700–3809	Hi-V motors	ACF	1910–11	
3810–3849	Hi-V motors	Standard Steel	1910–11	
3850–4024	Hi-V motors	Pressed Steel	1910–11	
4025–4036	Lo-V Steinway motors	Pullman	1915	17
4037–4160	Lo-V Fliver motors	Pullman	1915	
4161–4214	Lo-V Fliver motors	Pullman	1915	
4215–4222	Lo-V Steinway motors	Pullman	1915	15, 17
4223–4514	Hi-V trailers	Pullman	1915	16
4515–4554	Lo-V trailers	Pullman	1916	
4555–4576	Lo-V Steinway motors	Pullman	1916	15, 17
4577–4699	Lo-V motors	Pullman	1916	
4700–4770	Lo-V Steinway motors	Pullman	1916	17
4771–4810	Lo-V motors	Pullman	1916	
4811–4965	Lo-V trailers	Pullman	1916–17	
4966–5302	Lo-V motors	Pullman	1917	4
5303–5377	Lo-V trailers with compressors	Pullman	1922	
5378–5402	Lo-V trailers	Pullman	1922	
5403–5502	Lo-V motors	Pullman	1922	4
5503–5627	Lo-V motors	ACF	1925	
5628–5652	Lo-V Steinway motors	ACF	1925	17
5653–5702	Lo-V World's Fair cars	St. Louis	1938	17

IRT R-33 unit. [NYCTA]

All of the above noted equipment has been retired from passenger service, although selected cars have been retained for nonrevenue service.
Note: PRR indicates Pennsylvania Railroad and ACF is the American Car and Foundry Company.

R-11 experimental unit, rebuilt as R-34. [NYCTA]

II: Equipment purchased by the New York City Board of Transportation and the New York City Transit Authority for service on the IRT Division

CAR NUMBERS	CONTRACT	BUILDER	YEAR	NOTES
5703–5802	R-12	ACF	1948	5, 27
5803–5952	R-14	ACF	1949	5, 27
5953–5999; 6200–6252	R-15	ACF	1950	5, 27
6500–6899	R-17	St. Louis	1955–56	6, 27
7050–7299	R-21	St. Louis	1956–57	6, 27
7300–7749	R-22	St. Louis	1957–58	6, 27
7750–7859	R-26	ACF	1959–60	6
7860–7950	R-28	ACF	1960–61	6
8570–8805	R-29	St. Louis	1962–63	6
8806–9345	R-33	St. Louis	1963	6
9346–9769	R-36	St. Louis	1964	7, 18
1301–1625	R-62	Kawasaki	1983–85	5, 13
1651–2475	R-62	Bombardier	1984–87	5, 13, 22
8001–8010	R-110A	Kawasaki	1992	13, 26

IND/BMT R-10 unit. [NYCTA]

BMT D unit. [NYCTA]

IND/BMT R-16 unit. [Author]

IRT Lo-V unit. [NYCTA]

IND/BMT R-44 unit. [NYCTA]

III: Equipment purchased by the Brooklyn Rapid Transit Corporation and the Brooklyn-Manhattan Transit Corporation prior to the 1940 unification

CAR NUMBERS	NAME OR DESIGNATION	BUILDER	YEAR	NOTES
2000–2599	Standard motors	ACF	1914–19	4, 25
2600–2899	Standard motors	Pressed Steel	1920–22	25
4000–4049	Standard trailers	Pressed Steel	1924	
6000–6120	Triplex	Pressed Steel	1925–28	4, 8
7003	*Green Hornet*	Pullman	1934	9
7029	*Zephyr*	Budd	1934	9
7004–7013	Multisection units	St. Louis	1936	9
7014–7028	Multisection units	Pullman	1936	9
8000–8005	*Bluebird*	Clark	1938, 1940	8

[Note: all of the above noted equipment has been retired from passenger service.]

BMT Multisection articulated unit. [Author's collection]

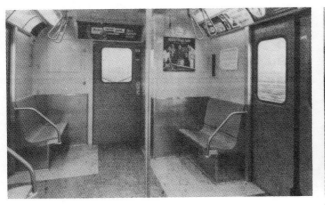
Interior of an R-32 unit, with operator's cab to the right of the end door. [NYCTA]

Interior: BMT/IND R-44 unit. [General Steel Industries — St. Louis]

IV: Equipment purchased by the City of New York for the Independent Subway System

CAR NUMBERS	CONTRACT	BUILDER	YEAR	NOTES
100–399	R-1	ACF	1930–31	4
400–899	R-4	ACF	1932–33	
1300–1399	R-6[1]	Pressed Steel	1936	
1150–1299	R-6[2]	Pullman	1936	
900–1149	R-6[3]	ACF	1935–36	
1400–1474	R-7	ACF	1937	
1475–1549	R-7	Pullman	1937	
1550–1599	R-7[a]	Pullman	1938	24
1600–1649	R-7[a]	ACF	1938	
1650–1701	R-9	ACF	1940	
1702–1802	R-9	Pressed Steel	1940	23

All of the above noted equipment has been retired from passenger service, although selected cars have been retained for nonrevenue service.

Interior view of an IRT car. [Author]

V: Equipment purchased by the New York City Board of Transportation and the New York City Transit Authority for service on the BMT and IND divisions

CAR NUMBERS	CONTRACT	BUILDER	DATE	NOTES
1808–1852; 3000–3349	R-10	ACF	1948–49	10, 5, 27
8010–8019	R-11	Budd	1949	11, 5, 26, 27
6300–6499	R-16	ACF	1955	5, 27
8020–8249	R-27	ACF	1960	6
8250–8351; 8412–8569	R-30	St. Louis	1961	6
8352–8411	R-30(a)	St. Louis	1961	6
3650–3949	R-32	Budd	1965	6, 22
3350–3649	R-32(a)	Budd	1965	6, 22
3950–4149	R-38	St. Louis	1966	12, 6
4150–4549	R-40	St. Louis	1967–68	12, 6
4550–4949	R-42	St. Louis	1968–69	13, 6
100–399	R-44	St. Louis	1971–72	13, 14
500–1278	R-46	Pullman	1974–78	13, 14, 19, 21, 22
2500–2924	R-68	Westinghouse-Amrail	1986–88	5, 13
5000–5199	R-68	Kawasaki	1988–89	5, 13
3001–3009	R-110B	Bombardier	1992	13, 26

First IND R unit, R-1 No. 100. [Author's collection]

NOTE: In 1954, thirty ex–Staten Island rapid transit cars were purchased for service on the BMT. Of the total, twenty-five were motor cars, and they were numbered 2900–2924. Five trailers never were used in passenger service by the TA. All were built by Standard Steel in 1925 and have since been retired.

NOTES

[1] Did not run in regular passenger service; nonrevenue equipment otherwise not included in this roster.
[2] Car No. 3352 preserved at Seashore Trolley Museum, Kennebunkport, Maine.
[3] Car No. 3663 preserved at Branford Trolley Museum, East Haven, Connecticut.
[4] Several representatives of this class preserved by the TA for historical purposes.
[5] Single-unit cars; cabs on both ends.
[6] Coupled into two-car sets; one motorman's cab per car.
[7] Permanently coupled into two-car sets, except Nos. 9306 through 9345, which are single units.
[8] Three-section articulated units.
[9] Five-section articulated units.
[10] R-10 units in the 1800 series renumbered into the 2900 series in 1970.
[11] Rebuilt under contract R-34 in 1964–65.
[12] Some of these cars air-conditioned.
[13] Air-conditioned.
[14] Includes cars with full-width cab on one end, no cab on the other end; also cars with no cabs at all.
[15] Converted from trailers to status shown in 1929.
[16] Nos. 4223–4250 converted to Hi-V blind motors in 1952.
[17] Designed for steep grades of Steinway Tunnels; could not operate with other cars.
[18] None of the postwar IRT cars before the R-62 units was built with air-conditioning. Retrofitting began in 1975.
[19] Nos. 1228–1278 include even-numbered cars only.
[20] R-9 unit No. 1801 on display in the New York State Museum, Albany.
[21] Prior to being delivered to the TA, R-46 No. 816 was shipped by Pullman to Caracas, Venezuela, in late 1976 in an effort to win a contract for rolling stock for that city's new subway. No. 816 traveled through the Port of Miami; Pullman failed to land the contract.
[22] For its day, was the largest order for railway passenger cars in the United States.
[23] No. 1801 preserved at the New York State Museum in Albany.

BMT experimental articulated units, built on the eve of World War II by the Clark Railway Equipment Corp. [Author's collection]

(24) No. 1575 reconfigured after an accident into prototype for R-10 series.
(25) All Standard motors delivered as single units; many later combined into three-car permanently coupled sets.
(26) Experimental trains.
(27) All cars in this series have been retired.

Left: It took a lot of muscle for a tower operator to work the handles on a manually operated interlocking plant. The operator here is leaning into the last such installation on the whole system, at the BMT's Rockaway Parkway terminal. *Right:* This more modern installation is at Euclid Avenue on the IND. [Both photos NYCTA]

APPENDIX B

SUBWAY SIGNALING

THE NEW YORK SUBWAYS HAVE NOT BEEN 100 percent free of collisions over the years, but the record is remarkably good. Credit on this score goes to many factors, not the least of which is the automatic signal system that protects the various lines and routes.

The signal system in use today is a simple one—simple, that is, compared to the many different kinds of indications and aspects a person must know to pass a book-of-rules examination on any standard American railroad. Excluding early BRT/BMT el operations, the BMT and IND have always used roughly similar signal codes. While the Interborough employed a different and more complex system through most of its history, including a generous reliance on semaphore-type signals, it is now being brought into step with the system used on the other two divisions.

There are two principal kinds of signals: automatic block and interlocking. Block signals contain green, yellow, and red indications, although in certain instances a fourth indication is used in conjunction with one of the three colors to inform a motorman of some special condition. Red means "stop," and if a train doesn't, a raised arm next to the signal at trackside exercises a simple but effective form of automatic train control. The raised arm trips a switch located on the lead truck, emergency brakes are applied automatically, and the train stops. All TA lines and trains are equipped with this fail-safe mechanism. (The term *fail-safe* is used advisedly; the circuits are designed so that any short circuit or malfunction in the system immediately throws the signal to red and raises the trip arm.) Except for some local tracks on some early lines—and most of the els—all rapid transit ever built in New York featured automatic train stop signals as original equipment. (The new Second Avenue line in Manhattan, when and if it is ever completed, will introduce a more complex and varied form of automatic train control. Plans call for coded electronic impulses to be transmitted to a monitor on board the train, providing a full range of speed controls, and not just simple stop protection. The R-44 and R-46 subway cars are equipped to run on such lines.)

Once a train pauses at a red block signal, the trip arm automatically lowers, and the train *can* proceed. However since 1970, the book of rules does not permit the motorman to do so. A red automatic block signal now means "stop and stay"; in past years it meant "stop and proceed," prepared to find the next signal also showing red or possibly even finding the block itself occupied. This maneuver—stopping at a red signal and allowing the trip arm to lower automati-

Here is the heart of the TA's automatic signal system. *Left:* A trackside trip is raised to engage a protruding device on a subway car and throw the train into an emergency stop. Such trips are in the raised position when an automatic block signal such as the one shown at right displays a red indication. [Both photos NYCTA]

cally—is called "keying by." The terminology dates to bygone days on the Interborough: when a motorman paused at a red signal, he had to get out of his cab, descend to trackside, and crank down the track trip with a keylike device. Keying by a signal still happens in the subway but only after a motorman has been given radio clearance by the dispatcher to execute the move.

A yellow block signal means "slow," since the next signal may be showing red. Green means "proceed." Variations occur chiefly in what is called "time signal" territory. Here block signals do more than protect trains from each other; they force motormen to observe permanent speed restrictions. Approaching a downgrade, say, on which the maximum allowable speed is 15 mph, a motorman will see ahead nothing but yellow and red block signals. Often, the red signals will also show an extra indication in time signal territory to distinguish the aspect from a conventional "stop" signal. The motorman must reduce speed. If the train is traveling at or under the allowable limit, the signals ahead will clear and permit it to continue—but only at a rate that will require the motorman to remain below 15 mph.

Interlocking signals are the second major species found at trackside. They contain two separate red-yellow-green signal heads and frequently other indications as well. They protect all junctions and can often be found at places other than junctions where a towerman or dispatcher might want to be able to exercise control over a train. A standard automatic block signal cannot be set at "stop" from a remote location, whereas an interlocking signal can.

A double-red indication on an interlocking signal means "stop and stay." No keying by is, or ever was, permitted in the face of such an indication. Interlocking signals also indicate the route for which an approaching switch is set. Green-over-green and yellow-over-green are, respectively, the "proceed" and "proceed

Interlocking signals contain two full signal heads. The upper one informs a train operator how fast the train should proceed, and the lower one tells which way an upcoming switch is set. [Author]

with caution" indications for the straight set; green-over-yellow and double-yellow are the equivalent indications for the diverging track.

Until the DeKalb Avenue reconstruction in 1958 eliminated its need, the BMT employed a special blue signal on an interlocking unit. It was used approaching a unique three-way switch and allowed the motorman to know which of three routes was set.

There are other kinds of signals and indications used in the subway system. Small ground-level dwarf signals are often used at switches to allow for occasional movements against the ordinary flow of traffic. They are manually controlled from a tower, generally do not include trip arms, and are not part of ordinary operations.

The Transit Authority maintains total respect for its signal system. In addition to obvious considerations of safety, it is a smoothly functioning signal system that permits optimum performance on any subway line. Passengers on the IRT may have been impressed by the new subway cars purchased for the old Belmont lines during the 1950s, but TA engineers were just as concerned about the part of the IRT improvement program that called for total replacement of all older signals so that the new equipment's full potential could be realized.

A simple but dependable signal system—now backed up by two-way radio—plus a management that insists upon near-religious observance of the book of rules: these are the elements that combine to produce safe and dependable transportation for almost 4 million passengers each day.

NOTES

CHAPTER 1

[1]As a result of McGraw's decision, Boston claimed, *and still claims*, the 1904 world championship of baseball by default.

[2]The amalgamation of 1898 had several milestones. Following earlier state legislation, a referendum was held on November 6, 1894, throughout the territory proposed for inclusion in what was then generally called Greater New York. It passed. Next, a special committee had to draft a charter, a document that was then submitted for ratification to both houses of the state legislature in early 1897; this too was successful. In November of the same year, a mayor was elected for the new metropolis, and he was Robert Van Wyck, a Tammany Hall Democrat. He defeated former Brooklyn mayor Seth Low, a Republican. (Low later was successful and was elected the new city's second mayor in 1901.) And then, at the stroke of midnight when December 31, 1897, became January 1, 1898, the new City of New York began its formal existence.

[3]For a classic treatment of slum conditions in late-nineteenth-century New York, see Jacob A. Riis, *How the Other Half Lives* (New York: Scribners, 1890).

[4]The control handle was inscribed: "Controller used by the Hon. George B. McClellan, Mayor of the City of New York, Thursday, Oct. 27, 1904. Presented to the Hon. George B. McClellan by August Belmont, President of the Interborough Rapid Transit Company."

[5]Later called the Allied Chemical Tower, it was from atop this building that an illuminated white ball (and later an illuminated "big apple") descended as midnight approached on December 31 to mark the start of each new year for crowds assembled below in Times Square, and in later years for a nationwide television audience as well. Were the white ball ever to have continued descending through the sidewalk, it would have wound up in the middle of the Interborough's southbound local track.

[6]McClellan (1865–1940) was the son of Civil War General George Brinton McClellan (1826–1885), the man who unsuccessfully ran against Abraham Lincoln for president when the latter stood for reelection in 1864. McClellan-the-younger served in the U.S. House of Representatives (1895–1903) and after his political days became a professor of economic history at Princeton University. His academic field of expertise was the history of Venice, but he wrote widely, including an autobiography that remained in manuscript form in the care of the New York Historical Society for many years. See *The Gentlemen and the Tiger*, ed. Harold C. Syrett (Philadelphia: Lippincott, 1956).

CHAPTER 2

[1]I have written elsewhere of the Boston subway. See *Change at Park Street Under* (Brattleboro, Vt.: The Stephen Greene Press, 1972). An excellent study of several important world subway systems is Benson Bobrick, *Labyrinths of Iron* (New York: Newsweek Books, 1981). The subway system of London has been described in many books, the definitive study being T. C. Barker and Michael Robbins, *A History of London Transport*, 2 vols. (London: George Allen & Unwin, Ltd., 1974, 1975).

[2]For a detailed description of the development of the Manhattan elevated lines, see Robert C. Reed, *The New York Elevated* (South Brunswick, N.J., and New York: A. S. Barnes & Co., 1978).

[3]Sprague (1857–1934) was born in Milford, Connecticut. He graduated from the U.S. Naval Academy at Annapolis in 1878 (seventh in a class of fifty), was appointed an ensign in 1882, and served on the U.S.S. *Lancaster*. He resigned his commission in 1883 and joined the fledgling Edison organization at Menlo Park, New Jersey, but soon tired of his assignments there since they primarily involved street lighting projects while his own interests were in the field of transportation. He left Edison in 1884 and established the Sprague Electric Railway and Motor Company. His initial efforts were aimed at the New York elevated lines, since he felt replacing their steam locomotives would be the most appropriate first step for the concept of electric transportation. But the els weren't ready for electrification quite yet, and thus he turned to street railways. His success in Richmond in 1888 ushered in a period of tremendous growth for street railways; these companies quickly electrified their operations and abandoned the animal power that had been the industry's source of energy until then. For his reflections on all of this, see Frank J. Sprague, *The Electric Railway* (New York: Century Co., 1905). This work is a reprint of two articles originally published in *Century* 50 (July and August 1905): 434–451, 512–527. Sprague was also a contributor to a special series of articles in the trade magazine *Street Railway Journal* with a personal remembrance of his own role in the onset of electric transportation; see "The History of the American Street Railway Association," *Street Railway Journal* 24 (1904): 515–600.

[4]For a thorough description of the electrification of the railroad lines operating into Grand Central, see William D. Middleton, *Grand Central* (San Marino, Calif.: Golden West Books, 1977). There have been many books written about Pennsylvania Station and its electric-powered trains, including a small one by me; see *Rails Under the Mighty Hudson* (Brattleboro, Vt.: The Stephen Greene Press, 1975). For an excellent study of the entire American railroad industry and its use of electric trains and locomotives, see William D. Middleton, *When the Steam Railroads Electrified* (Milwaukee: Kalmbach, 1974).

CHAPTER 3

[1]Belmont (1853–1924) came from a distinguished line. His father arrived in New York in 1837 as the North American representative of the House of Rothschild and quickly became an important figure not only in the world finance but also in Democratic party politics, the circles of fashionable high society, and the developing sport of thoroughbred horse racing. Belmont Park and the "third jewel" of racing's Triple Crown, the Belmont Stakes, memorialize the family name. His mother, Caroline Perry, was an actress whose uncle, Oliver Hazard Perry, won the Battle of Lake Erie in 1813 and whose father, Matthew Calbraith Perry, initiated U.S. relations with the empire of Japan in 1854. Belmont-the-younger, John McDonald, and William Barclay Parsons teamed up again after their New York venture on the Interborough subway and in 1905 began a nine-year effort that culminated in the building of the Cape Cod Canal. Their enterprise was called the Boston, New York & Cape Cod Canal Co.

[2]Parsons (1859–1932) graduated from Columbia College and quickly earned a worldwide reputation as a premiere engineer in the field of railway construction. Prior to taking the assignment in New York with the Board of Rapid Transit Commissioners in 1899, he had been working on the construction of a railroad from Hankow to Canton in China. He resigned his subway post soon after the Interborough opened in 1904 and went to Panama, there to prepare a report for President Roosevelt on the practicality of a canal across that narrow isthmus. Parsons worked with Belmont on the Cape Cod Canal beginning in 1905 and joined the U.S. Army Engineers in 1917 after the United States entered World War I. Upon leaving the army after the war, he retired—but hardly to a life of inactivity. Rather, he devoted his energies to research, writing, and lecturing. His publications are many; his major work is *Engineers and Engineering in the Renaissance* (Baltimore: Williams and Wilkins, 1939).

[3]The development of American railroad passenger cars from wood to steel, including the importance of Interborough car No. 3342 in that evolution, is told in John H. White, *The American Railroad Passenger Car* (Baltimore: Johns Hopkins University Press, 1978).

[4]For further information on the development of New York's first subway, see *Interborough Rapid Transit: The New York Subway* (New York: Interborough Rapid Transit Co., 1904; reprint ed., New York: Fordham, 1991); Joseph Cunningham and Leonard De Hart, *A History of the New York City Subway System*, pt. I (New York: Authors, 1976); Stan Fischler, *Uptown, Downtown* (New York: Hawthorn, 1976), pp. 36–48. For an unusual perspective on the city's first subway by a major participant in its construction, see William Barclay Parsons, "Twenty-five Years of the New York Subway," *New York Times*, October 27, 1929, sec. X, p. 4. In 1902, an important news magazine of the engineering profession published an eight-part series on the subway; see "The New York Rapid Transit Railway," *Engineering News Record* 47 (1902): 83–86, 106–107, 127–129, 161–164, 199–201, 236–239, 318–320, 374–377. There was also a series of articles on the new Interborough subway at the time of its opening in a journal of the urban transit industry: "The New York Rapid Transit Subway," *Street Railway Journal* 24 (1904): 464–471, 601–659. These articles from the *Street Railway Journal* formed the basis of *Interborough Rapid Transit*, published by the Interborough at the time of the subway's opening. A more recent study provides insight into the early development of rapid transit in three cities: New York, Boston, and Philadelphia. See Charles W. Cheape, *Moving the Masses* (Cambridge: Harvard University Press, 1980). Cheape's New York treatment runs from pages 19 through 101 and contains extensive bibliographical citations to primary and secondary materials.

CHAPTER 4

[1]Many of these converted cars remained in service into the 1950s and were essentially unchanged; they featured manually operated end doors but remotely controlled center doors. They were able to operate in trains of more modern cars by always being placed at either end of a train, where a conductor would also be positioned, i.e., two conductors per train, if necessary. The conductors operated the doors in the newer cars with remote controls, as well as the center door in the front or rear car. The doors at the front and end platform on a train weren't used at all—standard Interborough practice with all its vestibule running stock. Thus, a single manually operated door was positioned next to the conductor's station and could be operated manually.

[2]See Epilogue for details on McAdoo's Hudson & Manhattan.

CHAPTER 5

[1]Hedley (1864–1955) is a man whose name is more identified with the IRT than anyone else's, including August Belmont. At one point, he attempted to prevent the BRT from using the term *subway* to describe its underground transit system; only the IRT was a real subway, in his view. Born in England, Hedley came to the United States and rose to important positions with both the Manhattan and Brooklyn elevated railways. From 1893 until 1903, he lived in Chicago and headed up key elevated railways there. Then, he went back to New York and a stint on the Interborough from 1903 through 1934. He was an explosive man who fought hard and often with those who disagreed with him, but his talents and his enthusiasm were boundless when it came to running, and improving, the Interborough Rapid Transit Company. Apparently this predilection ran in the family too; his brother worked for William Gibbs McAdoo's Hudson Tubes, and a nephew, Sidney Bingham, was a New York subway executive of a later generation;

both his father and grandfather were railwaymen back in England as well.

[2]The Fulton Ferry is reputed to have been established in pre-Revolutionary days using sailing craft. Known for certain is that in 1814, Robert Fulton introduced the line's first steam-powered vessel, *Nassau*, whose single paddle wheel was located between two separate hulls. *Nassau* was a catamaran, in other words. Soon after, the line became part of a ferryboat empire controlled by the Union Ferry Company of Brooklyn, the largest of all the East River operators and one that was truly dominant on the East River south of the point where the Brooklyn Bridge now stands. Bridge and tunnel construction eventually did in the Union Ferry Company, though, and in 1922 its three remaining routes, including the Fulton Ferry, were purchased by the City of New York for operation under municipal auspices. But even municipal operation failed to save the Fulton Ferry; on the evening of January 19, 1924, the 1862-built wooden sidewheeler *Union* made the last crossing. For further information about this important element in the overall mass transit picture of New York, see my book *Over and Back: The History of Ferryboats in New York Harbor* (New York: Fordham, 1990).

[3]A conventional view holds that vibrations from reciprocating steam engines could weaken and even destroy a suspension bridge. Washington Roebling, the Brooklyn Bridge's chief engineer, disagreed. He said the small elevated steam engines could certainly traverse the bridge without fear and pointed out that conventional (i.e., much larger) railroad steam engines regularly plied the suspension bridge his father, John Roebling, had built over the Niagara River. There was even talk, at one time, of hauling regular railroad passenger cars across the bridge to permit through service from Brooklyn to Buffalo. Nonetheless, Roebling was ignored, and until electric traction was available, the Brooklyn Bridge ran cable car shuttles and not steam-drawn trains. See David McCullough, *The Great Bridge* (New York: Simon & Schuster, 1972), pp. 518–519. The cable cars used on the Brooklyn Bridge, incidentally, although they looked much like conventional elevated railway rolling stock, were actually much larger and were not able to be absorbed into the BRT's el fleet. Many were sold to interurban railway companies, electrified, and lived out their days on country lines far from New York.

[4]Most American railroads are bewildering amalgamations of underlying companies, predecessor agencies, one-time competitors, paper corporations, and the like. In the case of the LIRR, its original investors had little interest in serving Long Island points at all, and so they built a main line through the island's sparsely settled midland so trains could more quickly get from Brooklyn to Greenport on the eastern extremity, there to connect with steamboats for New England points and rail connections on to Boston. Other companies were organized to serve Long Island's more established communities; the South Shore Railroad was one of these. For further details on this now publicly owned and operated railroad, see Vincent F. Seyfried, *The Long Island Rail Road: A Comprehensive History*, 7 pts. (Garden City, N.Y.: Author, 1961–1975); also see Ron Ziel and George H. Foster, *Steel Rails to the Sunrise* (New York: Duell, Sloan and Pearce, 1965).

[5]For details on the Triborough Subway System, see "A New Subway Line for New York; Its History," *Engineering News Record* 63 (1910): 288–289.

[6]It is thought that certain "nonrevenue" moves were made over this connection, including trips aboard a special Interborough subway car called *Mineola*, the private car of August Belmont. A plausible journey for the boss on such occasions would have been from a spur track in the basement of the Hotel Belmont on East Forty-second Street that connected with the subway to a Nassau County racetrack served by the LIRR's third-rail electric network, Belmont Park. Belmont also served on the board of directors of the LIRR. His private subway car, the *Mineola*, was built by Wason and carried on the Interborough's roster as No. 3344. The only New York subway car ever to be equipped with a restroom and a kitchen, it was later used by the IRT as a construction car and finally sold for junk. The story has a happy ending, though. Rescued from a farm in New Jersey, *Mineola* now sits in splendid retirement at the trolley museum in Branford, Connecticut.

CHAPTER 6

[1]One can find slightly different dollar figures for the cost of building the Dual Subway System in various sources, as well as slightly different splits between the city and the two companies. This can usually be explained by whether merely Contracts Three and Four are being discussed or the full spectrum of agreements beyond the two basic documents.

[2]The Triborough Subway System involved generous tunnel dimensions to permit the operation of full-sized standard railroad equipment, as discussed in Chapter 5. Once it was determined that conventional railroads would not be connecting with the subway, these specifications were relaxed a bit when technical specifications were developed for the Dual Contracts. The Interborough necessarily had to continue to use smaller equipment, since its system was built around the smaller dimensions of the Contract One and Contract Two lines. But the BRT began its subway career with tunnel and equipment dimensions larger than the Interborough, but not quite as large as the original Triborough.

[3]There is only one station left in the whole New York City subway system today where trains regularly operate that are longer than the platform can accommodate: South Ferry on the IRT's Broadway local. The others have been expanded or closed.

[4]For further information on the trolley cars that operated across the Manhattan Bridge, see George V. Arnoux, "Manhattan Bridge Three Cent Line," *Electric Railroads*, no. 32 (December 1962). An excellent study is available that discusses the construction of all the major bridges in New York City. See Sharon Reier, *The Bridges of New York* (New York: Quadrant Press, 1977).

[5]Company men originally called the Standards "steel cars." In later years, when large numbers of single units were permanently coupled into three-car sets, the resultant lash-up was called a B unit; cars that remained single units were designated A units. As a result, the fleet itself was sometimes called the ABs. Of the company's roster, 900 were motor cars (Nos. 2000–2899), and 50 were motorless trailers (Nos. 4000–4049). The motorless trailers were permanently coupled between two motorized units; this lash-up was called a BX unit. BX units were supposed to be restricted from operating over the Manhattan Bridge because of its steep grades, but every so often one did.

[6]For further information on the Dual Contracts, see *New Subways for New York: The Dual System of Rapid Transit* (New York: Public Service Commission for the First District, 1913); Peter Derrick, "Catalyst for Development: Rapid Transit in New York," *New York Affairs* 9 (Fall 1986): 29–59. A series of articles on the Dual Contracts originally published in *Engineering News Record* in 1914–1915 were republished in book form; see Fred Lavis, *Building the New Rapid Transit System of New York City* (New York: Engineering News Record, 1915). This book includes a separate treatment on the reconstruction of the elevated lines by Maurice E. Griest ("Design of the New Elevated Railway Lines," pp. 67–73).

CHAPTER 7

[1]In addition to the Brighton line, three other steam-powered suburban railroads ran to Coney Island and were eventually merged into the BRT. Andrew Culver opened the Prospect Park & Coney Island R.R. in 1875, the beginning of what later was called the Culver line. The oldest of the three dates to 1864, was known for most of its early days as the Brooklyn, Bath & West End R.R., and ran between Coney Island and a ferry slip at the foot of Thirty-ninth Street in Brooklyn where passengers transferred to ferryboats of the New York & South Brooklyn Ferry and Transportation Co. for the final leg of their trips to Manhattan. The New York & Sea Beach

R.R. opened in 1879 and linked Coney Island with a connecting steamboat line at the foot of Sixty-first Street. Despite recent efforts of the Transit Authority to adopt a simplified letter code for all its transit lines, these latter two routes, very much in existence, are still called in Brooklyn, respectively, the West End line and the Sea Beach line. All three of these once steam-powered suburban railroads were later electrified, linked into the BRT's Fifth Avenue–Myrtle Avenue elevated line, and eventually tied into the Fourth Avenue subway at the time of the Dual Contracts. For further details, see Joseph Cunningham and Leonard De Hart, *A History of the New York City Subway System*, pt. II (New York: Authors, 1977), esp. pp. 9–20. Also see Alan Paul Kahn and Jack May, *The Tracks of New York, No. 2* (New York: Electric Railroaders' Association, 1975), passim; Karl Groh, "Above the Streets of Brooklyn," *Headlights* 37 (September–November 1975): 2–20.

[2]Hylan (1868–1936) was born in Ulster County in upstate New York. His father was an Irish immigrant and farmer; his mother traced her roots to pre-Revolutionary America. With little education, he came to New York City in 1887 and found work as a track layer on the Brooklyn elevated railway. He advanced to fireman on the steam-powered line, then engine hostler, and finally engineer. When a younger brother who had been studying law suddenly died, Hylan felt compelled to undertake legal studies, and it was this that set him on a course that eventually led to elected politics. Hylan drew support from the Hearst organization on the strength of his stands on issues, as well as from the fact that, as a Democrat from Brooklyn, he was not a product of the Tammany Hall organization. His two terms as mayor were marvelously hectic times, with considerable attention being paid to local transportation matters. He greatly expanded the municipal ferryboat fleet by taking over many failing private companies; he instituted a municipally operated electric trolley bus service on Staten Island; but he reserved his choicest passions for battles on behalf of improved city subway service. After leaving City Hall, he was appointed to a judgeship and had written an autobiography, although it is just a short pamphlet: John F. Hylan, *Mayor Hylan of New York: An Autobiography* (New York: Rotary Press, 1922).

[3]Beyond confusion about where he was supposed to be going, Luciano's operation of the train was later described as reckless. One passenger claimed he took the curve at Sands Street "as if the body of the [first] car was attached to the wheels on springs so that it could snap back."

[4]Lead car No. 726 was built in 1888 by the Pullman Palace Car Co. for service on the BRT behind steam locomotives and rebuilt with electric motors in 1905. Trailer No. 80 was built in 1887 by Gilbert Car Co. Trailer No. 100 was built in 1887 by Gilbert. Power car No. 725 was built in 1888 by Pullman Palace and rebuilt with electric motors in 1905. Power car No. 1064 was built in 1903 by John Stephenson Co.; electric motors were installed in 1904. Subsequent investigations by the BRT into the train and its equipment failed to develop evidence that any mechanical flaws or failures contributed to the crash. A letter dated November 20, 1918, from the Westinghouse Traction Brake Company, for example, addressed to W. G. Gove, the BRT's superintendent of equipment, concluded that "it is our opinion that the braking apparatus, so far as could be determined by the equipment as it existed after the wreck, was in proper working order in every respect."

[5]I have continued to study the Malbone Street Wreck. (See a paper I presented at the May 1991 Subway History Conference sponsored by the New York Transit Museum, "The Malbone Street Wreck; a Moment in the History of Urban Transportation.") From an examination of official New York City death records, I have positively identified 93 fatally injured victims—92 passengers and one BRT crew member. Unfortunately, there is some confusion as to the exact number of fatalities. Newspapers typically settled on a number on the day after the accident—anything from 89 to 105—and continually referred to that number in all subsequent stories, including those written months later during the various trials. (The trials themselves technically involved manslaughter indictments for the wrongful death of but two victims, Edward Erskine Porter and Thomas F. Gilfeather.) Of the 93 victims, 52 were men and 41 were women; the oldest was a 70-year-old man, the youngest a 14-year-

old girl; all fatally-injured victims were residents of Brooklyn except for two sisters from Michigan who were visiting a third sister in Brooklyn, a sailor from Charleston, South Carolina, who was assigned to the Brooklyn Navy Yard, and two individuals whose addresses were listed as in Manhattan. The actual death toll from the Malbone Street Wreck may be somewhat higher than 93; I can say with certainty, however, that it is at least 93. My mother lost two cousins in the Malbone Street wreck.

[6]There is some confusion over the motorman's real name. In fact, he was Edward Luciano, and he lived in Brooklyn at 160 Thirty-fourth Street, a short distance from the BRT's shops and yards at Thirty-ninth Street and Fifth Avenue. He is identified in early press accounts of the accident, as well as in official BRT reports, as Edward Lewis. It is reasonable to speculate that an obviously Italian-sounding name was changed to something less so since it was simply more comfortable in 1918 to do so, although whether this was an initiative of the BRT or Luciano himself is unclear. The March 1917 issue of the *BRT Monthly*, an employee magazine, contains a joke whose only point is the supposed ignorance of a streetcar passenger whose speech is rendered in an effort to imitate an Italian accent. The Lewis-Luciano confusion is compounded by the fact the Kings County district attorney who prosecuted the various Malbone Street cases was Harry E. Lewis, and an important witness at the trials was the BRT's supervisor of instructors, Wilbur Lewis.

[7]For further details on the decision of the War Labor Board and the BRT's reaction to it, see "Company's Action on Decision of War Labor Board," *BRT Monthly* 3 (November 1918): 2–4, 19.

[8]Despite all the precautions, the Malbone Street wreck "repeated itself" on December 1, 1974, fifty-six years and one month after the first crash. No lives were lost. The train of Budd-built R-32 units was traveling dead slow, but it derailed and hit the tunnel wall at the same spot the 1918 tragedy took place.

CHAPTER 8

[1]When the BMT was chartered in May 1923, "a great deal of thought," in the words of the *Times*, went into selecting a name for the new corporation. The word *Brooklyn* had to be included in the title, and "in a preferential position."

[2]The Rosoff company was headed by "Subway Sam" Rosoff, a high-wheeler of extraordinary proportions who frequented racetracks and gambling casinos the world over. The movie *Saratoga Trunk* was based on his life. Interestingly, another Samuel Rosoff was one of the guards on the ill-fated BRT train involved in the Malbone Street wreck.

[3]Subway advertising had become a major industry by 1932. Artemas Ward sold his franchise to a man named Barron G. Collier in 1925, and Collier's company continued to place ads in the subways until 1940. Among the young copywriters who at one time produced persuasive prose for Collier's clients were F. Scott Fitzgerald and Ogden Nash.

[4]Walker (1881–1946) was born in New York and attended New York Law School, where he distinguished himself not at all. Indeed, his legal career was always overshadowed by his ambitions to be a song writer. "Will You Love Me In December," his best-known piece, can probably be called a popular classic. It is small wonder, then, that his dual roots in law and entertainment led him to a synthesis of the two in the world of politics. He was a man of impeccable style, and while the revelations of corruption within his municipal administration eventually led to his downfall, many say that he was an honest man who did not personally profit at public expense. See Gene Fowler, *Beau James: The Life and Times of Jimmy Walker* (New York: Viking, 1949).

[5]The double el fare to Coney Island was dropped with the advent of the Dual Contracts. It continued on certain BMT-controlled streetcar lines to Coney Island until after World War II.

CHAPTER 9

[1]Until it was rebuilt in the 1970s, one could manage a fleeting glimpse of the action at Yankee Stadium from passing IRT trains. Also, the 161st Street station was one of the last sites on the entire system where preturnstile ticket choppers were used. As late as 1948, arriving fans were encouraged by megaphone to purchase a ticket for the trip home. Use of the long-outmoded system eased congestion at game's end, although regular turnstiles handled day-to-day traffic.

[2]These figures were valid when the Independent was built. New signals and new rolling stock have since improved BMT and IRT performance.

[3]For additional information on the Independent subway, see Groff Conklin, *All about Subways* (New York: Julian Messner, 1938). Although this might be called a children's book, it is an excellent work on the construction, outfitting, and operation of the city's third subway system. See also Joseph Cunningham and Leonard De Hart, *A History of the New York City Subway System,* pt. III (New York: Authors, 1977); Frederick A. Kramer, *Building the Independent Subway* (New York: Quadrant Press, 1990).

[4]For an excellent detailed treatment of the original IND subway cars, see Karl F. Groh, "Farewell to the 'R-9s,' " *Headlights* 39 (July–September 1977): 5–13.

[5]The full code: A, Eighth Avenue–Washington Heights; B, Sixth Avenue–Washington Heights; C, Eighth Avenue–Grand Concourse; D, Sixth Avenue–Grand Concourse; E, Eighth Avenue–Queens; F, Sixth Avenue–Queens. Each of the six options was operated, although each did not necessarily run both local and express service.

[6]Purists could fault this statement, since the terminal used in 1908 later became a trolley car facility, and the permanent route of the Centre Street subway line is to the north of the original underground station.

[7]Although Stillwell Avenue may be the busiest *terminal* in the country, it is not the busiest *station* on the New York subway system. That honor goes to the West Fourth Street station in Manhattan, part of the Independent system, where more than a thousand trains stop, but do not terminate, every twenty-four hours. West Fourth Street has eight tracks—two local and two express on each of two levels.

[8]See *First Annual Report: Federal Works Agency* (Washington, D.C.: U.S. Government Printing Office, 1940), pp. 136–137.

CHAPTER 10

[1]There was confusion over what to call the once-private systems after unification. An effort was made to find new three-word titles that could still be abbreviated BMT and IRT, but with no luck. One Bronx politician suggested calling the two old lines the La Guardia Lines but didn't press his point in that the North Beach Airport in Queens had recently been renamed to honor the mayor. A Manhattan judge suggested calling the BMT and IRT the Triborough Subway System. In the end, the terms *BMT Division* and *IRT Division* were settled upon.

[2]Quill (1905–1966) was born in County Kerry in Ireland and fought against the British in the effort that led to the establishment of the Irish Free State in 1922. In 1926, he immigrated to the United States and landed in New York, where he went to work on a pick-and-shovel job with one of the contractors building the new Independent subway. Later that year, he hired on with the Interborough as a gateman, became a U.S. citizen in 1931, and then moved into union work. A story still told among TWU old-timers claims Quill joined the Communist party not out of any strong ideological conviction but because the Communists were willing to rent

his fledgling transit union a meeting room from time to time. For a biography of Quill, see L. H. Wittemore, *The Man Who Ran the Subways* (New York: Holt, Rinehart and Winston, 1968). For a more encompassing work on labor-management relations on the New York subways, including a wide array of tables, see James J. McGinley, S.J., *Labor Relations in the New York Rapid Transit Systems, 1904–1944* (New York: King's Crown Press, 1949).

[3]A novel, three-section articulated design based on the then new PCC streetcar and the many innovations it pioneered.

[4]For details on the New York, Westchester & Boston, see Roger Arcara, *Westchester's Forgotten Railway* (New York: Quadrant Press, 1972).

CHAPTER 11

[1]The Polo Grounds was long served by elevated trains of both the Sixth and Ninth avenue lines; indeed, for many years, a storage yard and maintenance facility for trains was located behind the third-base grandstands of the park. The el station behind center field was the northern terminal of the lines until the time of the Dual Contracts, when trackage was extended across the Harlem River to connect with the Jerome Avenue elevated line. Onward from 1933, the Polo Grounds was also directly served by the IND Grand Concourse line. Yankee Stadium continues to be served by the same Concourse line, as well as by the IRT Jerome Avenue line.

The home of the Brooklyn Dodgers until 1957, Ebbets Field, was situated close by the Prospect Park station of the BMT Brighton Beach line. (Baseball fans walking from that station to the ballpark virtually crossed right over the tunnel site of the 1918 Malbone Street wreck.) Ebbets Field was also but a quarter-mile away from the IRT station at Franklin Avenue and Eastern Parkway. A recent study has attempted to justify the still-controversial move of the two National League teams to the West Coast after the 1957 season and cites poor highway access to Ebbets Field as a clear and obvious shortcoming. The fact that is overlooked, however, is that there is equally poor highway access in New York to the American Museum of Natural History, the Empire State Building, and the entire Times Square theater district. Places are accessible in New York if you can get there by subway; both Ebbets Field and the Polo Grounds were. See Neil Sullivan, *The Dodgers Move West* (New York: Oxford University Press, 1987), esp. pp. 28–44.

[2]Although the Rockaway line *opened* in June 1956, it was not really *finished*. Electrical substations were incomplete, and full traction power was not available. For several months, the line operated under these restrictions: reduced speed, short trains, and a complete ban on the IND's four-motor R-10 units. Only two-motor prewar R units could travel the Rockaway line at first.

[3]The service pattern on the West Side IRT had been this: trains that branched off on the Lenox Avenue line at Ninety-sixth Street were identified as Seventh Avenue services, while trains that continued due north along Broadway were called the Broadway–Seventh Avenue line. There were many variations, but as a general rule, the Broadway–Seventh Avenue express ran from 242d Street and Broadway to New Lots Avenue in Brooklyn; the Seventh Avenue express ran from 180th Street in the Bronx to Flatbush Avenue in Brooklyn; the Seventh Avenue local ran 145th Street and Lenox Avenue to South Ferry; and the Broadway–Seventh Avenue local from 137th Street and Broadway to South Ferry.

[4]Rapid arrival of large numbers of new IRT cars allowed for some novel car assignments in the late 1950s. A group of mechanically sound IRT Lo-Vs were fitted with extension plates at the door sills and operated on various BMT shuttle lines until that division received new rolling stock.

CHAPTER 12

[1] Despite the creation of the MTA, it remains both common and correct to refer to the city subway system as the New York City Transit Authority—the TA, for short.

[2] Original plans also called for relatively few Manhattan stations, and this too would have compensated for the "no express" design. But as community groups from bypassed neighborhoods began to apply pressure, more stations were added.

[3] On July 30, 1982, an advertisement appeared in the *Wall Street Journal* that read, in part: "The Metropolitan Transportation Authority is interested in soliciting proposals from qualified firms for the temporary use of certain areas within partially completed subway tunnel structures located beneath Second Avenue in the following areas: 1. East 99th Street to East 105th Street, 2. East 110th Street to East 120th Street."

[4] Any annual issue of the MTA's Annual Report spells out the financial and operational relationships of the city government, the Transit Authority, and the MTA. Particularly illuminating are footnotes to the financial statements of the MTA's various subsidiary agencies.

[5] Annual subway patronage for a number of benchmark years is as follows (in thousands):

Year	Passengers	Year	Passengers
1905	448,000	1947	2,051,000
1910	725,000	1950	1,681,000
1915	830,000	1955	1,378,000
1920	1,332,000	1960	1,345,000
1925	1,681,000	1965	1,363,000
1930	2,049,000	1970	1,258,000
1935	1,817,000	1975	1,054,000
1940	1,857,000	1980	1,009,000
1945	1,941,000	1985	1,010,000

[6] Operating revenue for both bus and rapid transit operations of the New York City Transit Authority are derived from the following sources:

Passenger fares	50%
Local assistance	24%
State assistance	23%
Federal assistance	2%
Other sources	1%
Total	100%

[7] After completing the R-46 order, Pullman withdrew from the passenger car business.

[8] Shoe beams are the insulated material mounted on the outside of the trucks to which the third-rail shoes are attached.

[9] The Transit Authority, together with the City of New York, who helped fund the R-46 purchase, brought suit against both Pullman-Standard, the prime contractor for construction of the cars, and Rockwell International Corporation, Pullman's subcontractor for the manufacture of the cars' trucks. The TA and the City were awarded $72 million from Rockwell in December 1980, and the defective trucks were all replaced by 1983.

EPILOGUE

[1]At the end of World War II, electrified commuter railroad service into New York City from the surrounding suburbs was provided by four separate railroads: the New York Central; the Long Island; the New York, New Haven & Hartford; and the Pennsylvania. The Delaware, Lackawanna & Western also operated electrified suburban service, but it terminated in Hoboken, New Jersey, across the Hudson River from Manhattan. These railroads, plus others, also operated nonelectrified suburban passenger service in and around New York. All of these electrified services are now in the public sector under the following alignment: the Long Island Rail Road is a separate arm of the MTA; both the Pennsylvania and the DL&W are operated by New Jersey Transit; something called the Metro North Commuter Railroad, yet another arm of the MTA, operates both the New York Central and the New Haven services, the latter in conjunction with the Department of Transportation of the State of Connecticut. For further details, see William D. Middleton, *When the Steam Railroads Electrified* (Milwaukee: Kalmbach, 1974), passim.

[2]McAdoo (1863–1941) was born in Georgia, educated in Tennessee, and practiced law in Chattanooga until 1892, when he moved to New York City. After supporting the presidential campaign of Woodrow Wilson in 1912, he was appointed secretary of the treasury in 1913 and was instrumental in the formation of the Federal Reserve in 1914. He also served as director general of all U.S. railroads when they were brought under government control during World War I. His two presidential efforts were in 1920 and 1924, and his single term in the U.S. Senate was between 1933 and 1939 when he was elected from the state of California. McAdoo has written an autobiography: *Crowded Years* (Boston: Houghton Mifflin, 1931).

[3]The Newark subway was opened in 1935 and today runs from Pennsylvania Station on Raymond Boulevard in downtown Newark to Franklin Street, more than 4 miles away. Of this distance, something over a mile is underground, and the rest is on grade-separated private right-of-way; the route largely follows the path of an old canal. Originally, the line served as a feeder into Newark for streetcars of the Public Service Company coming from many points. That is, trolleys reached Newark via the subway but operated beyond the subway route as conventional streetcars. As these street-running routes were converted to bus after World War II, the subway was cut back to simply the 4-mile portion running on private right-of-way. Its future began to look grim in an automobile-dominated era, and talk of its total abandonment was heard. But such was not to be the case. In 1953–1954 secondhand PCC streetcars were purchased to replace older deck-roof cars; carefully maintained, they continue to serve the route to this day. Now part of New Jersey Transit's statewide and publicly operated network of mass transit services, its future appears assured. For further information, see John Harrington Riley, *The Newark City Subway Lines* (Oak Ridge, N.J.: the author, 1987).

[4]For a treatment of the H&M and its evolution into the PATH system, see my book, *Rails Under the Mighty Hudson* (Brattleboro, Vermont: The Stephen Greene Press, 1975). See also Anthony Fitzherbert, " 'The Public Be Pleased,' William G. McAdoo and the Hudson Tubes," *Headlights,* supp. (June 1964); Paul Carleton, *The Hudson & Manhattan Railroad Revisited* (Dunnellon, Fla.: D. Carleton Railbooks, 1990).

[5]There is little published material on the SIRT. See Middleton, *When the Steam Railroads Electrified,* pp. 290–292, 429–430.

[6]The SIRT R-44 units carry numbers that are a continuation of the TA's own series. Currently running on Staten Island are units 400–437, and even-numbered units 438–466.

[7]Information taken from *Jane's Urban Transport Systems,* ed. Chris Bushell, 11th ed. (London: Jane's Transport Press, 1992), pp. 236–240.

INDEX